GIVE YOUR OTHER VOTE
TO THE SISTER

by
**DEBBIE
MARSHALL**

GIVE YOUR OTHER VOTE TO THE SISTER

A WOMAN'S JOURNEY INTO THE GREAT WAR

UNIVERSITY OF
CALGARY
PRESS

© 2007 Debbie Marshall

University of Calgary Press
2500 University Drive NW
Calgary, Alberta
Canada T2N 1N4
www.uofcpress.com

LIBRARY AND ARCHIVES CANADA CATALOGUING IN PUBLICATION

Marshall, Debbie, 1959-
  Give your other vote to the sister : a woman's journey into the Great War / by Debbie Marshall.

(Legacies shared ; no. 26)
Includes bibliographical references and index.
ISBN 978-1-55238-228-8

1. MacAdams, Roberta, 1881-1959. 2. Women politicians—Alberta—Biography.
3. Canada. Canadian Army. Royal Canadian Army Medical Corps—Nurses—Biography.
4. Nurses—Alberta—Biography. 5. Alberta—Politics and government—1905-1921.
I. Title. II. Series.

FC3672.1.M32M37 2007   971.23'02092   C2007-902298-7

The University of Calgary Press acknowledges the support of the Alberta Foundation for the Arts for our publications. We acknowledge the financial support of the Government of Canada through the Book Publishing Industry Development Program (BPIDP) for our publishing activities. We acknowledge the financial support of the Canada Council for the Arts for our publishing program.

This book has been published with the aid of a grant from the Alberta Lottery Fund — Community Initiatives Program.

Printed and bound in Canada by Houghton Boston
∞ This book is printed on Rolland Enviro 100 acid free paper

Cover design, page design and typesetting by Melina Cusano

To Heather

CONTENTS

ACKNOWLEDGMENTS

As this book goes to press, news of the first female Canadian soldier to die in combat has reached the front page of newspapers across Canada. Capt. Nichola Goddard died in the midst of a firefight near Kandahar, Afghanistan. While many women have served in the Canadian military, she was the first to die in a combat role. Her death is a reminder of the changing nature of women's participation in the armed forces, as well as the price that women — past and present — have been willing to pay in the service of their country.

The book that you are about to read is about a woman from a much earlier war than the one in which Capt. Goddard served. Lt. Roberta MacAdams was an officer in the Canadian Army Medical Corps during the Great War (1914–1918). Like Goddard, she and other women serving overseas often put themselves at risk to represent their country. Although MacAdams would survive the war, forty-seven of her female colleagues would not. These women lost their lives from disease, drowning (several died in the German sinking of the hospital ship Llandovery Castle), or from wounds sustained as a result of enemy bombing raids.

Researching the life of MacAdams has been personally enriching. I have forged new friendships, deepened my understanding of the role that Canadian women played in the Great War, and gained a special appreciation of the contribution made by MacAdams and the women of her era. Many individuals and groups have helped me in my research. While all of them have played an important role in the development of this biography, I have had the pleasure of producing it and therefore I am responsible for any of the mistakes and shortcomings that may be found within its pages.

Many libraries, archives and individual archivists provided me with invaluable and gracious assistance. These included the National Archives of Canada, Ontario Provincial Archives, Provincial Archives of Alberta (Marlena Wyman), Imperial War Museum Archives, British Coledale Newspaper Archives, Glenbow Archives (Lynette Walton), Alberta Legislature Library, Lambton Archives (Anne Ashton), Royal College of Nursing Archives (Susan McGann), Women's Studies Library, Ohio State University (Linda Krikos), Guelph McLaughlin Archives at the University of Guelph (Darlene Wiltsie), Moore Museum (Laurie Mason), Sarnia Public Library (John Rochon and Jeffrey Beeler), Edmonton Public Schools Archives and Museum (Lori Clark), and the Orpington Public Library.

The Canada Council for the Arts and the Alberta Foundation for the Arts provided the funding that allowed me travel to England and France to do my research. We are indeed fortunate to have funding bodies dedicated to the support of Canadian writers and artists.

Professors Catherine Cavanaugh and Susan Mann were my "history mentors." They patiently read most of the chapters, providing critical and insightful comments and helpful suggestions. Cathy is passionate about Alberta's female politicians and was the first to encourage me to write about Roberta. Our "history lunches" often kept me going when I needed encouragement. Susan and I kept up a lively e-mail correspondence that enriched me personally and intellectually. When I had a question about the military nurses of the Great War, she was always willing to provide an answer. Maurice Doll, formerly of the Royal Alberta Museum, provided useful information about military insignia and uniforms. Writers Erna Paris and Myrna Kostash read early drafts and gave invaluable editorial advice. Heather Boyd, a long time journalist and editor, did the initial edit of the entire manuscript. Scott Anderson copy edited the book and caught some of my most egregious errors. John King, senior editor of the University of Calgary Press, recommended and oversaw the final revisions. It is a much stronger book as a result of their efforts. It has also been a pleasure to work with such creative people as producton editor Peter Enman and designer Melina Cusano. And Judy Dunlop reminded me that indexing, like writing, is a type of art. Grants Coordinator Kellie Moynihan worked hard to raise the necessary funds to ensure the publication of *Give Your Other Vote to the Sister.* Carol and Rae Allan, Margaret and Jim Robertson, and Diane Buchanan provided some of that funding, for which I am deeply grateful. I am also indebted to Walter Hildebrandt, former director of the University of Calgary Press, for encouraging me to write and submit this manuscript, and to the current interim director Geoffrey Simmins for ensuring its publication.

My mother and stepfather – Rosemary and Herb Heidinger – took me to see the home of the first Women's Institute in Stoney Creek and to the University of Guelph Archives. They also kept their eyes open for information about early Ontario women in addition to taking me to Sarnia for the first time. My mother-in-law Corinne Marshall was always willing to share her father's Great War records and mementos with me. These helped me gain a sense of what the conflict was really like for the Canadians who fought in France. My daughter Rachel Culbertson was a supportive presence who tolerated her mother's obsession with all things WWI to the point that she could sing a very favourable rendition of "Tipperary."

Lesley, Brian, and Terri Stanger provided my daughter, my partner and I with a place to stay during my research trip to Britain. Their warm welcome and wonderful sense of humour often reminded me that I needed to pay attention to the world beyond the dusty halls of archives and museums. James Wheeler, owner of what was once Harry Furniss' house in Hastings, kindly showed me through his home and garden. It was wonderful to see the place where Roberta and Beatrice spent many happy weekends during the war.

Robert Price (Roberta MacAdams' son) and his family provided me with information, papers, and artifacts about Roberta. I especially appreciated the loan of Roberta's purse and military insignia. Monica Newton (Beatrice Nasmyth's daughter) shared the many letters, photographs, and articles written by her mother. Monica's friendship continues to be one of the best results of my research work. Harry Furniss (Beatrice's son) provided useful information and helpful advice. Sheila Gormley (Leslie MacAdams' granddaughter) was always ready to look for information when I needed it. Her warmth and friendship made my research trips to Sarnia very pleasant. Douglas MacAdams provided useful background information and photographs of his grandfather William MacAdams. Neil and Tom Spaulding (Maud Hanna's descendants) found and shared photographs, letters, and memories of the Hanna family.

Several people gave me helpful information. Roger Gallaway (MP for Sarnia-Lambton) sent me copies of articles about Sarnia's political past. Norma Geggie and the Gatineau Historical Society shared their research on Wakefield, Quebec. Bud Squair provided me with a wonderful booklet containing recipes from World War I. Peter Gann and Alan Mustoe sent me useful facts about Orpington. Military historian Laurel Halladay kindly sent me copies of correspondence between an Alberta soldier and his wife during the Great War. Seonaid Laidlaw provided an interesting article about Maud Hanna and her horticultural contributions to Sarnia. I am also grateful to Elaine Waisglas for showing me through the former Toronto home of the Hanna family.

Finally, my deepest thanks go to my partner Heather, who supported me through the writing of this book. She patiently listened when the Great War and Roberta MacAdams seemed to be my only topics of conversation, encouraged me when I struggled to unravel the mysteries of Roberta's life, read and corrected early drafts, and most important, never lost her faith in my ability to write this book. For once, words really aren't enough.

INTRODUCTION:

THE PHOTOGRAPH

Step up to the mahogany and brass camera and look through the viewfinder. When you open the shutter, she fills the lens.

Her face is a soft pale oval underneath a starched white nurse's veil. Wisps of grey hair emerge from under her austere head covering. Her nose is straight and long; beneath it, a slight, tentative smile. But the clear, strong eyes that look out from her face are anything but shy. They stare through you like the blade of a bayonet.

Her name is Roberta MacAdams and she is posing for her election flyer. It is London 1917, a time when soldiers on leave at night struggle to find their way along pitch-black streets while German zeppelins drop bombs and the phrase "air raid" enters the common language.

Hundreds of thousands of Canadians are in Europe to help shore up Britain's and France's defences against a seemingly unbeatable enemy. Roberta is one of those Canadians. She has served at a military hospital; now she is running for election as one of two soldiers' candidates to the Alberta provincial legislature. Her photograph will be printed on seven thousand campaign circulars and sent to prairie soldiers occupying boggy trenches and broken cow sheds along France's front lines. It reads:

> *Soldiers and Nurses from Alberta! You will have two votes at the forthcoming Election under the Alberta Military Representation Act.* **Give one vote to the man of your choice and the other to the sister.** *She will work not only for your best interests but for those of your wives, mothers, sweethearts,*

The photograph of Roberta that started my journey into the Great War.
Provincial Archives of Alberta; A13185

sisters and children after the war. **Remember those who have helped you so nobly through the fight.**

I first saw that yellowing flyer at Calgary's Glenbow Archives more than eighty years after the Great War ended. I was doing research for the "Great War" section of a CD-ROM on Alberta history. That work involved finding information for a short biography on the Great War politician Roberta MacAdams. The archivist didn't need her usual steel-wheeled cart to roll out the "R. MacAdams Collection." Instead, she handed me an oh-so-thin file folder. Inside, on top of a handful of documents, was the campaign circular. I looked it over and set it aside, planning to read through the other materials first. Despite my best efforts, my attention kept being pulled back to it, and to the face of the woman at its centre.

In the weeks following my visit to the Glenbow, the words "Remember those who have helped you so nobly through the fight" began to haunt me. I needed to know more about the woman whose resolute gaze disturbed my sleep. I asked a historian where I might find more information. "You won't discover much about her. Very little has been preserved," she told me. It was a verdict I was unwilling to accept. It would be up to me to reclaim Roberta MacAdams' life.

I had personal reasons for wanting to find her. In the 1980s, I had been a graduate student living in a Victorian walk-up in Toronto. Every March, I would put my books aside, tuck my baby into a stroller, and join the long procession of women protesting against violence and calling for pay equity, racial justice, and reproductive choice. I sang "Bread and Roses" alongside young women with shaved heads and spike collars as well as cane-carrying grandmothers who had been marching before I was born. As we walked arm in arm, I wondered if the women who had fought for our rights at the turn of the century would have recognized themselves in our faces.

Decades after those protest marches in Toronto, sitting in that quiet corner of the Glenbow Archives, it struck me that maybe *we* were the ones who were failing to recognize the women of the past. Their faces were disappearing, and along with them, a vital piece of our own identity and history.

One group of women seemed particularly absent from our collective memory. In my work on the Alberta CD-ROM project, I had spent months scanning library shelves and databases for information about the Great War. I discovered that over the previous twenty years there had been a publishing boom in Great War books. Doorstop-size books by John Keegan, Niall Ferguson, and Margaret MacMillan had crowded onto bestseller lists. Biographers such as Dominic Hibbard and Jean Wilson had drawn compelling new portraits of the Great War writers, and memoirists David Macfarlane and Stephen O'Shea had charted their own journeys "back to the front." Novelists had also plowed the fertile fields of Flanders. Pat Barker's *Ghost Road* series, Sebastien Faulks's *Birdsong*, and Jack Hodgins's *Broken Ground* were all critically acclaimed explorations of the war's wrenching impact on the lives of individuals and communities.

With few exceptions, men were the main subjects of these books. Despite a surge of scholarly interest in women's experience of the Great War, most historians and writers focused on the strategies of generals and politicians, and the battles, mud, blood, and anguish of front-line soldiers. Women were usually only present in short chapters or footnotes describing how they nursed the wounded or "kept the home fires burning." In fiction, they were devices used to help readers understand the male protagonist – rarely the other way around. Some writers left them out entirely, making it hard to believe that women of any nationality ever walked on the martial fields of France and Belgium, sold their bodies on the edges of military encampments, or sailed in the hospital ships that plied the Mediterranean. It was as though the men who lined the trenches had no "before" or "after," and the women who gave them up to war were just so much background music.

Roberta MacAdams was only briefly mentioned in a few history books, notably Jack Granatstein and Desmond Morton's *Marching to Armageddon*. Yet, for a brief period in 1917, her simple campaign flyer would succeed in making her internationally famous as a groundbreaker in women's rights and as a symbol of women's contribution to the Allied cause. In September of that year, she became one of the first two women elected to a legislature in the British Empire and the only female soldier's representative. Her election victory was celebrated in the pages of the London *Times*, Toronto *Globe*, London's *Daily Mail*, *The New York Times*, and the Paris newspaper *L'Illustracion*. Suffrage newspapers such as Boston's *Woman Citizen* championed her election and front-line soldiers read about her success in *The Canadian Daily Record*.

Roberta's absence from the pages of most history books was yet another reminder of the great void in our understanding of women's experience of the Great War. It was a void that would be difficult to fill, as my historian friend had predicted. Roberta was not a prolific writer like suffragette Nellie McClung or a scrapbook keeper like Judge Emily Murphy. Instead, she chucked out every bit of correspondence she received as soon as she had penned a reply. But luck was with me. The obituary of her friend and campaign manager Beatrice Nasmyth revealed that Beatrice's daughter had lived in Vancouver. What's more, the account included her married name – Monica Newton.

As it turned out, Monica was still living in Vancouver. A warm, white-haired woman who would soon become a dear friend, she had boxes of scrapbooks filled with her mother's magazine articles and newspaper clippings. Together we pored over this archive, reading and commenting on prose that still seemed fresh and relevant nearly eighty years after it had been written. Monica had also preserved stacks of Great War letters between Beatrice and her parents. Some described Roberta's election campaign, as well as the friendship shared between the two women. The letters and clippings would soon lead me to articles by other journalists based in the United States, Britain, and France.

Research at the Alberta Legislature Library gleaned articles in which Roberta's speeches were reproduced word for word. Through the miracle of the Internet, I also found Roberta's descendants scattered across the country. Some, like the offspring of her sister Maud, had preserved ancient photo albums and Great War correspondence.

Over a two-year period, I compiled thick file folders filled with evidence of Roberta's presence. Yet something seemed to be missing. Like the families who waited for loved ones to return from overseas service, I felt cut off from what Roberta had experienced in Great War Europe. I needed to see for myself where she lived and worked. In the spring of 2001, I retraced Roberta's footsteps to Britain and France. Even there it wasn't always easy to find her. In busy London pubs and musty archives, she glided ahead of me like some elusive phantom, leaving only dim signs of her passage. Then, just as I would despair of ever finding her, I would come face to face with evidence of her life and work. In a modern hospital in Kent and a rolling graveyard among the sand dunes, Roberta would suddenly seem as close to my skin as the rain that soaked my clothes on a wet spring day in Flanders.

～～～

In May 2001, I was in Boulogne. Roberta had arrived in the port city in December 1917, a few months after her election victory. She was leading the first group of Canadian female journalists to visit France during the Great War (male journalists had already been allowed official visits to the war zone). The women were planning to tour the lines of communication – a vast network of hospitals, ambulance convoys, convalescent homes, roads, supply depots, veterinary hospitals, training grounds, repair shops, laundries, prisoner of war camps, postal services, and cemeteries. Arranged along the northwest coast of France, these vital services were linked by railways, roads, canals, and rivers.

I began my own first day in Boulogne by looking for the site of the Hotel Christol, the first stop on Roberta's tour. In 1917, it was the headquarters for the various branches of the Red Cross, including Canada's. "The Canadian Red Cross offices proved a little oasis for the Canadians whose duty took them to the base, and to the many going on leave or returning to the Front," wrote *Saturday Night* journalist Mary Macleod Moore. "Through those rooms during the war must have passed thousands of officers and men and nurses, who always received a cheery greeting and whatever help could be given to them by the Red Cross before proceeding on their road. Many of them never passed that way again."[1]

Roberta was well acquainted with the Canadian Red Cross. As a dietitian in a major military hospital, she knew that the preserves, fresh fruit, and chocolate it provided were vital supplements to the meagre menu which military hospitals were forced to offer. After her tour in France was over, she would go on a cross-Canada speaking tour, promoting the organization and encouraging Canadians to keep supporting it. Shortly before Roberta and her party arrived in France, the Red Cross had won the Nobel Peace Prize for its work during the first few years of the war.

At the tourism office on the Boulevard Gambetta overlooking the busy harbour, I asked if the Hotel Christol was still standing. Making a sweeping motion with her arm, the staff person replied, "It is all gone – everything was bombed in the Second World War. You will not find it." She sold me a guide to the British military cemeteries of Boulogne and gave directions to a bookstore where I might find more information about the area.

It started to rain as I made my way along the boulevard. The woman at the tourism office was right, of course. How could I expect Boulogne to appear anything like it had when thousands of troops marched along its narrow streets? A glance along the dock revealed a jumble of hotels and restaurants, their square lines and blank facades clearly indicating post–World War II construction. Yet as I turned and made my way up the hill, away from the harbour, I was immersed in the city as Roberta might have seen it. The wrought-iron balconies, tall windows, and stone houses had been constructed just before the beginning of the Great War.

It was important not to lose oneself in such meditations. Crossing the crowded streets was dangerous, since the French seemed to view driving as a contact sport. After yet another narrow escape at a crosswalk, discouragement set in. Here I was, doing research about a seemingly obscure woman in a country where I didn't know the language and lacked a detailed map to the sites that she had once visited. But I was there, and so was she.

At the bookstore I purchased some local histories, including one that contained a series of old postcards. Walking back towards the pier, with rain running down my neck, I opened the book. It fell open to a photograph of the Hotel Christol.

〜 〜 〜

I took the train to St. Omer. That was the station nearest the small Village of Arques, where "Number 7 Stationary Hospital" operated in an abandoned mill during the Great War. It was one of the many hospitals that Roberta visited during her tour of the French coast. In what marked the beginning of a series of coincidences, I arrived on May 14, the anniversary of the day that the small hospital was established. Leaving the train station, I crossed an old stone bridge and walked along the quiet canal that connected St. Omer and Arques. It was overcast, with a soft spring breeze rustling the branches of the heavy chestnut trees that hung over the water. The only people I met were fishermen sitting quietly along the shore, their lines taut.

When I finally reached the old stone buildings that lined the main road of the village, it began to pour with rain. I huddled under a narrow awning, eating sweet, custardy "mille feuilles" purchased in a closet-sized patisserie. Most of the buildings appeared to predate the war, and I imagined Roberta and the other women, their skirts swishing on the mud and snow, their curious faces scanning the aged buildings. But the physical signs of their passage remained elusive. I did not find the mill that Roberta and her friends toured, and the only chateau worthy of the name belonged to the owner of Cristal d'Arques – the local maker of fine leaded crystal. The building was a pile of tan stone at a busy intersection, across from a cemetery that contained both war graves with their simple white headstones and garish stone angels, memorials to the longer dead.

A few days later, I stepped out of a bus onto another quiet street, this time in the Village of Etaples. I stopped at a café and ordered a cup of thick espresso before hiking back to the Boulogne Road and on to the Etaples Military Cemetery.

The cemetery was located on part of what was once the site of the largest complex of military hospitals that any country has ever built abroad. At any one time, as many as twenty thousand wounded men filled its beds. Here, Roberta visited with Canadian women who nursed, volunteered as "Volunteer Aid Detachments," and drove ambulances. Their bravery under fire would shift, once and for all, her understanding of male and female roles. "I don't know what is the work of women and what is the work of men," Roberta told an interviewer. "I don't think we'll ever be able to straighten it out again."

One of the hospitals that Roberta toured in Etaples was Number 1 Canadian General. I wondered how she felt when, a few months after her visit, the hospital was bombed into oblivion and three Canadian nurses were killed. It began on the night of May 19, 1918. That evening, fifteen German planes attacked the hospitals. Within two hours, 116 bombs were dropped. One made a direct hit on the nurses' quarters, setting it on fire. Canadian Nurse Katharine MacDonald died instantly. Nurses Gladys Wake and Margaret Lowe were terribly injured. Wake, probably recognizing that she was unlikely to survive, begged black-faced stretcher-bearers to leave her and save themselves. Despite her protests, they pulled her from the burning hut. Above them, German planes flew low, sending a spray of machine gun fire among the rescuers. Throughout the raid, nurses aided the wounded, rigging up makeshift operating theatres. Some assisted with surgery, taking the place of orderlies who had just been killed.

While most patients and nurses were instructed to lay beneath their beds for protection from flying glass, the three hundred men in Number 1 Canadian General who were anchored to their beds with fractured femurs had to remain where they were. Many nurses chose to stay nearby, calming their patients' fears. As morning dawned, sixty people were dead or dying. Katharine MacDonald, Gladys Wake, and Margaret Lowe were among them.

I was in Etaples Military Cemetery on the anniversary of that May raid. From the wide concrete platform overlooking the cemetery, I looked down on a vast, rolling green hill, banked with the railroad tracks that once transported soldiers and supplies. In front of me were nearly twelve thousand identically shaped white headstones, arranged in neat rows like the hospitals that once stood nearby. In one of the stone monuments overlooking the graves, there was a compartment with a copper door. Inside were books with the names of the dead and directions to where I could find the location of the graves of the Canadian women who were mortally wounded on that May evening in 1918.

The words on the simple white stone cross that marked Gladys Wake's grave read: "The noble army of martyrs praise thee." The epitaph seemed appropriate for a woman whose last words were "Tell them not to be sorry, but glad, and tell them to carry on."[2] It was the kind of stiff-upper-lip response that was embraced by Roberta and many of the women who served overseas. In the visitor's book at the entrance to the cemetery I scrawled an epitaph of my own, dedicated to Gladys and Roberta and all the Great War women: "We remember you."

Late that afternoon, sitting in an out-door cafe off the Place Charpentier in Boulogne, I scanned curling photographs and faded newspaper accounts of the women's tour of France. Once again Roberta stared back at me, this time in her dress uniform, all bundled up against the damp December cold. Someone touched my elbow and I looked up to see a woman standing near my table. She was wearing a long blue dress and her hair was wrapped in a white scarf. Over top was a starched white apron with a red cross emblazoned on the bib. For a few seconds I was convinced I was hallucinating. Then she held out a tin can with the "Croix-Rouge Francaise" label on the outside. She was collecting for the French Red Cross. I emptied my pockets.

PRELUDE:

THE SPEECH

A tall, slender woman with grey-streaked dark brown hair and Irish blue eyes is speaking in the hushed legislature. One of her black-gloved hands holds her speech in front of her. The other rests in a soft fist behind her back. She wears a navy blue dress uniform with a double row of gold buttons down the front. On her shoulders are the twin stars of a lieutenant in the Canadian Army Medical Corps. It is Edmonton, Alberta, February 27, 1918. Her name is Roberta MacAdams.

> *"Mr. Speaker: As a beginning member and as one quite unversed in the manners and customs of legislators, it would be naturally my inclination to remain seated for a season at least, to sit at the feet of those of ripe experience and finished proficiency. But in this time of stress, one's inclinations go to the wall. The signal honor and the very grave responsibility which is mine to represent Alberta's overseas fighting men, seems to impose upon me the responsibility to say at least a few words on matters directly affecting them. And therefore, Mr. Speaker, I must crave your indulgence and the indulgence of the House, towards any errors or transgressions which I, in my ignorance, may commit."*

Roberta's voice is as clear and sharp as the ice that hangs from the columned porch of the domed legislature. The men who fill the assembly chamber listen intently, some with slight smiles on their faces. It's only the second time a female representative has made a speech in a legislature anywhere in the British Empire and the first time that one has done so wearing a military uniform. Most of the members of the assembly are enjoying the spectacle. It's a bit like watching a dog walk on its hind legs – possible, but rare. Some may detect a note of irony in her words, but brush it off as highly unlikely coming from such a feminine and distinguished-looking woman.

What these black-suited politicians do not realize is that the woman they see before them is a mass of contradictions. Roberta MacAdams is a groundbreaking female politician who, until her election campaign, had not seen the necessity of women obtaining the vote. As a professional woman, she has benefited from the women's rights struggle, but she has never supported it. Yet here she is, ready to fight for the rights of soldiers, nurses, and the families who wait for them.

Newspaper articles portray Roberta as being without political ambition. What they do not say is that she has deep political roots. She's the granddaughter of Irish Protestants – one of Canada's largest immigrant groups, and one of its most political. Her paternal grandfather was a soldier fervently loyal to the British crown. Roberta's father was a political "backroom boy" who used his newspaper business to promote the Conservative Party, and her famous brother-in-law – William Hanna – was a member of Prime Minister Borden's cabinet. She has spent a lifetime watching her family's political exploits from the sidelines. Now it is her turn to enter the political ring.

CHAPTER 1

AWAY FROM THE FAIR ISLAND

Oh, it being in the month of August, eighteen hundred and thirty-three
My parents they forced me for to leave my count-r-y
To leave this fair island where my first breath I drew
They forced me to Americay, my fortune to pursue.

The reason that they banished me I mean to let you hear
Because I would not break my vows I made unto my dear
'Twas on the Monarch of Aberdeen from Belfast we bore down
We hoisted English colours, to Quebec we were bound.

Sailing on the ocean, no danger did I fear
My mind was on the one I love, my charming Sally Greer
The wind blew from the mountains, it tossed us to and fro
Our ship she struck against a rock, to pieces she did go.

Oh, it was on St. Paul's Island for three long days we lay
The cold ground being our bed, and our covering was the sky
Of three hundred and fifty passengers, only thirteen reached the shore
rest of them to the bottom went; they sank to rise no more…

It's now I'm in a strange country, my sorrow to bewail
No friends or relations to hear my mournful tale
But I hope to be in Ireland before another year
Where I can rove in splendour with my charming Sally Greer.

(Sally Greer, Traditional Irish Canadian Folk Song)

The ship creaked and groaned as the waves beat against its solid wooden hull. Inside her cabin, Mary McAdams cradled her sleepy son Robert while her eight-year-old daughter Margaret leaned against her shoulder. Mary's husband William was out on the deck, escaping from the claustrophobic confines of the room that had been their home for three weeks. The night sky was as black as the inside of a coal bin, the stars and moon as bright as a hundred oil lamps. Rolling seas surrounded the ship, an endless expanse of water that could be calm one moment and violent the next. Tonight, the sea seemed to have made a compromise. It heaved like a pan of water on a low boil, bouncing just enough to make queasy passengers fill their slop buckets, but calm enough to allow the captain to really enjoy his nightly shot of brandy.

Standing on the shifting deck, William must have wondered about his decision to move his family to Canada. Everything he owned and treasured was sailing within this great floating woodpile. Ahead of him lay a wilderness he'd never seen. Behind him was Britain, and before that, his native Ireland. In between was this long voyage on an uncertain sea.[1]

In the 1840s, immigrants to North America needed strong constitutions to survive the Atlantic crossing. Food was often poor and sanitation impossible. William and Mary were more fortunate than most. They probably had enough money for a private cabin. Ninety-eight percent of passengers travelling to North America made the trip in steerage. They were assigned bunks in the dark, foul-smelling space beneath the ship's deck. Each family was allotted approximately ten square feet of space per adult and five feet per child. Unlike cabin passengers, who ate the same food as the captain, those in steerage had to bring their own provisions and cook them over open grates on the ship's deck. The only items the captain was required to provide were fresh water (it was often anything but) and a ration of rancid biscuits.[2]

All passengers – rich or poor – shared some fears in common. Shipwrecks (as the famous song "Sally Greer" attests) were not infrequent[3] and cholera and typhus were common shipboard illnesses.

Only the strong and the lucky survived an ocean voyage; 10 to 20 per cent of those who set out for Canada died before the end of the trip. Their bodies were wrapped in homespun sheets, laid on planks balanced on the edge of the ship's deck and allowed to slide down into the hungry waves.

These were grim thoughts. Those struggling to survive the harsh journey were better off closing their eyes and trying to imagine better things. William's mind may have turned to his hometown of Londonderry, a long, pear-shaped strip of land in Northern Ireland, set in the crook of the winding River Foyle. Londonderry's narrow northern tip was surrounded by a mile-long, red-tinted seventeenth-century wall. It enclosed the original town, founded sometime in the Middle Ages.[4]

Londonderry was famous for St. Columb's Cathedral, a pile of weathered stone that soared upward, culminating in a spire as delicate and high as any found in London or Paris. It was an Anglican cathedral in a very Protestant town. In 1613 King James had declared the county a "London Settlement" and settlers from Scotland and England were encouraged to move there by merchants based in London. Many of these immigrants prospered, the result of preferential treatment by the British government. In the late seventeenth century, Irish Roman Catholics were not allowed to own land or lease it for long periods. By the time these laws were abolished in the 1770s, most of the best land was in the hands of Protestant "Anglo-Irish" and "Ulster Scot" landowners.[5]

These landowners were intensely loyal to Britain and embraced many of the worst qualities of British aristocracy. They lived the lives of country squires on rambling estates with well-stocked pantries and large staffs of servants while their land was divided into tiny plots and leased to poor tenant farmers. The farmers – about 80 per cent of Ireland's population – were mostly Roman Catholic. It was small wonder that many of them resented the landowners and began to fight back against the unfair ways they were treated.

Mary and William were members of the Church of England[6] and may have grown up in privileged landowning families. If this were so, it would not have guaranteed their fortunes. In the decade before Ireland's Great Famine, 25 per cent of Irish landlords were insolvent, the result of poor management and changing tax laws.[7] Younger sons of upper-class parents sometimes found themselves with few prospects and hoped that emigration would offer them new opportunities.

Whatever the reason, William pursued a career in "Her Majesty's Royal Engineers."[8] The Engineers were responsible for the design and construction of all military buildings in Britain and her colonies, including barracks, storehouses, chapels, and offices. All officers in the corps were trained at the Royal Military College in Woolwich, England, and that may explain why William, Mary, and their four-year-old daughter Margaret moved to Britain sometime around 1840.

The family wasn't alone. Between 1780 and 1845, roughly 1.75 million people left "the fair island."[9] The majority were Roman Catholic farmers and labourers, seeking their fortunes anywhere but on the shrinking scraps of land available to them in their homeland. But Protestants also left, hoping to expand the possibilities open to themselves and their families. Most migrants went to Britain, but many also made Canada their destination. So many, in fact, that between the 1830s and 1880s, the Irish made up the single largest ethnic group in English Canada.[10]

Around 1844, the McAdams family joined the exodus to North America. Family records don't reveal what motivated them to make the journey, but William may have been among the Royal Engineers dispatched to oversee the building of fortifications to protect Kingston's harbour and the Rideau Canal.[11] The British government, nervous about a potential invasion of its colonies by the United States, was sending its engineers to help shore up Canada's defences.

The McAdams' survived their long ocean voyage. The next mention of the family places them in the Township of Wakefield, Quebec, just north of Ottawa (known as Byfield at that time). According to historian Norma Geggie, Wakefield was a large farming community bisected by the La Peche River and bordered on the east by the wide, fast-flowing Gatineau. Pine-covered rolling hills ran down into sloping valleys and plains.[12]

Wakefield had been largely settled in the 1830s by newcomers from Northern Ireland, a fact that may well have appealed to William and Mary McAdams. By the time they arrived, the township had a gristmill "manufacturing Oatmeal and Flour of a superior quality." A woollen mill and sawmill went up soon after. By the late 1840s, the community had a general store stocked with bolts of fabric, lace tablecloths, and the latest men's collarless shirts. There was a one-room school (with thirty-five pupils by 1849) and a Presbyterian church. Most people in the township were living on established farms, roughly one mile apart. However, the census for 1851 also records that there were shoemakers, coopers, a carpenter, tavern keeper, and tailor living in the area.[13]

The evidence that recorded the McAdams family connection to Wakefield was a sampler sewn by Margaret McAdams. It was an alphabet, inscribed "Below som[e] repeated alphabets – Margaret McAdams, February 10 1846, Wakefield."[14] Another of her samplers, carefully framed, had "religion" as its theme – a sombre faith expressed in tiny multicoloured stitches:

> *Holy source of purest pleasure*
> *Bliss that never knows alloy*
> *Be thy precepts all our treasure,*
> *And thy practice all our joy.*
> *Lead us through this vale of sorrow,*
> *Safely to the darksome tomb,*
> *There is an everlasting morrow,*
> *Dawning shall dispel the gloom.*

The sampler revealed a child who knew the meaning of death, gleaned from a nightmarish ocean voyage.

During the next eight years, four more children were born to William and Mary – Daniel, William, Arthur, and Isabelle. Little is known about the movements of the family during this time. They resurfaced in the historical records in 1863 when William

McAdams purchased a 125-acre lot in Minto Township and cleared the land with the help of his family.[15] It wasn't an easy task. The area had only been settled six or seven years before. Llewellyn and Leonidas Chaloner, two Welsh brothers living in Minto at the time, observed that the local soil was made up of a rich loam containing clay, sand, and isolated spots of gravel. "(T)he progress made under disadvantageous circumstances is certainly creditable and praise-worthy," wrote the brothers.[16]

Minto Township was also very isolated. Only a few rough roads had been cut through the bush, and its main centre, Harriston, barely qualified for the label "village." It had one general store, two taverns, a church, and a school. A far cry from well-settled Ottawa and pastoral Wakefield, where neighbours were usually only a mile apart. Yet, despite the "disadvantageous circumstances" described by the Chaloner brothers, William did manage to prosper, becoming an "influential citizen" according to *Biographical Sketch of Wellington County*. Unfortunately, William wasn't able to enjoy his success for long. In 1867, only six years after the family settled in Minto, William McAdams died at the age of sixty-seven.

The farm passed into the hands of the patriarch's youngest son, Arthur. Leaving land to the youngest or second youngest son was a common practice among Irish immigrants.[17] While their fathers were still alive, older sons were given money or other types of support to help them get out on their own and start a living. By the time the head of the family died, the youngest son was often still at home, helping with the family farm. The land would be left to him, along with the responsibility of caring for his widowed mother.

This arrangement suited William's eldest son Robert. The toddler who had made the rough Atlantic crossing with his parents in 1844 was now twenty-four. Robert was an ambitious, intellectual young man with more interest in books than ploughs. He had begun work as a reporter for the *Advocate*, a newspaper in Mount Forest, ten miles northeast of Harriston. It was the beginning of his lifelong passion for the newspaper business.[18]

✌ ✌ ✌

The year his father died was also the year that Robert McAdams married Catherine Brown, a soft-spoken woman from Aberdeen, Scotland. She was tall and slender, with prematurely grey hair and deep-set eyes that her children would inherit. Little is known about her personality, except that she had an open and positive disposition that endeared her to a wide circle of friends.[19]

Between 1868 and 1872, Catherine gave birth to three daughters – Mary, Maud, and Margaret. With a growing family to support, Robert moved from being a reporter to a publisher. It was a smart move – journalism in the nineteenth century was an uncertain career with poor salaries and long hours. In the age before television and radio, many former journalists made their fortunes as newspaper and magazine publishers.[20] Robert began by purchasing the *Advocate* and selling it a year later to buy another – the *Petrolia Advertiser*.[21]

It was a time when newspapers were clear about their political loyalties. Robert – like his father before him – was a staunch Conservative. His newspapers provided him with a ready forum to promote his political views. Being politically active was a typically Irish thing for Robert to do. According to historian David Wilson, Irish immigrants to Canada had a "widespread knowledge of how to organize collectively to achieve political ends."[22] Irish Anglicans had a long history as the controllers of local government in Ireland and Irish Catholics had long fought to gain their rights in the political arena. In Canada, these experiences resulted in high numbers of men like Robert McAdams playing influential roles in local, regional, and even national politics.

Robert and Catherine were now living in Petrolia, a booming town in Lambton County on the southwestern edge of Ontario, near the border with the United States. Just a few years before, Petrolia had been a backwoods settlement. However, the discovery of oil in the area in 1866 had drawn investors, entrepreneurs, and workers eager for jobs in the new industry. Soon Petrolia became a town, complete with banks, churches, schools, barbershops, fire department, not to mention lawyers, real estate agents, and doctors. The *Advertiser's* fortunes reflected the boom. Before long, it had over one thousand subscribers.[23]

The prosperity of his business helped Robert establish his family among the ranks of Ontario's growing middle class. But his path to a life of genteel serenity was still haunted by the ghosts of his family's Irish past. In the late 1860s and early 1870s, the yawning gap between Catholics and Protestants back in Ireland made itself felt in the comfortable parlours of southwestern Ontario. Newspapers reported that Canada was about to be invaded by the Fenians, a group of Roman Catholic Irish-Americans who opposed British rule in Ireland. In Lambton County, rumours flew from town to town. One "eyewitness" maintained that a seven-hundred-man army was massing just outside Port Huron, ready to invade Sarnia. Another claimed he'd seen a group of Fenians crossing the ice to the Village of Froomfield.[24]

It's hard to understand how such a rag-tag group could provoke such panic. The Fenians often had more bravado than brains, as one of their drinking songs suggests:

> *Many battles we have won, along with the boys in blue,*
> *And we'll go and capture Canada, for we've nothing else to do.*[25]

Yet there were some reasons to be concerned about the Fenians. Few Canadians believed that the American appetite for new territory had decreased since the War of 1812. Fenian border raids fuelled suspicions that the United States government was using the Irish conflict as a cover for its own interest in gaining a foothold in Canada. Lambton County, on the border with the United States, seemed particularly vulnerable to attack. In 1866, the federal government sent their first armed detachments to Sarnia and over the next few years about four thousand men were lodged in the town. Trains were kept ready to evacuate the town at a moment's notice.[26]

As it turned out, no shots were ever fired in the defence of southwestern Ontario. Yet people in other parts of the country did pay a high price for opposing the Fenians. Nine Canadians were killed in Fenian attacks along the Niagara River,[27] and in 1868,

D'arcy McGee – a prominent Irish Canadian nationalist living in Montreal – was assassinated by Fenians for speaking out against Irish Catholic aspirations.

McGee's death must have been unsettling for Robert McAdams. Like McGee, he was a Conservative Irish Canadian publisher who was unafraid of airing his political views in the pages of his newspaper. That such views could possibly make him a target for extremists might have been an uncomfortable revelation. The Fenian uprising may also have been a potent reminder that the divisions that his parents had left behind in Ireland had followed them across the ocean.

⚬⚬⚬

In 1872, Robert sold the *Advertiser* and became co-owner of the *Sarnia Canadian*, another Conservative newspaper (he would eventually take sole ownership when his partner, Stuart MacVicar, died). He and Catherine moved their young family to Sarnia, little realizing that it would be their home for over fifty years. The town was set on the banks of the St. Clair, not far from where the waters of Lake Huron emptied into the river. Early in the nineteenth century, the densely forested area had been home to the Chippewa. But by the mid-1800s, waves of settlers had changed both the landscape and the face of those who occupied it. French, English, and Scottish newcomers flooded in, building houses and farms. A village emerged from the dark Ontario soil to serve them. After much debate, it was named Port Sarnia after an English channel island which bore little resemblance to the raw pioneer community of rough dirt roads and high boardwalks, wood frame houses, square-fronted stores, a sawmill, blacksmith shop, two taverns and a scattering of churches.

By 1857, the village had become a town that, according to early resident Charlotte Nisbet, wasn't much to look at. "There was nothing very imposing about any of the buildings in the 1860s. I suppose that the Durand block was the only large building in the whole length of [Front Street]. There were a few other brick

Front Street, Sarnia, at the turn of the twentieth century.
Courtesy John Rochon.

buildings but most of the shops were of wood, and some of them very small."[28] In this rural backwater, cows and pigs wandered the streets, grazing in unfenced yards until chased away by wide-skirted women wielding shovels and brooms.

Unknown to Nisbet, Sarnia would soon be transformed by an economic boom. In 1858 and 1859, two railway lines – the Great Western and Grand Trunk Railways – linked the town eastward to London, Toronto, and Montreal. Steam ferries had already stretched the trade route westward to the United States. These were barge-like ships built and operated by the Grand Trunk Railway; each could take as many as nine passenger cars or twenty-one freight cars across the lake between nearby Point Edward and the American town of Port Huron.

Sarnia's entrepreneurs quickly seized the opportunity to ship their goods into the United States and across Canada quickly and cheaply. Within a few decades, the town was a busy manufacturing centre. The King Flour Milling Company, the Doherty Manufacturing Company (makers of stoves), and the John Goodison Thresher Company provided jobs for hundreds of Sarnians. Yet even these businesses would be eclipsed by the wealth shifting uneasily beneath the rich southwestern Ontario soil. In the mid-1800s, oil was discovered in nearby Enniskillen Township. Before the end of the century, refineries would be built in Sarnia, giving birth to the town's petrochemical industry.

Soon, the ramshackle wooden shops that Charlotte Nisbet so despised were being torn down to make way for more permanent structures. The year that the McAdams family moved to Sarnia, the town was undergoing a construction boom. Along fashionable Christina Street, rambling brick mansions decorated with bay windows, wide front porches, and brightly painted cupolas were being built for the town's leading families. By 1876, the street also boasted a three-storey city hall with a central bell tower that overlooked a busy market square where farmers gathered twice a week to sell their produce.

A block away from Christina was Front Street, the town's main avenue. By the 1870s, it was as stylish as any Toronto business district. Solidly built banks, hotels, drug stores, furniture and clothing shops lined its wide dirt avenues and high wooden boardwalks. Catherine could buy the latest fabrics from Toronto and browse glass cases filled with diamond, opal, and turquoise rings at Turner's Jewellery Store. If the family's budget allowed, she could go to El-lis' Dry Goods Emporium to buy a sable fur to wear to parties and "at-homes" during the harsh Canadian winter. Robert, who loved a good cigar, could buy his favourite brand from specialty stores offering "foreign and domestic tobacco."

Front Street overlooked Sarnia's busy harbour on the St. Clair River. On weekends, sightseers crowded the docks to catch glimpses of the paddle-wheelers, ferries, and double- and triple-masted sailing ships that regularly docked in Sarnia Bay. Mail, passengers, and freight were regularly shipped to and from the port. A train station was conveniently located so passengers debarking from the ferries only had to walk a few yards to the station to continue their journeys on land.

Christina Street, home to Sarnia's most fashionable families.
Author's Collection; Postcard.

Sarnia was also part of the federal riding of West Lambton, represented by Liberal leader Alexander Mackenzie – a well-liked local stonemason – since 1861.[29] Mackenzie and the Liberals were overwhelmingly popular. They would hold on to the West Lambton seat for over three decades. Their success was championed in the local Liberal newspaper, the *Sarnia Observer*, the *Canadian's* chief competition.

The fact that his new hometown was a Liberal stronghold didn't deter Robert McAdams or his partner Stuart MacVicar from using the pages of their newspaper to promote the Conservative Party, feature the activities of the Orange Lodge (to which Robert almost surely would have belonged), and criticize what they considered to be the "Romish" leanings of the Liberals.[30] At the same time, both men were pragmatic enough to know that in Liberal Sarnia, they couldn't rely solely on their newspaper to guarantee their financial success. In 1872, the partners expanded their business to include a job printing plant.

That same year, Canada's most popular Conservative, Sir John A. Macdonald was fighting for re-election. Macdonald was a hard-drinking lawyer from Kingston who had a gift for building political alliances among widely diverse groups. He headed the "Liberal-Conservative Party," a coalition of Conservatives, Reformers, and French Canadians. In his first administration, Macdonald made it his mission to build Canada as a nation. He helped bring Manitoba and the North-West Territory, British Columbia, and Prince Edward Island into confederation, and embarked on an ambitious plan to build a railroad that would unite Canada from sea to sea.

Despite Macdonald's tremendous popularity across Canada, Sarnians preferred their own candidate for prime minister – Alexander Mackenzie. On August 21, 1872, the two men met for the debate in Sarnia's market square on Christina Street. Robert and Catherine might well have had ringside seats. They lived only a few blocks from the square and it was improbable that Robert, representing the town's Conservative newspaper, would have missed the contest between the two leaders. Macdonald was in fighting form. He had arrived at the Sarnia docks the night before in the gunboat *Prince Edward*. Crowds poured into the square early in the day. Everyone wanted to be within hearing distance of the two titans. Horse-drawn wagons filled every available space. In a May 2003 article in the *Sarnia Observer*, journalist George Matthewson, describes what happened next:

> Mackenzie opened the showdown with a point-by-point denunciation of Macdonald. Here was a prime minister, Mackenzie thundered, whose spending was out of control, who had given British Columbia six representatives for 10,000 people while Lambton had one for 30,000 who had sullied his hands with double dealing, who had bought votes with public housing. 'That's another falsehood,' retorted Sir John, his face enraged.... The insults and accusations went on all afternoon to the delight of the assembled townsfolk and visitors.[31]

Macdonald would win the election of 1872 with a much smaller majority than he had received in 1867. The victory was anything but sweet. He would resign a year later following disclosures that he had accepted hundreds of thousands of dollars in campaign money from railway giant Sir Hugh Allen. After the election, Allen was awarded the contract to build the Pacific railway, with the proviso that he remove American control from his board of directors – a difficult task, since the Americans had provided him with the money he used to fill Macdonald's campaign coffers. When the Liberals made the scandal public, the government fell and another election was called.

In 1874, the Liberals swept into power and Sarnia's Alexander Mackenzie became Canada's second prime minister. Mackenzie was to serve only one term. His administration inherited the enormous challenge of completing the railway and a nationwide economic depression. While the Liberals were occupied with putting the country back on its feet, Macdonald was spending his time redesigning his party's platform. He fashioned a national policy that rejected the free trade approach of the Liberals and protected Canadian industry through tariffs. Macdonald's new policies appealed to manufacturers, workers, and consumers alike. In 1878, the Tories were returned to power, an unstoppable tide that would only be turned back with Wilfrid Laurier's Liberal Party victory in 1896.[32]

While politicians were busy building the country, Robert and Catherine were building their family. In the years immediately following their move to Sarnia, Catherine gave birth to two more children – William in 1874 and Johnston in 1876. Leslie, the last of the boys, would be born in 1883.

During this period, the family began to spell its name differently. McAdams gradually gave way to MacAdams (both spellings were used by the family for nearly a decade). Popular mythology claimed that "Mac" was a Scottish spelling, while "Mc" was Irish. Perhaps Robert and Catherine were making a concession to Catherine's Scottish ancestry. A less savoury answer may have been that they were simply "re-branding" the family as more Scottish than Irish and – given the Fenian upheavals – eminently more respectable.

Sometime between 1872 and 1880, tragedy overtook Robert and Catherine. Their daughters, Mary and Margaret, died. Today their bodies lie in small, unmarked graves in Sarnia's Lakeview Cemetery. Cemetery records don't provide the exact dates or reasons that their lives were suddenly cut short, but the nineteenth and early twentieth centuries were precarious times for children. Disease, accidents, and hunger took a great toll on society's most vulnerable members. In the late nineteenth century, approximately one half of all the deaths in Canada were of children under fourteen years of age.[33]

The sudden loss of two of their eldest children must have been a terrible shock to Robert and Catherine. They would have known that those children who survived their first few years had a better chance at making it to adulthood. To lose two children who had both safely passed through infancy must have been terribly tragic. The couple kept the memory of the younger of the two girls alive. When Catherine gave birth to another daughter in 1878, they named her Mary.

In addition to Johnston, William, Leslie, Maud and the second Mary, one other daughter would survive to adulthood. On July 21, 1880, a one-line announcement appeared in the births section of the *Sarnia Observer*, right above a large advertisement for lady's horse drawn carriages. The simple statement read "In Sarnia, on the 21st of July, Mrs. Robert McAdams, of a daughter." The name of that anonymous daughter was Roberta Catherine. It was a quiet beginning for a woman who would one day become internationally famous.

CHAPTER 2
CANADIAN BORN

We first saw light in Canada, the land beloved of God;
We are the pulse of Canada, its marrow and its blood;
And we, the men of Canada, can face the world and brag
That we were born in Canada beneath the British flag.

Few of us have the blood of kings, few are of courtly birth,
But few are vagabonds or rogues of doubtless name and worth;
And all have one credential that entitles us to brag –
That we were born in Canada beneath the British flag.

We've yet to make our money, we've yet to make our fame,
But we have gold and glory in our clean colonial name;
And every man's a millionaire if only he can brag
That he was born in Canada beneath the British flag.

(Canadian Born, E. Pauline Johnson, 1903)

The old #39 highway flowed past sprawling farmhouses with pink Rose of
Sharon trees on vast emerald lawns, grey-timbered barns and silver silos, row
upon row of square-baled hay and fields with chest-high corn banked by rows
of evergreens. Sarnia emerged from the corn like a shimmering urban oasis,
spread over a curve of land bordered to the west by the St. Clair River and to the
north by the fingertip of Lake Huron.

On my first day in the city, I walked along the public pathway that lay
between the St. Clair River and Front Street, once the city's main avenue. A
faint, acrid odour hung in the air. It came from "Chemical Valley," the stretch

of oil refineries and industrial towers that lined the river like a cityscape from a science-fiction movie. Billion-dollar plants established here by Amoco, Suncor, and Imperial Oil had long fed the city's flourishing economy. Recently, however, Sarnia's boom had gone bust. Some of the city's largest petrochemical plants had closed or downsized. Their decline had a ripple effect on the city's economy; in 2003, Sarnia City Council posted a $373,000-dollar deficit.[1]

The economic insecurity was reflected in the uneven fortunes of Sarnia's downtown core. A block away from the waterfront, many of the graceful brick shops that lined once-elegant Christina Street were closed, the paint on their battered facades cracked and peeling, their windows scrawled with graffiti. A few businesses remained open; a cluster of pubs, a flea market, tattoo parlour and some second-hand stores. They catered to an uncertain clientele. With the exception of two elderly shoppers pulling wheeled carts, the street was empty. A gust of wind made a fast-food cup bounce along the sidewalk.

Not all of the businesses in Sarnia's downtown core had fallen on hard times. The Front Street waterfront had been renovated as a retro shopping district. Storefronts were restored, and fashionable businesses like Grace Brothers Antiques, Harbour Bay Clothing, and Sincerely Gifts were luring shoppers away from outlying malls. In the windows of LaCache, expensive cornflower-print dresses with matching straw purses and bucket hats filled windows where bolts of fancy sateen and taffeta, lacy handkerchiefs, and lady's calfskin gloves were once displayed to discerning customers.

Inner-city homes were being resurrected, too. A stone's throw from Front and Christina, young families and retirees, eager to escape the cookie-cutter sameness of suburban housing, had moved back into the city's oldest residential neighbourhoods. They purchased dilapidated century-old Gothic Revival homes, removed the warped sheets of plywood that covered their curving windows, replaced the elaborate lacy wood trims that once edged their roofs and painted wraparound porches in muted greens and pale yellows.

One of the streets reclaimed by these urban pioneers was Brock, a quiet road lined with hundred-year-old chestnut trees arching over wide lawns and hedges cut low so that neighbours could still see each other while they weeded their flower beds. Brock Street was the neighbourhood where Roberta MacAdams lived between 1884 and 1908. I had been told that her childhood home still stood, and as I counted the numbers leading me there, I wondered what it would tell me about her life.

The MacAdams' house on Brock Street North, Sarnia.
Author's Collection.

The building at 233 North Brock Street turned out to be a white-sided, two storey house with a wide veranda in front. This porch was flanked by two large screened windows with fluttering white lace curtains and matching green shutters. At the top of the steps leading up to the veranda were two Greek-style plastic urns overflowing with red geraniums, and behind them, two olive green double front doors. The veranda roof provided the floor of the second-storey balcony directly above. An old-fashioned wooden screen door with a half-moon transom overhead led into an upstairs hallway. The door was framed with long, slender windows. On each side of the balcony were two more windows, the twins of the two on the main floor. The roof peaked above the balcony and then spread out on each side like two wings, ready to fly.

It was a large, comfortable, middle-class home, for a large, comfortable, middle-class family. I closed my eyes and imagined Roberta and her sister Mary sitting on a porch swing on a sticky summer afternoon with the scent of lilacs soaking the air. In my mind, Mary — a round-faced twelve-year-old with a long nose and rosebud mouth — sat with her back ramrod straight and unconsciously smoothed her skirt, in case someone should suddenly take a notion to walk up *the path for a visit. Roberta sat next to her sister, her glossy thick brown hair trying hard to escape from a large satiny bow tied at the back of her head. She was slender, with a soft oval face and deep-set blue eyes. Her long fingers held open the pages of a new book by Harriet Beecher Stowe. Roberta hunched over the thick volume — partly to shut out the rest of the world, partly to disguise the height that was already making the ten-year-old feel self-conscious. As the swing shifted, her long, full cotton dress swept the floor of the porch. A warm breeze streamed over the two sisters, as though they were sailing on one of the paddle-wheelers on Sarnia Bay, neighbours waving as they floated by along Brock Street.*

I walked up the steps to the veranda and rang the many doorbells on the side of the house. No one answered. It wasn't a surprise. The house had been divided into apartments for upwardly mobile young professionals, most of whom were at work on that sticky Tuesday afternoon. I walked back down the steps and around the outside of the building, along the long narrow centre wing that jutted out in the back. It once housed the kitchen, pantry, and upstairs bedrooms. At the back of the house, the trap door that led down into the coal cellar butted up against what was once the original kitchen. A large square window overlooked a shady backyard, now partially paved over for tenant parking. When the MacAdams lived here, anyone peeping through the window into the house might have seen Roberta — who loved to cook — sliding heavy pans filled with puffy bread dough into the black interior of a mammoth silver-edged wood stove. The kitchen would have been filled with the heavy aroma of yeast and wood smoke.

Standing outside the kitchen window over a hundred years later, the only smell in the air was the sweet scent of fresh laundry. Yet there wasn't a sign of a clothesline within a mile of the house. Perhaps I had breathed in the scented apparition of the ruffled shirtwaist blouses, collarless men's shirts, and billowing white cotton sheets that were once hung here on a taut rope between two sturdy wooden posts.

⊂⊃ ⊂⊃ ⊂⊃

When Roberta was a teenager in the late 1890s, servants were as basic to the running of an upper-middle-class home as a refrigerator and stove would be to the life of a similar family a hundred years later. The MacAdams family had at least one maid[2] and it would

Roberta in her late teens.
Spaulding Collection.

have been this woman who toted the heavy baskets filled with the family's wet laundry out to the line to dry. She would have also ironed, dusted, swept, blacked the wood stove (and made sure it was kept stoked), and done endless other large and small jobs.[3]

As one of her teachers later observed, Roberta was raised with little experience of the "pots and pans side" of domestic life.[4] In other words, having a family servant freed her and her sisters from the dirtiest and heaviest household responsibilities. This did not mean that they lived lives of leisure. It was a time when homemaking required many hands. Fresh fruits and vegetables had to be grown or purchased, foods preserved for the winter, and meals prepared.

Most young women also sewed – in many Sarnia households a few evenings each week would be set aside for darning, patching, knitting, and crocheting. While "Sitlington's Ladies Dry Goods" on Front Street had begun to offer ready-made blouses and dresses, most women still found it more economical to make their own clothes from yards of crisp cotton, soft, expensive cashmere and serviceable gingham. Although she would never be an enthusiastic seamstress, Roberta would have been expected to make everything from her white cotton petticoats to her thick woollen skirts. Even her best hat was probably her own creation, with its silk pom-poms and wide fabric ribbons arranged on a broad straw brim.

Not every skill, however, was as tangible as a straight seam or a well-made loaf of bread. In their teens, the MacAdams girls gained a reputation for being refined and self-contained.[5] Roberta would one day be described as having "a quiet voice with a quality which readily commands attention, a tall graceful figure, grey hair over a young face, an expression of serenity, and withal, a sense of poise." Her impeccable manners, elevated speech and a dignified bearing were qualities carefully nurtured by her mother. Catherine MacAdams worked hard to prepare her daughters for lives as gracious hostesses, loving wives, and caring mothers. It was, after all, the Victorian age.

According to historian Wendy Mitchinson, late-nineteenth-century Canadians were "inundated with powerful and at times maudlin descriptions of the concept of sexual separation at every level – intellectual, physical, moral and emotional."[6] Sermons, poems, articles, and books celebrated and reinforced women's "natural" role as wives, mothers, and homemakers. No one summed it up more succinctly than Tennyson, in his poem "The Princess:"

Man for the field and woman for the hearth,
Man for the sword and for the needle she,
Man with the head and woman with the heart,
Man to command and woman to obey...

Of all the MacAdams girls, Mary and Maud seemed most destined for the "hearth." Nicknamed "Muddie," Mary was pretty, feminine, religiously devout and at times, stuffy and prudish.[7] Maud was extremely beautiful – tall and graceful, with slightly sloped shoulders, blue eyes and curling dark brown hair. According to her brother Johnston, Mainie (as she was affectionately nicknamed) was "the most human and the most lovable of the clan, and the most self-effacing in good deeds."[8]

Older than Roberta by nearly a decade, Maud frequently had to act as a second mother to her sisters. Catherine MacAdams was in fragile health, perhaps the result of her many pregnancies. During periods when she was confined to bed, Maud took most of the responsibility for supervising the busy household. Only Roberta – like the boyish sister "Jo" in Louisa May Alcott's *Little Women* – seemed not quite able to fit the Victorian ideal. Nicknamed "Bert," she was tall and awkward, shy and intellectual.

The three sisters were growing up at time when deeply ingrained views about male and female separation were reflected in equally entrenched laws denying women the right to vote or hold political office. Laws concerning property and marital rights put women at an economic and social disadvantage. Middle- and upper-class women who craved an independent life found themselves locked out of many universities and barred from most professions. Some perceived them as biologically unfit for intellectual work.

There were of course, women and men who fought to change prevailing attitudes and laws limiting women's rights. In 1876, Dr.

Emily Stowe – Canada's first female physician – established the Toronto Women's Literary Club, the country's first suffrage organization. In 1893, Lady Aberdeen helped found the National Council of Women of Canada (NCWC). This group was a non-partisan federation of voluntary women's organizations, devoted to improving the status of women and children. Another group dedicated to advocating for change was the Women's Christian Temperance Union (WCTU) – an organization that believed that women's participation in government and society would bring an end to the social and economic problems caused by alcohol.

Little of this activism seemed to trickle down to the MacAdams family. Roberta would later tell reporters that she had only ever been to "two suffrage meetings in my life"[9] and that she had "not always been especially anxious"[10] for the vote. She was a privileged young woman who believed that men and women were equal in dignity but had distinctly different roles in society. The Great War would eventually alter her views, just as it would for many women of her generation.

〰 〰 〰

While Maud, Roberta, and Mary were being prepared for lives as homemakers, their brothers were finding out if printer's ink ran in their veins. Like other young men of the period, Johnston, William, and Leslie helped their father run the family business.[11] The print shop was probably the most profitable part of that enterprise. "The Canadian Job Rooms are supplied with the most modern styles of type and most efficient machinery and possesses every requisite for the turning out of first class job work. Estimates furnished on application," declared one of the company's advertisements.[12]

Only one photograph survives of the interior of the print shop. Taken sometime early in the new century, it shows three young men posed in various locations in the shop. The ages of the men correspond to those of Johnston, William and Leslie and, if so, it may be one of the few surviving images of the three brothers. One stands proudly next to Robert's well-oiled press. A sign dangles from one end, declaring "Capacity: 10,000 Per Hour." Robert MacAdams' penchant for order and discipline is reflected in another sign hanging above a tool rack. It states: "A Place For Everything and Everything in Its Place." It was a message that his daughter Roberta would also absorb. Throughout her life she would have little tolerance for disorder or waste.

Of his three sons, William MacAdams most resembled Robert in appearance and personality. Tall and lean, with a long narrow face and square jaw, he was fiercely independent, choosing to set his own path in life rather than have one chosen for him. In 1900, he would leave Sarnia to move west to seek his fortune.

William's departure would leave Leslie and Johnston to carry on their father's work in Sarnia. Today little is known about Leslie MacAdams. According to his granddaughter, Sheila Gormley (who still lives in Sarnia), he was the youngest child in the family, a friendly, outgoing young man who would one day become a town councillor. Of the three boys, he would show the most interest in running his father's business. Robert trained him to be a printer and, by the 1920s, Leslie would be the only brother still running the "Canadian Print Shop."

Much more was known about Johnston, the eldest of the three boys. By the time he reached the end of his teens, he was six feet tall, broad-shouldered and handsome, with a cleft in his chin, blue eyes and brown hair. Johnston was also cool and rational, an intelligent and articulate young man who could speak four languages fluently.[13] In his early twenties, he would win a writing competition offered by the *London Post* on the "Best Reasons for Tarriff Reform." The prize was a trip to Britain and Europe. According to Johnston, he found himself "addressing great political meetings all over England – with an offer of a constituency if I could have financed it."[14] As events would prove, his sister Roberta would share his keen political sensibility.

≈≈≈

Roberta (with hands behind her back) out for a swim.
Spaulding Collection

In one of her few existing childhood photographs, a smiling Roberta stood on a sandy beach. She wore dark cotton stockings, a wool bathing dress with brass buttons, cotton edging and built in corset. Her unruly hair was stuffed into a ruffled mop cap and there were white bathing shoes on her feet. The photograph was probably taken at Wees Beach, on Lake Huron, one of the area's most popular swimming spots. Roberta faced the camera, her arms crossed behind her back, shoulders bent slightly forward, eyes looking straight into the camera. She was about fifteen years old. Standing beside her was another girl, looking shyly to her right, her bathing costume covered by a cosy-looking jacket. The girl may have been Mary or a friend of Roberta's, out for a day at the beach. After a discreet five-minute plunge into icy cold water (few women knew how to swim in the late nineteenth century) the pair walked together along the sandy beach, basking in the feeling of air on legs that were deliciously free of heavy skirts and petticoats.

Children of the nineteenth century knew pleasures that have been almost forgotten in the twenty-first. In the winter, Roberta could go sleighing with a crowd of friends bundled up against the sub-zero temperatures, or skating at St. Andrew's Rink, a large covered arena in the town's centre. The rink was the place to be for many social events. In mid-February 1897, a masquerade carnival was held there, with costumed skaters swaying across the ice to waltzes played by local musicians playing fiddles with fingers so cold they could barely feel the strings.[15] On Thursday evenings, the rink was reserved for hockey. Scores were posted on the front pages of *The Canadian* and the stands around the ice were filled to capacity as local boys faced off against teams from Stratford, Toronto, and even Detroit.[16]

In spring and summer, cycling was popular, especially among the men of the area. The "Wheelmen's Club" of Sarnia sponsored mass cycling meets drawing crowds of cyclists from as far away as Toronto. They gathered at the market square before setting off on twenty-five-mile races. It is not known whether any of the MacAdams were among the racers, although it would not have been surprising. They were all avid sportsmen who loved to curl and

St. George's English Church,
Sarnia, Ont., Canada

The church attended by the MacAdams family.
Author's Collection; Postcard.

golf. Johnston was also a superb horseback rider and crack shot. There was plenty to hunt – in the summer, the skies above Sarnia were sometimes black with flocks of ducks and geese.

As the town matured, Sarnia developed a thriving cultural scene. Given her interest in the arts, Roberta may have been in the audience for some of the dramas of the Sarnia Little Theatre. It produced lavish plays such as *The Mistletoe Bough*, with a large cast dressed in seventeenth-century court clothes – the men in knee breeches and tails and the women in lacy gowns and powdered wigs.[17] Later, she may have preferred to crowd into the tent set up in Sarnia's market square to watch silent movies such as *How a Wife Gets Her Pocket Money* and *Wedding by Correspondence*. It would have been a daring thing to do. Sarnia's mayor frequently accused theatre operators of showing "disgusting" movies.[18] One operator retaliated by offering a reward to anyone who could prove that the films they were showing were immoral in any way, shape, or form.

The concern about morality wasn't confined to the content of moving pictures. A Boys Brigade Hall, with a swimming pool and track, was built in 1893, as part of a response to the problem of underage drinking and smoking among the town's youth. "The mayor made a statement to the council and asked for the assistance of all the members of the council and of every moral man in Sarnia, to put an end, if possible, to an evil of which many complaints had been made to him, namely, lads frequenting the Chinese laundry and Jim Higgins store and getting cigars and whiskey there," wrote Robert MacAdams on the front page of the *Canadian*. Although Robert was a temperance enthusiast, he wasn't as worried about cigar-smoking – all three of his own sons would take up his cigar habit.

The most important center of social activity and public morality in the late nineteenth century was the church. Sarnia had many – St. Andrew's Presbyterian, Central Methodist, and the Church of Our Lady of Mercy. The MacAdams attended St. George's, the newly built Anglican church just around the corner from their Brock Street home. Robert had strong religious convictions. He became the church's Vestry Clerk, taught Sunday School and helped a local Anglican missionary translate the Bible into Chippewa for the Native people in the area.

There was another reason that Robert wanted his family to attend the prominent congregation. Its members included the Pousettes, Salters, Pardees and Gurds, the small group of families who formed the thick cream of Sarnia society. They were the doctors, lawyers, land speculators, and politicians who donated the church's altar, ornate carvings, and stained glass windows. As a prominent local publisher, Robert wanted his family to take their rightful place among other movers and shakers.

Each Sunday morning, the MacAdams family filled a pew at the cathedral-style Anglican church while white-bearded Rev. Davis stood in the high oak pulpit, preaching the law and gospels in a velvety Irish brogue. Born in County Kilkenny in 1850, Davis was a member of the Masons and Knight's Templar, semi-secret groups that drew men together to explore their moral and religious values and to do charitable work in the community. He was also chair of the local school board and was the main speaker at the opening of the Sarnia Collegiate, the high school that Roberta attended.[19]

The MacAdams children were expected to pay close attention to what Davis had to say. As Sara Duncan says in her turn of the century novel *The Imperialist*, the words of most religious leaders of the late nineteenth century were taken very seriously by their parishioners.

> [The priest] had what one might call prestige; some form of authority still survived in his person, to which the spiritual democracy he presided over gave a humorous, voluntary assent.... A particular importance attached to everything he said and did; he was a person whose life answered different springs, and was sustained on quite another principle than supply and demand.... [The church] was his dominion, its moral and material affairs his jealous interest, and its legitimate expansion his chief pride.[20]

Davis was known as a "true shepherd... an ever active worker both in Sunday School and Church."[21] It may have been his blend of high Anglicanism and educational fervour that would influence

Roberta to one day plead for more inspiration in educational life. "Patriotism and citizenship cannot be taught in the abstract," she would argue, "they must be the outcome of good teaching of all the virtues."[22]

Davis was also a constant visitor to the homes of his parishioners.[23] When he came to tea at the MacAdams', all the women in the family would pitch in to make the house presentable. The family servant was likely handed a wicker basket and sent to the downtown market to barter with farmers for the freshest vegetables and fruits to grace the gleaming dining room table. The regular late afternoon meal would expand into something a little more elegant than usual and Catherine and her daughters would prepare special delicacies – perhaps scalloped oysters, chicken salad, pickled pears, white rolls and butter, and thin slender slices of cold tongue. Catherine would pour hot tea from a silver pot into wafer thin-china cups, while one of her daughters would offer cream and sugar in a matching pitcher and bowl. On those days Roberta may have made and served fat slices of the tangy-sweet lemon pie that would become a well-known specialty of hers. One-half cupful of lemon juice, grated rind of one lemon, one and one half cupfuls sugar, five tablespoons cornstarch.[24]

❦❦❦

I had made a full circle of the house and was standing in front of the screen window leading into what had once been the dining room. There was a breeze and the white lace curtains parted to reveal a large, leggy spider plant obscuring the view into what was once the dining room. Looking through the same window on a late summer afternoon in 1893, one might have seen a tidy Victorian clutter, heavy draperies pulled back, a silver tea service on a long sideboard on one side of the room, plates filling a rail high above. The tea dishes would have been cleared away and the family would still he gathered around the table. Maud might have placed a cut-glass vase filled with light purple asters on the table, and the dusky light from the window would have poured around the blooms and sent long shards of petal-shaped shadows down the table towards

Robert. He would be holding his lapel with one hand and sweeping the air with the other, reciting in his Ontario accent, with its touch of the Irish, one of the many poems locked in his memory. "Half a league, half a league, half a league onward, all in the valley of death rode the six hundred. Forward the Light Brigade."[25]

Robert was passionate about literature. In the 1870s, he had been elected president of the Sarnia Mechanic's Institute, a type of club for local business-men who wanted to improve themselves by sharing books and newspapers. The Institutes resembled the "Reading Societies" that developed in northern Ireland in the late eighteenth century. As historian Donald Akenson suggests, these Societies enabled those who wanted to improve their social standing to "smooth down roughest edges of a harsh society."[26] Similarly, the Mechanics' Institutes prepared upwardly mobile newcomers to Canada to take their place in the genteel parlours of their new homeland. Such institutes promoted Victorian morality, self-sufficiency, and intellectual life, three causes that Robert's daughter Roberta would also one day champion.

In 1899, Robert was asked to chair a committee to build Sarnia's first public library.[27] After it was built, he lobbied town council to keep its services free, despite the fact that many public libraries operated on the basis of paid memberships. The library was for the people and must be made available to the people, he argued. "The idea is to get the public to realize that the Library is their Library," he told an interviewer. "(T)hat the books which it contains are their books; and that the employees and members of the board are at their service for any information or assistance which they require."[28]

Roberta shared her father's love of books. Throughout her life, she was devoted to the promotion of literature and education. According to one writer, she became an insatiable reader whose homes were always "full of books, good friends, good food, laughter and love."[29]

Robert's other great passion – politics – would also be embraced by his youngest daughter. In the years that Roberta was growing up, her father be-came more active in the back rooms of Sarnia's Conservative riding association, using his newspaper as a launching pad for some of the area's rising political stars. One of these was a young, charismatic Sarnia lawyer named William "Jack" Hanna. Jack would provide Roberta with her first lessons about the public side of political life – its triumphs and its costs.[30]

CHAPTER 3

FAMILY MATTERS

How sweet it is to sit 'neath a fond father's smile,
And the cares of a mother to soothe and beguile!
Let others delight mid new pleasures to roam,
But give me, oh, give me, the pleasures of home!

Home! home! sweet, sweet home!
There's no place like home!
To thee I'll return, overburdened with care,
The heart's dearest solace will smile on me there.

No more from that cottage again will I roam,
Be it ever so humble, there's no place like home.
Home! home! sweet, sweet home!
There's no place like home!

Mid pleasures and palaces though we may roam,
Be it ever so humble, there's no place like home.
Home, home, sweet, sweet home!
There's no place like home! there's no place like home!

(Home Sweet Home, John Payne, 1822)

I was getting to know Sarnia. I could find my way around Roberta's old neighbourhood as easily as the one where I had spent my own southern Ontario childhood. My street had been a lot like Roberta's — rambling brick houses with long lawns and narrow pathways, rose bushes pushing against picket fences, tall trees shading pebbled sidewalks, kids on bikes looping back and forth from the road to the sidewalk and back again. Even the library – a ten-minute walk from Roberta's house – was like the one where I worked as a teenager.

The Sarnia Public Library was a rectangular box with glass and chrome doors. As I walked inside, I could smell the familiar scent of pine floor cleaner hanging in the air and see long rows of bookshelves and reading tables surrounded by worn wooden chairs. I had come to look at back issues of the **Sarnia Observer** *to see if there was any sign of Roberta or her family in the pages of the one-hundred-year-old newspaper. I would have preferred to look at Robert MacAdams'* **Canadian**, *but only four issues out of a few thousand had been preserved.*

I was soon spinning the dial of a manual microfilm reader, watching as years of Sarnia history whirled past. It was like sitting at the controls of my own time machine, moving backwards and forwards through time and space. Women's gowns magically grew wider, men's shirt collars thrust higher. At times the themes in the headlines – free trade, military funding, and political patronage – seemed so familiar, it was as though I were reading current newspapers. Then a headline about votes for women or railway scandals would remind me that I was living in Roberta's past – not my own.

The dial slowed as I spotted an article that read: "The new Collegiate Institute was formally opened yesterday afternoon. The splendid programme arranged for the occasion by the committee was successfully carried out in the large hall which takes up the whole of the upper flat of the building."[1] More spins of the dial and a photograph of the Collegiate emerged – three storeys tall, with six peaks and countless tall windows.[2] This sprawling Victorian building was the high school Roberta entered in 1893.

～ ～ ～

Roberta glanced at the frost-coated window and shivered.[3] Her soft green wool skirt, lamb-chop sleeved blouse, and fitted jacket[4] were no match for the forty-below chill that was freezing the thin glass panes.[5] The mammoth furnace of the Collegiate was as inadequate as the pot-bellied wood stove that had been the sole source of heat in the small elementary school she had graduated from the previous June. The only saving grace was that the frigid weather kept her awake during Mr. Grant's endless lecture on

The Sarnia Collegiate.
Author's Collection; postcard.

Latin verbs. He stood at the front of the class, hair neatly parted in the middle, small oval glasses pushed close to his eyes. A stiff white collar was wrapped snugly around his neck and beneath it was a tight-fitting black jacket with small brass buttons. He looked to all intents and purposes like a slender black beetle. Yet if Roberta or any of her classmates fell asleep to his monotonous chirp, they would find themselves rudely awakened by the swift smack of his thin wooden ruler across their desks.

Grant was not only the Classics Master, he was the school's principal.[6] The Collegiate was Sarnia's flagship school – concrete evidence that the town was no longer a rural backwater. The four-storey building had been constructed in 1891 at a cost of $40,000.[7] According to administrators "every facility for the proper instruction of pupils" could be found within its walls.[8] Its gleaming wooden floors, wall-to-wall blackboards, and multi-peaked roof were proof that no expense had been spared in producing a school of which all Sarnians could be proud.

Students were expected to live up to their expensive new school by following a rigorous academic program. Roberta studied Latin, French, mathematics, European and British history, science, physical education, grammar and rhetoric.[9] Of all her subjects, English literature was Roberta's favourite. Within the stiff green embossed covers of her *Ontario High School Reader* she encountered the romantic poems of William Wordsworth, Matthew Arnold, and Alfred Tennyson.[10] Arnold's "Rugby Chapel" was required reading and the extravagant language in this excerpt was typical of both the poet and the time in which he lived:

> *Weakness is not in your word,*
> *Weariness not on your brow*
> *… at your voice,*
> *Panic, despair, flee away.*
> *Ye move through the ranks, recall*
> *The stragglers, refresh the outworn,*
> *Praise re-inspire the brave!*
> *Order, courage, return.*
> *Eyes rekindling, and prayers,*
> *Follow your steps as ye go.*
> *Ye fill up the gaps in our files,*
> *Strengthen the wavering line,*
> *Stabilize, continue our march,*
> *On, to the bound of the waste,*
> *On, to the City of God.*

Roberta didn't know that within twenty years, anyone reading Arnold's words would take for granted that the poet was describing the superhuman efforts of soldiers going over the top in the gory mud of Passchendaele. They would be wrong, Arnold's father had been a schoolmaster; in *Rugby Chapel*, the poet was simply describing his father's commitment to inspire his students. In the sunset of the late nineteenth century, "gaps in our files" and "wavering lines" were still only problems for rugby players and teachers trying to foster a love of Latin among bored young students.

Although she excelled at all her subjects, Roberta was a quiet and unobtrusive student. She was a teenager when women – however gifted – were expected to hide their intellectual light under a bushel lest potential marriage partners find their intelligence threatening or simply unattractive. While she lived in a household where the printed word was revered and intellectual discussion part of daily life, Roberta was also the daughter of conservative parents who placed a high value on respectability and traditional male-female roles. Like most intelligent young women of her time, she adapted herself to the conflicting messages received from home and society. On the outside, she became the quintessential Victorian young lady – quiet, feminine, and self-effacing, a persona so deeply ingrained that over two decades later, a reporter would still be able to write: "Miss MacAdams is very modest about her achievements and desires notoriety least of all."[11]

On the inside, Roberta's mind remained uncorseted. She read widely and was shaped by many of the intellectual issues of the day and the rapid changes in Canadian society. It was an era of unprecedented optimism and national pride. For the first time, Canadians could grasp an image of themselves as one nation. The Canadian Pacific Railway connected east and west and settlers and entrepreneurs were flooding westward to create new lives for themselves. The telegraph was linking people together across provinces and the telephone was starting to connect people within their own communities. Roberta's parents were the first Sarnians to have their own telephone. By 1905, four hundred would be in use.

Intellectual and cultural progress rode alongside the engine of technological change. Canada was now producing its own poets and essayists, painters, and sculptors. The golden paintings of Waterloo's Homer Watson – dubbed "Canada's Constable" by Oscar Wilde – were internationally famous and Canada's history was now deemed important enough to be immortalized on canvas. Painter Robert Harris's mammoth mural "Fathers of Confederation" would soon hang in the Canadian Parliament Buildings in Ottawa and his pictures of domestic and rural life in Canada would be prized by art lovers and historians for generations to come.

By the time she graduated in 1898, Roberta could find the works of Canadians Sara Jeannette Duncan, Bliss Carman, Duncan Campbell Scott, and Pauline Johnson on the shelves of the Sarnia Public Library. While these writers were beginning to articulate what it meant to be Canadian, most children and youth were taught that England (not Canada) was "the most important country of the world, ruling over nearly one-sixth of the whole land surface of the globe and nearly one-sixth of its population."[12] Britain's system of government was to be admired and defended by *all* her subjects – this was what patriotism, duty, and nationhood were all about. These themes were echoed in the pages of Roberta's *Ontario Reader*; Steele's essay "On the Love of Country," Gladstone's "The British Constitution," and the nationalistic hymn "Rule Britannia" all emphasized loyalty to God, Queen, and Empire.

Not all Canadians appreciated the strong ties to Great Britain fostered in the nation's homes and schools. Political journalist Goldwin Smith argued that Canada had little in common with the varied peoples of the Empire and might be better served by a "commercial union" with its closest neighbour, the United States. Other thinkers took a more moderate approach, arguing that Canadians needed to develop their own national identity, one not based on romantic feelings about Britain but on a genuine love of the land in which they lived.[13]

Those debating Canada's status within the Empire little realized that within a few decades, Roberta and the other young students sitting at iron-legged desks across the country would be reconsidering Canada's place in the Empire from the uncomfortable confines of trenches and hospital wards in western Europe. Those soldiers and nurses, set loose on the world, would compare their country with Britain and find the latter wanting. At the end of that war, Roberta would tell a group of young women that "the patriotism of Canadians lay largely in dreams and ambitions. While that of Britain was bound up in history and tradition and fostered by the village church with its peal of bells, and the stately, ancient homes, that of Canada was not so much concerned with material things, but was rather a seeking after ideal citizenship."[14]

Yet on that cold December day in 1893, while Roberta struggled to keep warm in a drafty classroom, these events were still far in the future. She and her classmates were still very much like the land of their birth, a country Roberta described (in much the same way as Pauline Johnson) as a "clean, young, strong unwearied land, with all its big experiences before it."[15]

⁕⁕⁕

As the youngest daughter in a large family, Roberta led a protected life, surrounded by the love and care of her mother and two older sisters. In later years she would argue that "the pressure of modern life has deprived the home of that quiet restfulness which develops the serenity of the soul" – a serenity she had experienced in her own childhood.[16] However, as she entered her late teens, there were shifts in her family life that would disturb that "quiet restfulness" and profoundly affect her future.

The first change came on June 30, 1896. On that early summer afternoon, most of the members of the MacAdams family were gathered together in the front pew of St. George's Anglican Church. It was Maud's wedding day. She stood, her back to the congregation, wearing a beaded cream-coloured gown with a long, filmy train. Beside her stood a short, square man in a high collar and dress suit. The church was packed with well-wishers from as far away as Ottawa, ladies in elegant silk gowns with hats piled high with feathers and broad-bloomed flowers, men in morning coats despite the eighty-degree Fahrenheit temperature. The scent of lemon oil and Lily of the Nile perfume mingled in the air as they quietly watched the couple pledge a lifetime together.

The man that Maud was marrying was William "Jack" Hanna. Those sitting in the polished oak pews might have been forgiven for thinking that he was an unlikely match for the dignified and refined Maud. Jack was ten years older, a rumpled overweight lawyer with thinning hair and large glasses, an avid outdoorsman who loved to hunt and fish. Yet both came from well-established Irish Protestant families, were keenly intelligent and compassionate,

Maud MacAdams (Hanna). Spaulding Collection.

and shared a common political lineage. Jack was a prominent local Conservative and Maud was the daughter of his closest political mentor – Robert MacAdams.

·Maud and Jack had been brought together through a strange combination of politics and personal tragedy. Five years before, fresh out of law school, Jack had eloped with beautiful, red-haired Jean Neil of nearby Point Edward. The wedding was one of Sarnia's biggest political scandals. Jean was the great niece of former Liberal Prime Minister Alexander Mackenzie. Jack was a prominent local Conservative who was being considered as a future contender for a seat in Parliament. Party loyalties shaped one's social circle in the late nineteenth century, and it was sometimes said a mixed marriage was not between Catholic and Protestant but between Conservative and Liberal.[17] The marriage of Liberal Jean to Conservative Jack must have caused tongues to wag over teacups in parlours throughout the small community.

In 1894, Jean Hanna was pregnant. Childbirth in those days was a dangerous process. If the baby was in the wrong position or there was some other complication, both mother and child often died. In January 1895, Jean became one of the unlucky ones. She died a week after giving birth to the couple's only child, a boy who was named "Neil" after his mother.

Jack was devastated and ill-prepared to take care of his infant son. MacAdams family rumour suggests that Robert MacAdams came to his aid, proposing that his eldest daughter manage Jack's home and care for baby Neil.[18] If this was the case, Robert may have had ulterior motives. In an age when women were expected to marry young, twenty-five-year-old Maud was already nearing spinster status.[19] Robert may have hoped that his eldest daughter would make a good match with the grieving widower. Whether or not Maud did step into the breach, in the year following his wife's death, Jack found himself drawn to his mentor's daughter.

Following their marriage, Jack and Maud moved into an elegant two-storey yellow brick mansion directly across from the MacAdams home. Within its large drawing rooms with their gleaming Connemara marble fireplaces and dark oak floors, the

William "Jack" Hanna.
Spaulding Collection.

couple entertained some of the leading political and social figures of their time – from future prime minister Arthur Meighen to Princess Patricia.

With the gracious and well-connected Maud at his side, the political barriers that might have been thrown in Jack Hanna's path by his earlier marriage were removed and Sarnia's teacup gossip was silenced. But the ghost of red-haired Jean Neil would never entirely leave him. Her memory would long be reflected in the face of their son Neil.

∽∽∽

Roberta stood at the window of what had been her older sister's bedroom. It was early evening and the wilting leaves of the mature oak tree outside the window had not yet recovered from the day's humidity. Maud's wedding gown still lay on the bed, ready to be packed and sent to her new home. The wedding had gone well – Maud had looked lovely with her hair drawn back and her small pearl and gold cross hanging from its thin gold chain around her neck.[20]

George Bernard Shaw would one day write, "It is a woman's business to get married as soon as possible and a man's to keep unmarried as long as possible."[21] Maud had successfully completed her "business" and Roberta knew that her other sister, Mary, was intent on following her example. Feminine and pretty, Mary was most likely to catch the eyes of the boys that her brothers brought home. Roberta was another matter. Her interests tended more towards books and study than flirtatious fluttering. The only romance on her horizon was more to be found in the poetry of Pauline Johnson than in a tangible affair with a young man. Besides, Roberta was not yet sixteen. There was some time left before she needed to think about marrying and setting up her own household.

Maud and Jack's marriage would, however, influence Roberta in less traditional ways. Her father had always been involved in the back rooms of the local Conservative riding association and no doubt kept his family well-informed on the kind of debate and consensus achieved while cigar smoke hung heavily in the air. Now, with Jack as her new brother-in-law, Roberta could learn about the more public side of politics.

In late May 1896, just weeks before his wedding date, Jack Hanna had embarked on the first of two attempts at winning a seat in the federal government. Unfortunately for him, the halcyon days of Sir John A. Macdonald were over. The country's most beloved Tory had died in 1891. He was replaced by a series of ineffective leaders, including the aged political warhorse, Sir Charles Tupper, one of the original Fathers of Confederation. Tupper became prime minister on May 1, 1896, a time when the debate over the educational rights of the French-speaking minority in Manitoba inflamed public opinion. His attempts to introduce legislation protecting French rights were blocked by the Liberals and he was forced to call an election.

The Liberals were led by Wilfrid Laurier, a young French Canadian. With his flowing hair combed back, tailored suits, and tiny silver horseshoe pinned to his cravat, Laurier made a charismatic contrast to the gray, rumpled Tupper with his unfashionable sideburns and sagging chins. Laurier campaigned on his charm – astutely managing to avoid taking a definite stand on what was becoming known as the "Manitoba Question." In coming years, he would gain a reputation as a master in the art of compromise, particularly in issues related to language and religion. In Quebec, he would be seen as a traitor to the French, while in Ontario he would be accused of turning his back on the English. "In Quebec I am attacked as an imperialist, and in Ontario as an anti-imperialist. I am neither: I am a Canadian," Laurier declared.[22]

With a little over a month to get the vote out, Jack threw himself into canvassing the voters of West Lambton.[23] But Laurier's silver horseshoe proved to be overwhelmingly lucky. In June 23, just one week before Jack's wedding day, the Liberals swept into power. Jack received so few votes that he lost his deposit.[24]

When local reporters suggested his defeat was the result of his unappealing campaign photograph, Jack answered with characteristic humour. "That wasn't the reason at all. You see those photographs were sent through the mail. The wives and daughters of the voters naturally got them out of the post. They were so infatuated with them that they stuck them up on their dressers at home and spent an hour or so gazing at them. Then when the husbands and fathers came home, supper wasn't ready and they took out their revenge on me."[25]

In the months following the Liberal victory, revenge was also on the mind of Robert MacAdams. He wrote fierce editorials in his newspaper, accusing the new government of being a bunch of "carpet baggers," eager to sell Canadian interests to the United States while flip-flopping on the question of free trade.[26] Meanwhile, Jack licked his political wounds and returned to the booming law practice he shared with partners Richard LeSeur and William Price. Early in his career, Jack had gained a reputation as a successful criminal lawyer. Now his legal interests turned to financially greener pastures. He took on prominent commercial clients, including the Grand Trunk Railway and Imperial Oil.

Roberta watched quietly and learned from Jack's first attempt at political office. His equanimity and humour would be a model for the way that she would approach her own ground-breaking political campaign, and his defeat would remind her that no matter how well a campaign was waged, success was never guaranteed. Jack's growing wealth and political influence would also enable Roberta to one day embark on adventures of her own.

❦❦❦

The crowd filling the bleachers inside St. Andrew's Rink rose as the strains of "The Maple Leaf Forever" emerged from beyond the big double doors leading into the arena. The 27th Battalion military band stepped into view, leading a long and noisy procession of 150 costumed marchers. At the head of the line was "Britannia" carrying a shield and trident. "Canada" followed, her long gown wrapped in red, white, and blue of the British flag. Behind them wound a cavalcade of dancing marchers wearing the supposed national dress of Spain, Canada, Holland, the United States, Japan, Ireland, Germany, and Russia. Riding habits brushed against military uniforms, samurai swords, frock coats and powdered wigs.

Roberta MacAdams was among the marchers. She wore a buckskin shirt over a long plain skirt. Ropes of brightly coloured beads dangled from her neck and a three-feather headdress was pinned to her long brown hair.[27] She was dressed as Pocohontas, the famous Indian princess who had prevented her father from executing colonist Captain John Smith. It was May 23, 1898, and Roberta and the other marchers were celebrating the opening of the Grand Kirmess, a festival organized by local women to raise money for the Sarnia Hospital.

The Kirmess was a distant ancestor of the multicultural fair that would become popular in Canada less than a century later. "The Carnival of Nations: A Brilliant Spectacle at St. Andrew's Rink," read the front-page headline of the *Sarnia Observer* on the last day of the five-day spectacle. Booths were arranged around the arena, each representing a different country. Two large British flags were hung from the ceiling, with a large American flag sandwiched in the middle. Canada's relations with the United States had warmed considerably over the years since the Fenian raids. In 1890, an underground railway tunnel had been built under the St. Clair River connecting Sarnia with the American town of Port Huron and Sarnians now received frequent cordial visits from their American neighbours across the lake.

Roberta was volunteering at the Canadian booth. Her job was to sell miniature canoes and bric-a-brac made of birch bark. In her fringed dress, she made a captivating contrast to her surroundings. The booth was designed to look like a typical red brick home with peaked roofs and wide windows hung with heavy draperies. It was also decorated with all the ambiguities of Canadian patriotism. Framed paintings of Queen Victoria, Alexander Mackenzie, and Sir John A. Macdonald were nailed to the outside of the "building." Perched on the centre of its roof was a stuffed beaver, framed by two small American flags. Hanging from the ceiling above was a banner made from a British flag to which was pinned a shield emblazoned with the words "Canada Forever."

Mary MacAdams was volunteering at the Kirmess, too. She was one of the performers in the dance of "Our Lady of the Snows."

Mary MacAdams (McBurney).
Douglas MacAdams Collection

The dance described the appearance of the Virgin Mary in the midst of a miraculous August snowstorm. Several of the town's leading young ladies were "attired in gowns of sparkling white and carried long white boas around their shoulders and extending to each hand."[28] The intricate movements of the dance and the delicate way that the performers "glided about" were applauded frequently by the admiring crowd.

Not all of the performances were as dramatic. At one end of the arena, the "Kirmess Komedy Kompany" put on the one-act comedy, "Miss Madcap." Some individuals created their own comedy as well. In what was a parody of the Spanish American War,[29] Uncle Sam raided the Spanish booth and triumphantly carried off its bandwagon. When calm returned, the Orpheus Banjo, Guitar, and Mandolin Club "rendered a musical selection under the direction of Prof. Bainey, which was duly appreciated."

The Kirmess revealed the prejudices and the hopes of small-town Canada at a time when the British Empire still seemed to reign supreme and few dreamed of visiting the countries represented in the booths that lined St. Andrew's Rink. There were Irish jigs, Dutch clog dancing, Spanish serenades, a presentation by Japanese performing midgets [*sic*] and a display of a German family celebrating Christmas (with ornaments available for purchase). A sign on the English stall declared "England for her own boys. It is Britannia still."

⤳ ⤳ ⤳

I took a break from the microfilm reader and idly flipped through the pages of a book of photographs on life in early Sarnia. I was working on the "you never know" principle, hoping to find some childhood image of Roberta among the hundreds of images of more prominent Sarnians.

It hadn't been easy to find photographs of Roberta's early life. So far I'd only been able to uncover two – a formal portrait taken when she was about eighteen or nineteen, and a picture of her at the beach. Both were in a box of photographs that belonged to some of Maud Hanna's descendants. They were grainy and smudged, but Roberta's clear-eyed face leaped out at me the moment I saw it.

The difficulty in finding photographs mirrored the challenges of finding textual references to Roberta. It had taken hours in archives, cemeteries, and on the Internet, just to piece together a coherent picture of her early life. At times it seemed like a fool's errand. From the beginning of my research, I had been frequently asked why I wasn't reclaiming the life of someone more famous. A woman like Nellie McClung would make a much better subject for a biography than a woman who was in history's spotlight for such a short time. I should at least choose to write about someone who had left a large library of correspondence, photographs, and published works.

But it seemed to me that the lives of ordinary people who stepped out and did something extraordinary – often in times of national crisis – were much more interesting than the lives of people whose fame preceded them. Roberta was an ordinary young woman whose early life was conventional and respectable – just like the lives of thousands of Canadians who made the exceptional decision to serve their country during the Great War. I wanted to find out what made her suddenly depart from the path of predictability and safety.

While finding information about my "exceptional" woman wasn't easy, whenever I seemed to run out of patience or hope some new image or grain of information would appear and I'd be back in the race again. It happened again with the photography book that I was flipping through. A photograph on page 100 was labelled "Kirmess, May 23–27, 1898." A group had been carefully posed in front of the Canadian booth; young women wrapped in British flags, girls in white gowns hung with flowers and vines, and ladies in plaid blouses over long dark skirts. Sitting on the floor in front of them, looking away from the camera, was a tall young woman wearing an Indian costume. Roberta MacAdams had surfaced again.

❦❦❦

The Kirmess marked the end of an era for Roberta. A few months later, she graduated from the Collegiate. At this point, her education ground to a halt. Higher education was prohibitively expensive, even for many middle-class families. The MacAdams had not sent their older sons to university. It was unlikely they would send Roberta. After all, she would probably soon find a husband, marry, and embark on her proper life's work – managing a household.

Mary MacAdams did indeed fulfill that dream before Roberta. In 1901, she married local salesman Robert McBurney and moved into a home a few blocks away from her parents. With her sisters busily establishing their own families, Roberta had unwittingly become the dutiful spinster daughter living at home with aging parents. At first, she may have welcomed the opportunity to remain in the comfortable cloister of her parents' home. But as the months became years, the walls of the Brock Street house may have begun to feel more limiting than comforting. When Roberta finally began to think beyond the boundaries of her "home, sweet, home," it was her independent brother Bill who would come to her aid.

Although Bill could easily have followed his brothers into the family business, he preferred to achieve success on his own terms. In 1900, he moved to the rough gold-mining town of Sandon, in

British Columbia's interior. There he established his own newspaper, *The Sandon Paystreak*. Like his father, Bill was highly outspoken, airing his opinions freely in his newspaper's editorial pages. In 1902, that quality landed him in jail.

In the early 1900s, cases in the British Columbia justice system faced unacceptably long delays. In front-page editorials, Bill Mac-Adams laid the blame for the delays at the feet of its judges. "We pride ourselves on our British fair play but we maintain a string of judges who are corrupt, lazy, debauched, and prejudiced, and we permit them to conduct the business of the country in a manner that is simply outrageous," he wrote in an editorial in the May 17, 1902, issue of the *Paystreak*.[30]

The young publisher had taken on a tiger. Bill was charged with contempt of court and summarily sentenced to nine months in the provincial jail at Victoria, with four bonds of $1,000 as security or another year in jail. "British justice and it is 5000 miles to the nearest port in Russia," wrote Bill in a report on the trial. Newspapers across Canada, from *The Vernon News* to the *Toronto Telegram* wrote scathing editorials accusing the courts of being more about "law than liberty."[31]

The prison door didn't stay closed for long. Perhaps as a result of the national outcry, the judges granted Bill a pardon with the condition that he write and publish a letter of apology. On August 9, Bill wrote the letter. But it was immediately followed with a long editorial underlining the poor character of justice in the British Columbia courts. "At the price of my liberty I publish an apology," wrote Bill. "I have learned many strange things about courts and contempts of courts recently.... One of the strangest is that it still lies within the power of certain judges to charge and sentence anyone who offends their dignity."

Bill's brave words were his last kick at the justice system in British Columbia. Not long after his release from prison, he closed his newspaper and moved to Alberta to accept two new jobs – one as managing editor of the *Edmonton Bulletin*, the other as night editor for the *Bulletin's* rival newspaper, the *Edmonton Journal*. During the day Bill wrote scathing articles for the *Bulletin*. In the evenings, he rushed over to the *Journal's* offices and wrote editorials taking the opposite view. It seemed an abrupt about-face for a man who preferred to defend opinions one at a time. But working for two newspapers was probably a necessity. In those days, reporters were often paid poorly, if at all – even the paycheques written by the *Edmonton Journal* sometimes bounced.[32]

Bill wrote home to tell the family of his adventures, and his wealthy brother-in-law Jack may have helped him cover his escalating legal bills. But it was Roberta who would be most affected by his wanderlust. One day, a letter addressed to her fell through the brass letter flap in the front door. Bill wanted his youngest sister to join him in the west and seek her fortune. Roberta didn't have the skills or education that would allow her to be successful in such an unlikely venture. But as she turned his letter over in her hands, she began to wonder how she might be able to alter that situation. It would take a few more years, but Roberta would eventually follow the rail-lines westward and join her brother in Edmonton.

While Bill was establishing his name as a small-town newspaper publisher in British Columbia, his brother-in-law Jack was again doing battle with the Liberals. This time, however, he was contesting the provincial, not federal, election. Not only did Jack win his seat, but when his party achieved a majority three years later, he was appointed provincial secretary. For the next few years, he would become famous for championing prison reform, health care, and education. The latter two issues would also become fundamental concerns for his sister-in-law Roberta when she would enter the political ring.

Back in Sarnia, Maud Hanna was immersed in motherhood. On April 13, 1897, just over eight months after her marriage to Jack, she gave birth to a baby girl that she named Margaret.[33] Within a year, a second daughter – Katherine – was born. Maud also embraced the role of mother to Neil Hanna. Raising him was like raising a hurricane. As he matured into adolescence, Neil became the kind of tree climber and horseback rider who kept his parents constantly teetering between pride and fear. Maud shared word of her son's exploits with her sister Roberta, who followed his adventures with interest, becoming more like an older sister than an aunt to a child who was as rough and tumble as his father.[34]

~~~

As she grew older, Roberta began to long for adventures of her own. Before the clatter of milk cans and heavy shuffle of horses' hooves on dusty dirt roads broke the morning silence, she could hear the sounds of Sarnia Bay through the open window of her second storey bedroom. On those heavy, still mornings, her cotton nightgown limp from the heat of an Ontario summer, she listened to the low moan of ships docking and the whistle of the Tashmoo as the long, elegant paddle-wheel steamer eased its way along the St. Clair River.

In the first decade of the twentieth century, Sarnia was no longer the isolated outpost it had been when Roberta's parents had arrived there. It was now a booming port town connected by steamer and train to the United States, and by rail to London, Toronto, and Montreal. As the outside world became more and more accessible, Roberta's personal horizons began to expand. With free rail passes provided by her brother-in-law, she would head off to Toronto to visit friends and find breathing space away from a life that was becoming quiet and predictable.

Roberta's father was now frequently away from home. Robert had retired in 1907 to take a new position as Deputy Registrar-General of Ontario (appointed by his son-in-law Jack). The newspaper and printing operation had been handed over to Leslie and Johnston. It seemed as though the whole family was now busy with their careers or family responsibilities. Around this time, Roberta began to explore new options for her own life. It is not clear what led her to consider further education and a career. She was twenty-seven, single, and had never lived away from her parents. Perhaps she was simply looking for a respectable way to escape the limited life of the spinster daughter. Or maybe her parents encouraged her to set her sails outward. They may have hoped that some "womanly vocation" might bring her into touch with an eligible bachelor who might sweep her off her feet.

Another possibility might have been that Roberta hungered for more intellectual stimulation and was deeply frustrated with her life and wanted independence. She may have shared these concerns with her sister Maud, the only member of the family who had the financial resources to help Roberta get the kind of education that would allow her to escape into the wider world. But what kind of a career might a modern, conservative, respectable, middle-class woman pursue?

A new movement in women's education provided the answer. It was spearheaded by Adelaide Hoodless, a well-to-do wife and mother living in Hamilton, Ontario. In August 1899, Hoodless's fourteen-month-old son died as a result of drinking contaminated milk. Hoodless was shattered by her loss and deeply disturbed that her public school education had not given her the tools to safeguard her family against this tragedy. She feared that many other women shared that ignorance. For the rest of her life Hoodless would actively campaign for the establishment of a wide range of programs teaching the "household arts" to girls and women.

One of the most successful of Hoodless's efforts were the Women's Institutes (WI). This was a network of rural women's groups dedicated to improving homemaking through the study of domestic science.[35] Hoodless was one of several founders who nurtured this organization into being. The first chapter of the WI was established in Stoney Creek in 1897. Within seventeen years there would be 843 chapters in Ontario, with twenty-five thousand members.

In 1906, a WI group was formed in the village of Forest, near Sarnia. It is not known whether or not Roberta MacAdams attended any of their meetings, although she may have heard about the organization. What is known is that in 1908, another of Adelaide Hoodless' ventures caught Roberta's interest. Six years before, Hoodless had managed to convince tobacco tycoon William Macdonald to fund a college for women dedicated to domestic-science education. That college would be named the Macdonald Institute (after its benefactor), and located on the campus of the Ontario Agricultural College in Guelph.

Hoodless' original goal for the Macdonald Institute was not to create a new profession for women or to encourage women to abandon their traditional roles in the family. She was a reformer, not a feminist, who simply wanted women's work in the home supported and valued. "[Domestic science] calls for higher and higher ideals of home life and more respect for domestic occupations," she remarked. "In short, it is a direct education for women as homemakers."

By 1908, the Macdonald Institute had already gone far beyond Hoodless' vision. Programs still included short courses for homemakers and housekeepers, but the school also offered a demanding two-year program to train domestic science teachers and institutional dietitians.

A college dedicated to promoting traditional values of home life and domesticity while providing respectable career possibilities seemed like just the right mixture for Roberta. She applied to enter the two-year program, little realizing it would take her down pathways that were anything but traditional.

CHAPTER 4

THE "MACDONALD" GIRL

Queenly, fair and blooming lassie
Garbed in gown of sky blue hue,
Stately mien, and pose triumphant
Embryo queen of rare menu.

Goddess of spoon and platter,
Mistress of man's ways and means;
Fairy nymph of kitchen clatter
Caterer of pork and beans.

Enemy of germs dyspeptic,
Mistress of all household arts;
Minister of domestic comforts,
Soft'ner of hardened hearts.

Like a sunbeam 'cross the campus
Trips she fair as thistle down,
Pure as sparkles on the grass blades,
In her light-blue college gown.

Men shall falter at thy footstool,
For thy hand kings deign to sue;
Peerless, bright Canadian lassie,
Queen of the Macdonald blue.

Sound your "slogan," clan Macdonald,
Sound it far with thrilling skirl'
Till all people and all nations
Know the sweet Macdonald girl.

(The Macdonald Girl, Kerry O'Byrne, n.d.)

A small black cab pulled up in front of Macdonald Hall. A dozen or
so women dressed in an assortment of wide hats, light wool jackets,
and long stiff pleated skirts were already standing in front of the
building, some clutching baggage slips in their hands, others standing beside heavy leather cases. As her driver steadied the horse, a
porter helped Roberta step down onto the sun-baked drive. At
twenty-nine, she looked more like an instructor than a first-year
student.[1] She was sophisticated, intelligent, well-read and deeply
determined to make the most out of her two years at the college.

After she brushed the dust off her dress, Roberta took a long
look at the women who had gathered to register for rooms in the
rambling three-storey red brick residence. One or two were clearly
a few years older than she, but most were barely out of their teens.
And although the Macdonald Institute had a reputation for reaching out to the daughters of farmers, their fashionable clothes and
expensive luggage suggested that these prospective students had
more "city" than "country" about them. They were the daughters
of manufacturers, civil servants, engineers, Members of Parliament,
architects, and accountants, men who were usually more than able
to pay the high tuition charged by the Institute.[2] First-year fees
were roughly $600, equivalent to the average annual wage of a
female Ontario teacher of the time.[3] Room and board cost an additional $180.[4]

Roberta breathed in the heavy, crushed-leaf smell of autumn.
Macdonald Hall, the residence where she would live for the next two
years, stood on the north end of the five-hundred-acre campus of
the Ontario Agricultural College (OAC). In the distance, she could
see the sheer stone faces of the buildings where the male students
studied. The College was just outside the town of Guelph, the site of
the train station from which Roberta had emerged earlier that day.

The Macdonald Institute as it looked when Roberta was a student there.
McLaughlin Library, University of Guelph; REI MAC A0057.

During her short cab ride to the College, she had passed through broad streets lined with the same brown-grey limestone that had been used in the building of the OAC campus.

Between Macdonald Hall and the agricultural college were long green fields of potatoes, carrots, turnips, and beets, all carefully tended by male agricultural students working in five-hour shifts.[5] Her own school was only a short walk north of the women's residence and was easily the most elegant structure on the OAC campus. Tall Grecian columns and round shields etched in rust-coloured stone decorated the front and sides of the Macdonald Institute. Its three-storey centre block was flanked by two-storey side wings, their roof-lines edged with white wooden trim. Entrance to the school was through an imposing brick and stone portico at the front, with a wide stone porch stretching out on each side.

When the wagon with her trunk failed to materialize, Roberta followed the lead of the other women, who were by now making their way nervously into the Hall. Crowded into the large foyer, they faced a circular oak staircase lit by a square skylight a few floors above. Several doors opened off the bright entryway. One of these was opened by Katharine Fuller, the residence superintendent. Fuller was a short, slender, middle-aged woman, with a wide smile that seemed to extend to both sides of her small round face. She invited the women into a book-lined room where they could relax until their bags arrived.

"Then followed the weary wait in the library when we balanced ourselves circumspectly on the edges of our chairs and cast covert glances at each other. Would we ever become acquainted, and distinguished, one from another," wrote an anonymous member of the first year class. "Occasionally a senior – she must have been one from the confident way she walked upstairs without being invited – would meet some girl she knew and they would go off arm in arm with heads together."[6]

At last the "weary wait" was over. A porter from the train station arrived with the women's luggage and Superintendent Fuller assigned rooms and handed out keys. Roberta's new quarters were small and crowded with furniture. A dresser and mirror stood in one corner and a gleaming china jug and bowl sat on a wash stand near a long narrow bed. A square oak table and two pressed-back chairs sat in the centre of the room.[7] It wouldn't have taken long for Roberta to make the cluttered space feel more like home. From deep within her trunk she unpacked a soft feather pillow, hand-stitched pillowcases, and crisp sheets. She hung her laundry bag on one of the small hooks in the closet beside the towels brought from home and placed a cake of soap in the dish next to the jug and bowl.[8] (Bathrooms were located down the hall.)

Roberta pulled out the mandatory blue cotton work dresses that all students were expected to wear for work in the kitchen, carefully shaking them out and hanging them in the closet. Next came some blouses, a few thin wool skirts, and a dark tie – the uniform for regular classes. In her dresser drawers she laid four starched white aprons, two pinafores (for laundry and chemical lab work), a sweeping cap of white cotton, a pair of bloomers and a sailor blouse (for the required daily gym class). In her underwear drawer she folded some long muslin nightgowns, a few fine cotton corsets, some boxy cotton underpants (probably edged in popular Valenciennes lace), three or four pairs of stockings, several reusable "sanitary" towels, one or two petticoats and a full length slip.[9] She shut the chest of drawers firmly, her unpacking complete. Now she was ready to register for her courses and begin her new life.

⟨≈⟩⟨≈⟩⟨≈⟩

I had a few days to spare after my research trip to Sarnia and decided to visit Guelph to see Roberta's alma mater for myself. The town had turned into a city that had long since engulfed the campus and grown far beyond it. Roberta's old school had undergone many changes. In 1964, the Ontario Agricultural College (including the Macdonald Institute) was absorbed into the newly formed University of Guelph. The programs of the OAC were broadened to include degrees in the sciences, arts and humanities as well as agricultural studies. The Macdonald Institute became the University's College of Family and Consumer Studies — a school now attended by both women and men.

Macdonald Hall looked much as it did when Roberta lived there, but it no longer stood isolated on an open field. Pink and white flowering trees, shaded pathways, and modern university buildings with sharp corners and natural stonework surrounded it. Macdonald Hall was still a women only residence. Young women in low slung blue jeans and T-shirts rushed in and out of the building, clutching library books and spiral bound notebooks. As I watched the easy way they made themselves at home, I wondered how Roberta felt when she arrived on that mid-September day in 1909. Did she feel like an exile — the poor spinster sister shipped off to find a career because she hadn't found a man? Was she fearful of her newfound independence, or was she excited and hopeful, as though she'd been given the keys to the cell door and finally found freedom?

Roberta was an articulate, intelligent woman. It's hard for me to believe she could have seen her entry into the Macdonald Institute as anything but a chance to develop her own restless mind and leave behind the limitations of family life. Yet she was twenty-nine years old — middle-aged by the standards *of the day — and until her arrival at the college, she had led a privileged and sheltered life. Fortunately for her, the Macdonald Institute was the perfect setting for her transition to independence.*

≋ ≋ ≋

Roberta quickly discovered that her life at Macdonald Hall was protected and above all, regulated. A gong woke her each morning at 6:45. Breakfast was at 7:30 in the Hall's oak-panelled dining room. By 8:30, Roberta was attending mandatory prayers in the large assembly hall of the Institute. For the rest of the day she attended classes in the same building. Lunch was served at Macdonald Hall between 12:00 and 1:30.

Even Roberta's off-hours were carefully controlled. Students were allowed free time after 4:00, but had to be at the Hall for dinner no later than 6:00. At 7:30 another gong would sound, marking the beginning of study time. Between 9:30 and 10:30 the women were allowed to socialize before yet another gong would signal "lights out." Students were allowed out only one evening each week and had to return "suitably escorted" no later than 10:15. As the Macdonald "House Rules" read: "No resident may leave the College during the day without notifying the superintendent; nor after 7:00 in the evening, without arranging with the Superintendent for suitable chaperonage."[10]

While women who had previously lived independent lives might have found such restrictions claustrophobic, Roberta thrived on them. As the second youngest in a large family, she had grown up surrounded by older brothers and sisters who had cherished and protected her. She lived a comfortable and in many ways, privileged life. Macdonald Hall provided her with a similarly cloistered environment, with a resident superintendent (Katharine Fuller) to play the role of mother. The stable, rule-bound Institute further echoed the values of Roberta's father, who had raised her to appreciate order and organization ("a place for everything and everything in its place").

What Roberta and many of her fellow students didn't realize was that learning to follow the rules of the Institute would benefit

Students at Macdonald Hall in 1910.
McLaughlin Library, University of Guelph; REI MAC A0058.

them in unexpected ways. Obedience, adherence to regulations, organization, the ability to live with strangers under a communal roof and to follow a strict routine were also part of the job description for those who entered military service in the first decade of the twentieth century. In local militias and cadet corps across Canada, men were learning some of the same life skills that were being taught feminine-fashion at the Macdonald Institute. When Roberta and other Macdonald graduates entered the Canadian Army Medical Corps during the Great War, they would quickly discover that the regimented world of the Institute had prepared them well for life under military discipline.

In her first year, Roberta's courses included English, psychology, chemistry, physiology, child study, the history of education, elementary cookery, foods, sanitation, laundry, house administration, and sewing.[11] Laboratory work, lectures, seminars, practical demonstrations, and examinations filled her days. Every course, whether academic or technical, had some connection to life in the home; chemistry was "a study of the food principles, carbohydrates, fat, protein, etc; chemical study of vegetables, cereals, milk, meat, condiments,"[12] while elementary cooking was a "careful study of cooking methods – boiling, simmering, steaming, broiling, baking."[13]

While Roberta excelled at the academic side of school life, her lack of practical experience with heavier household work soon began to show. In laundry classes, she learned how to make soap with kitchen fats. Then she used the same soap as she scrubbed heavy sheets in steaming vats of soapy water, eventually forcing them through the dangerous rollers of the "mangle," two heavy rollers used to wring water out of wet garments. In her sanitation course, she was shown how to dispose of household wastes and deal with mice and insects – not the usual job for a comfortable, middle-class woman. Roberta's unease with the seamier side of household life did not go unnoticed. As teacher Grace Greenwood observed, "[Roberta's] household experience has been very limited however. This was apparent in all of her practical work, and she needs to increase it before she does the best work in any line of domestic science."[14]

Course work didn't exclusively focus on the practicalities of household life. Students were also prepared to take an active role in Canadian society – still a radical idea for women in 1909. Lectures on the disposal of household wastes included discussions about municipal sanitation; courses on home nursing raised issues about health care. During the two years that Roberta studied at the Institute, she was given many opportunities to consider public policy issues as diverse as education, poverty, and the conditions faced by factory workers. As she would tell a group of students in 1919, no women in the world were better prepared to contribute to their country than Macdonald students, who were "studying economics in such practical ways. Canada was fortunate in having such a large body of healthy, sturdy, clear minded women turned out from the Institute every year, going out to contribute, consciously or not, their share in the great work."[15]

During Roberta's years at the Sarnia Collegiate, boys had presided over most student activities, and it was their achievements that were celebrated by teachers, parents, and their peers.[16] Life at the Macdonald Institute was very different. Roberta lived in an all-female environment in which young women took on all leadership roles and responsibilities. Despite the strict rules guiding their conduct, Mac' students still managed to establish and lead their own drama, choral, and book clubs, athletic associations, literary and debating societies, and a branch of the YWCA. They also hosted sleighing parties, masquerade balls, winter carnivals, and the occasional mixed hockey or baseball game with the male students of the OAC.

Women were also the main role models for Mac' students, teaching nearly all of the courses. Of her many instructors, none would have a greater impact on Roberta's life than Mary Urie Watson, the short, white-haired principal of the Institute. Born in 1866 in Ayr, Ontario, Watson was the daughter of an agricultural implements manufacturer. In her early twenties, she had attended both the Philadelphia Cooking School and Adelaide Hoodless's Normal School in Domestic Science and Art (a Hamilton-based school that was closed soon after the Macdonald Institute was established).

After graduating from the Normal School, Watson taught domestic science for a short while and then returned to the United States for further study. She attended the Teachers' College of Columbia University in New York, earning a domestic arts diploma and passing her New York State teaching exams. She soon returned to Canada as principal of Hoodless' Normal School, leaving in 1903 to become director of the Macdonald Institute. In 1904, she was appointed its principal.[17]

Watson was a guiding force in the lives of her students. Many found themselves invited to relax in the large Morris chair in her comfortable office with its wide oak desk, vases of flowers and pictures of her family's farm in nearby Ayr. After a glowing fire had been lit in the brick-lined hearth she chatted with them about their studies and their hopes for the future. Watson actively encouraged students to seek positions across Canada, often writing letters on their behalf. In a sense, she created her own "old girls" network, helping young women pursue independent lives while keeping them in touch with their former school. Some graduates would return and take up teaching positions at the Institute; others would return for short visits.[18] In 1911, it would be her recommendation that would enable Roberta to get her first teaching position.[19]

Although she had studied under Adelaide Hoodless, Watson did not embrace her belief that academics were unsuitable for young women. Instead, she held her students to the highest standards, as was evident in this letter that she wrote to an interested applicant in the United States: "Our whole effort is toward helping the students who come to us to make the most of their time. We do our best to help a girl choose the right course and the one she is able to carry, before she enters; then if she fails to make the required standing in her first examination and is reported as a loafer, or mentally unready for the course, we either recommend her to drop out or insist upon her doing so."[20] Watson had no difficulty in maintaining her high standards. The school always received more applications than they could possibly accept.

Roberta had no problem living up to Watson's expectations. By the end of her first year, she had an 82 per cent average (first-class honours). Her highest grades were in chemistry, physiology, and household administration, with her lowest grades given – predictably – for sewing, foods, and house practice.[21]

$\approx\approx\approx$

When she returned home for vacation during the summer of 1910, Roberta was almost thirty. Except for a brief Christmas vacation, she had been away from home for almost nine months. I wonder if she felt a new confidence and sense of personal autonomy as she stood on the Sarnia train platform. It is not difficult to imagine her reunion with her family. It would have been sometime after June 28, the official end of term. If her father or one of her brothers met her at the station, the two might have awkwardly embraced (the MacAdams did not have a reputation for being

Mary Urie Watson meeting with a student.
McLaughlin Library, University of Guelph; REI MAC A0043.

physically affectionate). Then Roberta would have stepped up into the waiting democrat and the pair would have made the short journey home, where her mother and some of the Sarnia-based members of the family were waiting to welcome her back. Were they struck by a new maturity and confidence in "Bert," now a senior college student?

Sometime during the summer of 1910, the MacAdams family grew again. Leslie married Muriel Thom, daughter of a well-known Sarnia photographer. Muriel was a pretty young woman with a heart-shaped face and long curly dark hair. The couple moved into a home a few blocks away from Robert and Catherine. Within a year, Muriel would give birth to their first child, John Leslie (Jack) MacAdams.

Only one other experience of that summer vacation has been recorded, a meeting between Roberta and a young man named Harvey Price. As former Glenbow archivist Shelagh Jameson has written, Harvey had "come to Sarnia from the Price home in Manitoulin, Ontario, to visit his brother, W.H. Price, a partner in the law firm of Hanna, LeSeur, and Price. As William [Jack] Hanna was married to Maud MacAdams, it was perfectly natural that he should meet her sister Roberta."[22]

According to family lore, Harvey met Roberta while the two sat in the waiting room of Jack Hanna's office. Harvey was four years younger than Roberta – a short, tanned, muscular twenty-five-year-old with blue-grey eyes who was earning money for law school by working as a guide for hunting parties in the North. The two quickly discovered they had much in common. Both were from middle-class, Conservative, Anglican families. Harvey's father, like Roberta's, had been the editor and owner of a small-town weekly newspaper (the *Gore Bay Times*).[23]

It was a casual meeting, and neither Harvey nor Roberta expected it to be repeated in the near future. Yet Roberta would one day meet the young guide again, this time under radically different circumstances, in the summer of 1917.

～～～

Back home after my visits to Guelph and Sarnia, I sat at the kitchen table sorting through piles of photocopies, print-outs, and photographs related to Roberta's life at the Institute. While the coffeepot spluttered, I switched on the radio news and heard about the latest carnage in Iraq, the sadistic abuse heaped on two adopted children by their parents, and scandals on Parliament Hill. I listened to stories about the ongoing drought on the prairies and the fires destroying ancient forests in British Columbia and reflected on what Roberta might have said about the challenges facing us. What might she have thought about Canada's role in international conflict, our relationship with our southern neighbour, and the continuing fragmentation of human life in our fast-paced age?

It was easy to forget, sitting in my comfortable twenty-first-century kitchen, that Roberta's world was complicated, too. By the time she left home to study in Guelph, Canada was undergoing rapid change. No longer a land of scattered settlements, fur trade forts, and raw bush, eastern Canada was carpeted by cities, factories, and rolling farmland. Roberta was a child of this change – daughter of immigrant parents, raised in a city, not on a farm, a first-generation urban Canadian.

While her eastern Canadian homeland was now firmly settled, the rest of the nation was just beginning the cycle of settlement. Now it was the prairies' turn to be transformed from bush and grassland into farms and cities. At the turn of the century, federal politicians, eager to exploit the European hunger for wheat, began to promote the settlement of the West. Clifford Sifton, Laurier's minister for the interior, established an ambitious and far-reaching program to encourage Europeans and Americans to emigrate to Canada and settle in what would eventually become the new provinces of Alberta, Manitoba, and Saskatchewan. Canada's population soon swelled to over six million as immigrants from all over the world flooded into the young country.

Although the new immigrants helped boost the country's economy, many Anglo-Canadians responded to them with prejudice and fear. There was open distrust of those who spoke different languages, wore strange clothing, and practised strange religions. Frank Oliver, the politician who replaced Sifton as minister of the interior in 1905, began to place restrictions on immigration by Asian, Eastern European, and Black American settlers. Racism was alive and well in Canada.

There were other problems, too. If Roberta had been able to switch on the radio in 1909, she might have heard stories about tuberculosis epidemics in Native communities, anti-Chinese rhetoric during political campaigning in Alberta, problems of vice and crime in Winnipeg, labour unrest in the Maritimes, high infant mortality rates, and the growing number of women doing sweated labour in garment factories in Toronto. Poverty, disease, and social unrest had not been eradicated by "progress."

Education was seen as the answer to many of society's ills, especially for non-English immigrants. As historian J.M. Bumstead has written, "Regular school attendance would ensure a more suitable environment for children than roaming the streets or working in factories, help them to learn skills that would lift them out of their poverty, and – in the case of immigrants – enable them to assimilate the values of Canadian society. In most parts of the country 'Canadian society' meant Anglo-Canadian society."[24]

This movement to shape and reform society was the catalyst that helped bring about the domestic science movement that Roberta joined in 1909. Many reformers believed that an education focusing on strengthening women's traditional work as homemakers would help correct what they perceived to be the disintegration of the moral fibre of Canadian society. Programs like those offered at the Macdonald Institute were originally designed to elevate women's traditional domestic work to the same status as that of men, not to challenge society's conception of what was and wasn't women's work. In fact, Institute founder Adelaide Hoodless was against the vote for women. "A woman who has not succeeded in training her sons to vote so that they will guard their mother's best interests and the best interests of the nation is not herself worthy to vote," she said in 1904.[25]

Yet, while the domestic science program fostered a traditional understanding of male and female roles, it also promoted academic excellence and provided women with a socially acceptable way to advance intellectually and vocationally. In fact, it provided women with a new profession. Graduates like Roberta were able to pursue satisfying careers as teachers, adult educators, academics, researchers, and dietitians. Not quite what Adelaide Hoodless had in mind when she helped establish the Institute.

During her second year in Guelph, Roberta gained even more confidence. She began to do practice teaching with children at Macdonald Consolidated, a public school near the OAC campus. As one of her teachers commented, "Miss MacAdams is a clever student, knowing her own powers and capable of using them to the best advantage. She is an excellent teacher, presenting her subject vividly and clearly. Her demonstrating showed the same characteristics."[26]

In the fall of 1910, Roberta befriended a young first-year student named Gladys Caverhill. Gladys was an outgoing, talkative twenty-one-year-old from Tillsonburg, Ontario. She had earned her junior teaching certificate from the London Normal School the year before and had entered the teacher-training program at the Macdonald Institute in order to specialize in domestic science. (Students who had already completed a two-year "normal" program elsewhere only needed to take one year of study at 'Mac' in order to specialize in domestic science.) The two women became instant friends – Gladys appreciated Roberta's reserve and maturity, seeing her as a "fine capable woman" from whom she could learn much. For her part, Roberta seems to have enjoyed Gladys' open personality and sense of fun. Unfortunately, Gladys was unable to graduate with Roberta in the spring. Her academic file listed her "date of leaving" as May 15, 1911, just one month short of completing the program. On the bottom of her report card, is the neatly penned sentence "Miss Caverhill was obliged to drop out on account of a nervous breakdown." The phrase "nervous breakdown" covered a wide variety of problems – from emotional upheaval to pregnancy. It was difficult to know what happened to Gladys, but she would resurface a few years later and the two women would once again resume their friendship.

As Roberta's time at the Institute drew to a close, events were taking place in Europe that would have a large impact on her life and those of millions of others. Although no one seemed to suspect it was possible, the world was less than five years away from war. Since 1909, Germany had been expanding its navy, building new Dreadnought-class ships. The British government, anxious that its own navy not be outclassed by Germany, established a Navy War Council and embarked on an ambitious ship-building program of its own. In response, Canadian Prime Minister Laurier put forward a policy to support Britain by establishing a small, independent Canadian navy, using British expertise, but under Ottawa's control. Critics quickly responded that ships that had to carry the British White Ensign could hardly be distinguished from Royal Navy warships in the event of war. The Conservatives recommended that Canada pay for some Dreadnought class battleships to be given to the British government. The furor over Laurier's policies ultimately split his party and led to its defeat in the federal election of 1911. Robert Borden would lead Canada as the world slowly lurched its way towards conflict.[27]

Graduation day, 1911. Roberta is likely among the women in this photo.
McLaughlin Library, University of Guelph; REI MAC A0171.

Roberta took a deep breath as she stepped out of the front doors of Macdonald Hall. A crowd of friends and family had gathered outside in a roped-off area on each side of the entranceway, watching to catch a glimpse of daughters and granddaughters. Roberta walked past them in a slow procession with the other graduates, all dressed in identical white cotton gowns, each carrying a yellow bouquet of buttercups and a brown and gold shepherd's crook. Then they stopped and formed two parallel lines, raising the crooks above their heads to form an archway between them. Winkona Frank (the "May Queen," chosen by her fellow students), her attendants, and Principal Watson walked under the archway. All the women stepped up onto a raised dais decorated with flowers where their queen would be "crowned."[28]

After the queen had assumed her throne, some shorter course students performed several "dainty dances" around a tall maypole decked with flowers and hung with long fabric streamers. An OAC professor and one of his students carried out a tall heavy Victrola. He wound up the machine and lowered its heavy needle onto a spinning record. Roberta sipped tea and ate thin finger sandwiches as the ethereal voice of Adelina Patti, the opera diva who had once entertained Abraham Lincoln, emerged from the trumpet of the Victrola. Then some students sang their own solos and others offered readings. As the sun set, fireworks exploded into the air from atop Macdonald Hall and Principal Watson invited students and friends to the school gymnasium for an impromptu dance.

⋘ ⋘ ⋘

Looking through the photographs of that long-ago graduation, I hoped that Roberta's family was among the guests who watched her graduate and that her father or brothers asked her to dance as the evening drew to a close. She was the first in her immediate family to graduate from post-secondary studies (and the only woman in her class to graduate with first-class honours[29]). Roberta was also about to be the first and only MacAdams girl to leave Ontario and find her fortune elsewhere. She had finally accepted her brother Bill's invitation to move to the West. By mid-September she would be on the train to Edmonton.

CHAPTER 5
THE NEW COUNTRY

"On Tuesday night, a grand ball was held at Hardwick and Rossell's store to which a large crowd attended. An orchestra specially engaged from Edmonton played splendid music and an enjoyable time was spent by the dancers. Supper was served at 12:00 and dancing continued till early morning."
(Stony Plain Advertiser, February 3, 1912)

Hardwick and Rossell's store was filled with farmers and their wives, the men in cheese-cutter caps and their best collars, the women wearing heavy dresses that smelled like winter laundry, cold and fresh from the line. Stony Plain was just a small prairie town, but the women wore their hats fashionably high, their dresses barely revealing glimpses of ankle. As they talked and laughed with friends they hadn't seen since the fall harvest, some absent-mindedly ran callused fingers over bolts of soft white flannelette piled high on the scrubbed pine countertops. Red-faced men pulled at their stiff collars and eyed the warm knitted toques (25 cents apiece). Practical headgear for the bitterly cold February of 1912.[1]

The air smelled of peppermint and wood smoke and sweat. Glass jars filled with sticky red and white sweets were arranged on shelves, next to bins of cookies and mealy winter apples, tins of baking powder, coffee, and tea. To reach the stairs leading to the second floor ballroom, patrons stepped past a glowing cast iron stove, two barrels of nails, and a roll of chicken wire. On the floor above, an orchestra from Edmonton had started to play and piano and fiddle merged into an energetic waltz that swept over the guests rushing up the stairs. The floorboards creaked with the sound of feet more accustomed to walking behind a plow than floating across a dance floor.[2]

One woman stood out among the heavy-footed dancers in the second-floor ballroom. Roberta MacAdams stood self-consciously in one corner, shivering inside her full-length fur coat.[3] Despite all she may have heard about the advantages of Alberta's "dry cold," she probably wasn't yet accustomed to minus-forty-degree weather. In November, a few months after she had arrived in Edmonton, Duncan Marshall, Alberta's plump, clean-shaven Minister of Agriculture, offered her a job teaching "domestic economy" to rural women.

Roberta's new job involved travelling the province on a special "demonstration train" sponsored by the provincial government and the CPR. Each year, in the heart of the frigid Alberta winter, the train carried agriculture instructors to small prairie towns. In drafty town halls and churches, they taught the latest farming methods to rooms packed with red-faced, bearded men with keenly critical eyes. Their train also carried chickens and geese, wheat sheaves, giant heavy-footed Percheron horses, butter-making equipment, and Shorthorn, Ayrshire, and Holstein cattle. It was sometimes hard to tell what the farmers look forward to seeing most – the instructors or the healthy animals and new machines. Between January 15 and February 10 this farm on wheels visited the communities of Stony Plain, Claresholm, Gleichen, and Olds.

Roberta was one of only two women on the eleven-member teaching staff. "Miss Perkins," a fellow graduate of the Macdonald Institute, was her assistant.[4] Roberta's task was to teach domestic science to farm wives. It was the first time that a course specifically designed for women had been included in the program. She was also expected to make a survey of the province to decide if there was grassroots interest in government support for a network of Women's Institutes similar to the organization that Roberta was so familiar with in Ontario.

In Alberta, the Institutes were relatively new. The only branch was located in the small community of Lea Park, east of Edmonton, near the Saskatchewan boundary. Margaret Graham, a member of

Main Street, Stony Plain, decorated for the arrival of the agricultural instructors. Stony Plain Multicultural Centre.

an Ontario institute before she moved to Alberta, formed the Lea Park Institute in 1909. She and the other women at Lea Park saw the institutes as an avenue for agricultural education for women. They lobbied the Alberta government to support local branches with funding and staffing. In 1912, their wish came true. Roberta was hired. The first community she visited was Stony Plain.

On the cold February night in 1912, it seemed as though the whole town had come out for the dance. There is no record describing how Roberta reacted to the party. But she was thirty-one, single, and far from the expectations of small-town Ontario. It is not hard to imagine her leaving her coat on a chair, accepting an invitation from one of her fellow instructors, and taking to the floor in a spirited waltz.

෨෨ ෨෨ ෨෨

Roberta had arrived in Alberta in September 1911 after a five-day train journey across the country. She must have been a striking figure, standing on the busy Edmonton train platform, her high leather boots, long fall jacket and wide-brimmed hat. It would have been easy for her to scan the crowd for her brother Bill – at 5'8", Roberta now towered over most women and many men.

Compared to Ontario, with its brick and stone cities and long-established farms, Roberta's new home was a brash upstart. Alberta had been declared a province six years before, and its sandstone legislature overlooking Edmonton's river valley was still under construction. The premier of the province was Arthur Sifton, a fifty-three-year-old lawyer and former chief justice of Alberta. Sifton had a reputation for being autocratic and aloof, but he had become an effective voice for the West, championing Alberta's recognition as a province and later its control over its own resources.[5] Political ambition and an interest in the West seemed to run in the Sifton family. Arthur's brother Clifford was the former federal minister of the interior who had flooded the prairies with newcomers from half a world away.

By the time Roberta moved to the West, those newcomers had suffered through a decade of hardship, clearing and tilling the rich farmland. Scandinavians, British, Germans, Galicians [sic], Jews, Americans, French, and other groups from across Europe now peopled what had become known as the "last best West." Another kind of settler had also begun to appear on the train platforms of Edmonton and Calgary. Educated, middle-class eastern Canadians in pinstripe suits and flowing dresses were arriving in Alberta, eager to break their own kind of ground. Roberta was part of this new wave of urban "settlers."

One million three hundred thousand people now lived in western Canada.[6] Real estate advertisements jostled for space in Edmonton's three daily newspapers and people were willing to pay the high prices being charged for small lots in Alberta's capital.[7] Prosperity was in the sound of hammers and saws and in the crisp white pinafores of well-fed girls skipping on high wooden boardwalks. The dreams of Edmonton's middle and upper class were rubbing off on the new banks, hotels, theatres, department stores, and schools that now served them.

Over one-third of the population in the three prairie provinces lived in rapidly expanding cities. There were over thirty-one thousand people living in Edmonton alone.[8] Young, educated, urban men and women were carving out new lives in the city, far from the cliquish confines of middle-class society in Toronto and Montreal. Henry Marshall Tory, the principal of Alberta's first university, summed up this generation's attitude to the Canadian West. "There was wine in the air; a feeling of excitement; of expectancy," he wrote. "It was difficult to explain. Perhaps it was just that everything was new, the people young and the conviction grows that great things were bound to happen in this rich new country."[9]

Roberta arrived in this "new country" to build a future unlimited by expectation and tradition. As she walked down Jasper Avenue in her black wool skirt and high-necked white blouse, passers-by could be forgiven for thinking they were seeing a "Gibson girl" in the flesh. The invention of American artist Charles Gibson, "Gibson girls" were magazine illustrations of the new "professional" women who had begun to grace offices and schools. They were educated, independent and fashionable, famous for their upswept hair, long skirts, tight waists, and high necklines.[10]

Roberta may have been the epitome of the independent Gibson girl, but she still had to depend on her brother Bill to support her during her first few months in Alberta. By now, Bill was married; he and his wife Annie had a two-year-old son and a five-month-old daughter. With his trademark cigars and tipped-back fedora, Bill was a well-known and flamboyant figure in the community. A year before Roberta arrived in Alberta, he had left his jobs at the *Journal* and *Bulletin* and was the proud owner of the fledgling newspaper, the *Edmonton Daily Capital*. From his cluttered two-storey brick office building in the city's downtown core, he again wrote the kind of astute and inflammatory editorials that once challenged the most powerful members of the British Columbia judiciary. He had also embraced a new political tradition – by 1912 he was listing his political affiliation as "Liberal."

The Edmonton Daily Capital newsroom. Caption: Bill MacAdams
stands at the right, wearing his trademark fedora.
Glenbow Archives, NC-6-239.

While Bill's career was once briefly limited by scandalized
judges with a thirst for revenge, his sister faced even more powerful
obstacles. In 1911, women continued to be hemmed in by society's
expectations of their "proper place." Many universities barred them
from their programs, and only a handful of professions were open
to them. Although the number of women in the paid labour force
in Canada had grown from 237,949 in 1901 to 364,821 in 1911,[11]
they were still chiefly hired as housekeepers and domestic servants,
seamstresses, typists, bookkeepers, saleswomen, farm workers,
teachers, and nurses.[12] The great majority of women were not "employed" at all – working without pay as homemakers. Despite the
demands of "progress," their role in Canadian society remained
confined to caring for the family and playing supporting roles to
the men who occupied centre stage.

By virtue of money, social connections, or sheer determina-
tion, a few women in the Canadian West did manage to escape

society's expectations, living independent lives and breaking new ground in careers usually reserved for men. In British Columbia, a solitary Emily Carr was painting her spirit-filled impressions of remote Native villages. Journalist Cora Hind was the no-nonsense man-suited agricultural editor for the *Winnipeg Free Press*. And in Alberta, explorer and naturalist Mary Schäffer had just published her book "Old Indian Trails of the Rockies," describing her travels through the mountains.

Across the prairies, the murmurs of women's suffrage were being heard in clapboard churches, newspaper offices, and women's clubs. Organizations like the Alberta branch of the influential Women's Christian Temperance Union (WCTU) pledged to work more actively for the vote for women. Members believed that women's votes would translate into a reformed society guided by "purer" laws such as prohibition. Louise McKinney was the president of the organization. Louise – a woman with whom Roberta would one day share a singular political honour – was a seasoned temperance campaigner with a ramrod-straight posture and serious face who worked as a WCTU organizer in the United States before moving to Alberta early in 1903.

Temperance wasn't the only issue that galvanized women to press for the vote. Mills and factories in the burgeoning cities of the West were using women as sweated labour. The average daily wage for a female factory worker was 83 cents compared to $1.46 for men[13] and conditions were abysmal. Female factory workers worked ten- and twelve-hour days in airless rooms, where, according to Nellie McClung, floors were often "littered with refuse of apple peelings and discarded clothing... there was no ventilation and no heat." McClung, the popular author who moved to Manitoba in 1911, cut her political teeth on the issue of wages and labour conditions, lobbying Premier Rodmond Roblin to take action against the exploitation of women and children. She would soon move to Alberta, where she would press Premier Sifton to bring in the vote for women.

Activists McClung and McKinney wanted women to be able to shape the laws that affected them and their families. Not all women rushed to stand under their banners. Many were so busy raising children and eking out an existence on farms or in cities that they had little time to reflect on their situation or advocate for social and political change. Others, like Roberta MacAdams, were oblivious of the need for change. Roberta was a privileged middle-class woman who had so far managed to achieve a kind of professional life with little opposition. She didn't seem to see any need to challenge the status quo, taking for granted her own innate equality and comfortable position in society. As she would one day tell an interviewer: "You see, in the West, it was always rather taken for granted that men and women were equal. It wasn't a controversial question at all."

Roberta would one day discover that some aspects of women's equality were very controversial indeed. Her eventual embrace of women's rights would be shaped by the rural women with whom she worked, and tempered by her exposure to the fires of war.

≈≈≈

Each day as Roberta began to teach, the air was filled with the steamy breath of sixty women crowding into the second-floor meeting room in Stony Plain's town hall. Some had travelled through blizzards to attend class. Cornelia Railey, the town's teenage school teacher, watched closely as Roberta gave practical demonstrations in the "preparing and cooking of soups, meats, tough and tender cuts, vegetables, desserts, bread, cakes, pastry for the women of the district."[14]

Unlike Railey, most of the women in the audience were long-time veterans of prairie life. Looking out at their weathered faces, Roberta felt uneasy. It was clear that most of these motherly-looking women had a knowledge of household management far superior to her own.[15] Town midwife Iris Umbach was probably in the audience. Iris and her husband Israel had moved to Alberta from Ontario in 1892, settling on a homestead just north of Stony Plain. In 1906, the Umbachs left the homestead and moved into the town, where Israel found steady work as a builder. In a picture

Participants in the agricultural program in Stony Plain. The large building
is the hall in which Roberta delivered her domestic science lectures.
Stony Plain Multicultural Centre.

taken around the time of Roberta's visit, Iris sat on a stiff-backed
chair, dwarfed by her eleven children (two others died in infancy).
Soon Iris Umbach and Cornelia Railey would work together to
establish Stony Plain's first Women's Institute.[16]

There was little that an urban woman with little "pots and
pans" experience could teach rural survivors like Umbach. At a
time when two out of every seven deaths in the province were babies under one year of age, experienced farm wives were probably
more concerned with basic health care than how to prepare tough
cuts of meat.[17] Although Alberta's cities were growing rapidly, most
women still lived on farms or ranches. Their jobs were "wife" and
"mother" and they had few rights and many back-breaking responsibilities. For the first few years on the prairie, many lived with
their families in sod or tarpaper shacks. Few were fortunate enough

to have log cabins or mail-order wooden houses. Most juggled huge tasks – from harvesting to managing dairy cattle, poultry, and the essential family vegetable garden. They birthed babies, raised children, preserved food for the winter, cleaned house, and did laundry. Cooking was one of their major occupations – over a five-day period during harvest, a woman could prepare as many as five hundred individual servings of food for a twenty-man threshing crew. She would sweat in the kitchen from dawn until midnight, then lay her aching body on a corner of the kitchen floor while a group of workers shared the only decent bed in the house.[18]

Given their heavy responsibilities, Roberta wondered why so many women made the huge effort to come to her demonstrations, often driving miles over dangerous icy country roads in sub-zero temperatures to listen to a city-bred home economist with little exposure to rural hardship. As she chatted with the women over steaming cups of tea, the answer slowly emerged. These hard-working women craved connection with one another.

"Life must be made less rural if (women) were to be happy," Roberta would one day tell an interviewer. For Roberta, "rural" meant "lonely." Isolated in mail-order shacks and sod huts, do-ing back-breaking work alongside often silent and bone-weary husbands, farm women had deep needs for friendship. Elizabeth Mitchell, a Scottish woman touring Alberta in 1912, mirrored Roberta's views. She observed that isolated women sometimes be-came mentally unbalanced. "Then fancies come, and suspicions, and queer ways, and at last the young Mounted Policeman comes to the door, and carries her away to the terrible vast 'Sanitorium' that hangs above the Saskatchewan."[19]

~ ~ ~

Standing on Main Street in Stony Plain on a bitter January day, I saw an avenue that had almost completely changed since Roberta's visit more than ninety years before. Gone were the decorations made by the town's welcom-ing committee: the giant archway decorated with sheaves of grain, the mul-

ticoloured streamer proclaiming "Fertile Stony Plain," and the freshly cut fir trees forced into deep snowdrifts. A chrome and brick provincial building had replaced the wood frame town hall where domestic science classes were held and the creamy white circus tent where livestock was displayed had long since disappeared. Hardwick and Rossell's store, the site of the dance, had burned to cinders in a 1954 fire.

Despite the loss of these landmarks, the ghosts of 1912 were still on foot in this small prairie town. They stared down from giant murals painted on the square wooden facades of the "western wear" stores and gift shops that now lined Main Street. Along one giant wall, a family drove through a winter landscape in a horse and cutter. Near the entrance to the **Stony Plain Reporter**, a newspaper editor was bent over an ancient printing press. But the most eye-catching mural portrayed an elderly woman wearing an incredibly garish wide-brimmed hat.

That woman was Cornelia Wood (formerly Cornelia Railey) – the same woman who watched Roberta MacAdams teach domestic science in Stony Plain in 1912. Born in Boxford, Missouri, she moved to Canada with her family while she was still a child. At sixteen, she began to teach in Stony Plain's one-room school and became active in community affairs. As she would later relate in **My Memories**, Wood's own life was dramatically affected by the leadership qualities that she observed in women such as Roberta MacAdams. Following Roberta's visit to Stony Plain, Wood helped establish a local branch of the Women's Institutes, and eventually became a member of the Alberta legislature, a crusty and outspoken advocate for women during the long reign of Social Credit Premier Ernest Manning.

At the height of her political career in 1967, Wood and the Alberta Women's Institutes raised funds to commission a painting of Roberta MacAdams for the Alberta government. That painting hung in the legislature for decades and then was quietly removed and stored somewhere in the government's vaults. Unlike that painting, Wood herself had not been forgotten. She was memorialized at the Stony Plain Multicultural Centre, an eighty-year-old red brick schoolhouse a few streets away from the highway that edges the town. Stepping inside its double front doors, I smelled roast beef, Yorkshire pudding, and Brussels sprouts. The centre housed a museum, art gallery, and "homesteader's kitchen," a basement restaurant known for its twenty kinds of pies. I walked up a flight of stairs into the museum and encountered the life of Cornelia Wood.

*Gleaming wood and glass cases held framed portraits, Wood's famous col-
lection of over one hundred hats, formal gowns, awards, and the memorabilia
of a life in public service. But the display that captured my interest contained an
ornately framed photograph of young Cornelia Railey as a nineteen-year-old
teacher in Stony Plain. She stared out at me in a high-necked lace-trimmed
black gown, her brown hair framing a strong and uncompromising face. This
was the young woman who witnessed Roberta's first steps into public life in
that town hall in Stony Plain in 1912.*[20]

In Claresholm, Gleichen, and Olds, the turnout for the domestic
science demonstrations equalled that of Stony Plain. Roberta was
convinced that something concrete had to be done to help women
meet and support one another across the miles of farmland and bush
that so often separated them. Soon after her sweep through these
four Alberta communities, she wrote a report for the Department
of Agriculture. It would be her first successful attempt at government lobbying. Roberta argued that formal government support
and financial assistance was a necessity in order for Women's Institutes to thrive. The government agreed.

"With this in view, it is now proposed to organize a system of
women's clubs or institutes under departmental supervision, having as its object the consideration and simplifying of all problems
pertaining to the home, and consequent achievement of better
home conditions and the increase of the general fund of comfort,
health, and efficiency," declared the Alberta government's annual
report for 1912. Roughly translated, it meant that politicians and
bureaucrats recognized the importance of women's contribution to
the farm economy and were willing to put their money where their
mouths were. Roberta was appointed as the first superintendent of
the Alberta Women's Institutes. Her assignment was to develop and
promote the organization across the province.

For the next six months Roberta criss-crossed Alberta by train,
car, and horse-drawn carriage. During the long hot summer of
1912, she met with rural women in towns as far south as Pincher
Creek, Lethbridge, and Magrath. The situation in Magrath hinted

at the economic decline that would soon engulf the province. During the previous twelve months, high winds, drought, torrential rains, early frosts, and snowstorms had plagued farmers in the area.[21] Although crops were doing well in the summer of 1912, farmers would not benefit. The price of wheat was dropping rapidly. Land values, artificially inflated by real estate speculation, were also declining.[22] Unemployed young men began appearing in the streets of Alberta's towns and cities, looking for any kind of work they could find. It was the beginning of an economic depression that would last until the flames of war reignited the Alberta economy.

One of the women whom Roberta met during her sweep through Magrath was Merel Hethershaw, the wife of a farm machinery salesman. On July 31, Hethershaw wrote a letter to the province's superintendent of fairs and institutes:

> G.W. Heathershaw
> July 31, 1912
> Dealer in First Class Farm Implements
> Magrath, Alberta
>
> Supt. Fairs and Institutes
> Edmonton, Alberta
>
> Dear Sir:
>
> Miss Roberta MacAdams accompanied by Mrs. Elinor Burns and Mrs. Fanny Gordon of Lethbridge, visited Magrath, July 10th and organized a Women's Institute. Mrs. G.W. Heathershaw was elected chairman and Mrs. Ida Woods secretary pro tem, after which the following officers were elected: President, Mrs. L.S. Taylor, Vice President, Mrs. Dora Jensen, Secretary Treasurer, Mrs. Merel Heathershaw, Directors, Mrs. Lou Rasmussun, Agnes Turner, Nellie Watkins, and A. Peterson.
> An executive meeting was held July 17th, the time, place and program for the first meeting was planned. On July 31st, at 3:30 p.m. in the Magrath School Auditorium, the first general meeting of the Women's Institute was held, the Pres. Mrs. Taylor presiding:

Music: "Maple Leaf Forever" Audience
Reading: "A Slave to Fashion" Miss Wilda Green
Address: "Work of Women's Institute" Mrs. Taylor
Songs: "Selected" Mrs. Lamb

General discussion as to how to create an interest amongst farmer's wives in our institute was led by Mrs. Wyman. Adjourned to meet August 28th at the home of Mrs. A. Peterson.

Mrs. Merel Heathershaw
Secretary Treasurer

By the time Merel Heathershaw wrote her letter to the Alberta government, Roberta had already begun to look for another job. Despite her deep admiration and respect for farm women, she felt that someone with deeper rural roots would do a more effective job on their behalf. As historian Shelagh Jameson writes, "Roberta, new to the country and its conditions as she was, felt that she was not familiar enough with the problems that faced the Alberta farm women to give them the assistance they required. She decided to return to the sphere of work which she had chosen."[23] Roberta may have also been ready to find a new challenge and start something new. As she would later explain to an Edmonton friend, "I am always more interested in organizing and building than in carrying on a completed routine."[24]

In June 1912, Roberta applied for a position with the Edmonton Public School Board, aided by a reference letter from her old mentor, Mary Urie Watson.[25] On August 26, 1912, she began work as the Supervisor of Household Science for Edmonton's public schools. Roberta was to be paid the comfortable sum of $1,600 per year (a male supervisor was paid $1,900).[26] Her office would be located at Victoria High School in downtown Edmonton.

Warm September sunlight poured in through the high windows and bounced back from the gleaming linoleum floor of the domestic science classroom at Victoria High School. Inside, long wooden counters were arranged in a square. In the centre was a large table; a shiny brass and iron kitchen scale sat on top and a meat grinder was tightly anchored to one edge. All the counters were fitted with cutlery drawers and low cupboards for supplies, pots, and pans.

Young women wearing starched bibbed aprons covering their long dresses, stirred pots of thick white sauce or boiled coffee in large pots on the gas stoves on each countertop. At one end of the room, a flushed teenage girl opened the door of a large coal stove while another slid pans of bread dough into its dark, hot depths.[27] They were eager to impress their teacher Miss MacAdams — as student Grace Studholme would later recall, "She looked so lovely in her fresh white uniform and hair neatly coiled. She greeted us all as though we were the very ones she wanted to meet. We loved her at once."[28]

Roberta walked from one girl to another, checking that they were carefully following the recipes recorded in the notebooks scattered everywhere. Despite her own keen interest in cooking, she was tired and distracted. In September 1912, there were over twelve hundred students taking domestic science classes in city schools each month. As the coordinator of the program, she designed courses, supervised teachers, ordered supplies and equipment, and taught domestic science at Victoria High School.[29]

There were now seventeen schools in Edmonton, with over four thousand students enrolled in classes. Victoria, like Roberta's own Sarnia Collegiate, was the elegant centrepiece of educational progress in the city. The new $150,000 Renaissance style secondary school stood on a two-block site near the city's core. Designed to accommodate up to five hundred students, it had a gymnasium, auditorium, physics and chemistry labs, and twelve classrooms.[30] There was also a special domestic science suite, with a demonstration kitchen, dining room, and sewing room.

The world seemed remarkably hopeful to the young men and women who attended the modern high school. According to

"Town Topics," an Edmonton weekly, "We are living in the age of science and education, in a time when people have to think and act quickly, when the adoption of modern methods and modern machinery means advancement. We may be up-to-date today and behind the times tomorrow. We want men and women of broad vision. We want modern ideas and new systems."[31]

Girls were included in the new emphasis on scientific methods and innovation. A systematic approach was to be applied to the management of the home. Alberta's department of education expected girls and young women to be taught food composition, nutrition, sanitation, and disease prevention. In practice, however, domestic science classes turned out to be more domestic than scientific. Grade six girls spent forty-five minutes a week sewing buttonholes, hemming pillowcases and making blankets for their dolls. Older girls graduated to making doilies and table napkins, underwear and simple dresses. Cooking and preserving were taught weekly, with time spent learning the composition of foods and making recipes from books with catchy titles like *Fifty-Two Sunday Dinners* and *What to Cook and How to Cook It*.[32]

❧ ❧ ❧

The graceful stone high school where Roberta once worked was torn down in the 1950s and replaced by a sleek, modern building. I walked down one of "Vic's" crowded corridors on a wet September afternoon. Students were rushing to class; the well-worn linoleum floor was scuffed with mud tracked in from the puddles on the sidewalk outside and the air smelled like sweaty socks. I found my way to the school's one-room museum and archives. It was filled with a jumble of fading school jackets, costumes from past theatre productions, well-thumbed programs and yearbooks, piles of clippings, signed photographs of famous graduates, and a director's chair once owned by school alumnus Anne Wheeler.

Propped up at the back of a glass case reserved for artifacts of a more distant past was the photograph I was looking for – "Teaching Staff of Victoria School 1912." The people in the blurry black and white image were casually grouped together in two rows. Roberta MacAdams stood in the back, wearing a high-necked long-sleeved blouse and dark skirt, hair drawn away from her face, a slight smile playing at her lips. She was one of only three women in the fourteen-member staff. Seated front row centre, hands clasped primly on his lap, was Principal William Carpenter. By 1914 he would be superintendent of the Edmonton School Board. Seated to his right was a young, tousle-haired John Percy Page. Page, a teacher from eastern Canada, would one day become the province's lieutenant governor. His wife, the former Maude Roche, had trained with Roberta at the Macdonald Institute.

Frozen in time, they looked remarkably casual, unaware of the changes brewing in Europe that would engulf them and many of their students.

⬤ ⬤ ⬤

1912 and 1913 were demanding and exhausting years for Roberta. Single-handed, she struggled to place the domestic science program on a solid footing within a large and growing school district. Fortunately, more help soon arrived, the welcome result of Mary Urie Watson's "old girls network." In November, the Edmonton School Board hired Roberta's school friend Gladys Caverhill as assistant domestic science supervisor. Caverhill had returned to the Macdonald Institute in March 1912 to complete the program she had abandoned so abruptly. After graduation, she followed Watson's advice and applied to the Edmonton School Board. Gladys was quickly hired and was soon teaching domestic science classes across the city. Roberta helped her find a room in the rambling boarding house where she now lived with her friends Percy and Maude Page.

Gladys' help freed Roberta to immerse herself in the minutiae of administration. Every purchase made by the domestic science department – from canning jars to desks – had to be approved by William Bradey, the secretary-treasurer and supplies commissioner for the Edmonton School Board. Bradey demanded that MacAdams keep a rigid check on costs, guarding against expensive "frills" such as garbage cans. Although his penny-pinching was frustrating for Roberta, Bradey had good reason to keep a check on school finances. Times were tough. The completion of the Canadian Northern and

Some of Roberta's domestic science students at work.
Edmonton Public School Archives; P85-5-23.

Grand Trunk Pacific Railways had resulted in massive job losses throughout Alberta. In Edmonton, the sharp decline in the value of real estate had bankrupted entrepreneurs and householders alike while undermining the local economy. Taxpayers and city politicians insisted that the school board reduce its spending despite the fact that thousands of dollars had been committed to building new schools for a growing population. With few places to cut, the School Board eventually "discounted" teacher's salaries by 10 per cent.[33]

Facing a cut to her own salary and under constant pressure to economize, Roberta's correspondence with the secretary-treasurer was often strained. Her files bulged with voluminous records justifying every purchase she made. She kept meticulous inventories of all equipment and a constant record of the state of supplies in school kitchens. What Roberta didn't know was that the administrative skills she was developing would later help her overcome much greater hurdles than those posed by a stuffy school board administrator.

As each school year ended, Roberta packed her trunk and travelled east, continuing her regular practice of spending long, humid summers with her family in Ontario. The modern phrase "you can't go home again" held little meaning for Roberta. In the early part of the twentieth century, people often lived their entire adult lives in one house, rarely travelling beyond the community in which they were born or raised. Even though Roberta had established an independent life separate from her family, she was still drawn back to her childhood home as strongly as the geese that nested in the ponds of southern Ontario each summer.

Her visits home gave Roberta a chance to catch up on family news. Leslie's wife Muriel was pregnant with their second child. Maud and Jack Hanna were more prosperous than ever. Jack was now on the board of Imperial Oil and had invested heavily in the company. Within a few years those investments would make him a millionaire. His work often involved frequent travelling. Late in the summer of 1912, the Hannas and their two daughters left Sarnia for a train journey across the country, leaving Neil to stay with friends.

Seventeen-year-old Neil had graduated from high school the previous year. His parents felt that he was not yet old enough for university. Instead, Jack allowed his son to article at his Sarnia law office. By now, Neil was a husky, sandy-haired young man with a reputation for recklessness. Just a few summers before, he had badly injured his leg in an accident along the Sarnia railroad tracks. His father may have had that injury in mind as he wrote home to his son in July. "Now let me say in conclusion, if you are going to break an arm or a leg or do any horrible thing to yourself this summer, do not, under any circumstances, do so until I return. As to this be good enough to exercise very special care all the time, and it may be that you will come through the summer alive. You see what an awkward thing it would be to have to break up the whole trip to come home to a funeral. It would not be a square deal on us. Signed, Your daddy, W. J. Hanna."[34]

Roberta (back row) and staff of Victoria High School.
Victoria High School Museum.

❦❦❦

Roberta returned to Edmonton in early September. For the next eight months, teaching and administration occupied her days and sometimes her evenings. She spent her limited free time visiting Maude and Percy Page and her friend Gladys Caverhill. There is little evidence that Roberta became involved in the women's suffrage campaigns that were bubbling below the surface of life in Alberta's capital. However, in April 1913, it would have been impossible for her to avoid hearing about a major confrontation between feminists and the province's premier. That month, Emily Murphy, Nellie McClung, and the two hundred members of the Edmonton Political Equality League organized a meeting at the legislature with Premier Arthur Sifton. When they arrived, Sifton stood on the legislature's front steps and prevented them from proceeding any farther. Tapping the ash from his thick cigar, he listened quietly as McClung and Murphy made impassioned speeches in favour of the extension of the franchise to women. Then he looked around at the women and drawled, "Did you ladies wash up your luncheon dishes before you came down here to ask me for votes? If you hadn't, you'd better go home, because you're not going to get any votes from me."[35]

The women were furious, but could do little to persuade the premier to take their cause seriously. Within three years, the roles would be reversed. Sifton would court the women's favour by offering women the vote and by allowing them to run for political office. Roberta MacAdams would be one of the first women to take advantage of the latter opportunity.

CHAPTER 6

MARCHING AS TO WAR

Oh! We don't want to lose you
But we think you ought to go
For your King and Country
Both need you so;
We shall want you and miss you
But with all our might and main
We shall cheer you, thank you, kiss you
When you come back again.

(We Don't Want to Lose You, Paul Rubens, 1914)

July 1, 1914, was one of the warmest Dominion Days that most Edmontonians could remember. Across the city, factory and office workers, homemakers and school children thronged the city's parks. Some watched the early-morning baseball game between the home team and Moose Jaw, or participated in events celebrating the amalgamation of Edmonton and neighbouring Strathcona. Fifteen hundred holiday makers took the train to Lake Wabumun to swim in the cool summer water or compete in sack races at the Methodist Church picnic.[1]

Only a few months before in *The Chinook*, Victoria High School's magazine, student F.C. McConnell had written that the "basis of society has changed from the military and the domestic to the economic and industrial. The conquest of the world by aggressive people is now made rather through the steel bridge and the locomotive than the rifle."[2] On this Dominion Day, the city basked in the belief that the horizon of peace and prosperity described by McConnell extended before them, the product of hard work and fresh ideas. Within a few days, a slim column on the front page of the *Edmonton Journal* would be the first hint that such naïve hopes would soon be burnt to ash and blown away on the hot dry prairie wind.

"2 Victims of Assassin were Laid at Rest: Archduke Francis Ferdinand and his Wife Buried at Vienna" reads the title of the short article.[3] The story didn't generate much local interest. Few people were concerned about the death of a distant monarch or any conflicts the assassination might have provoked. "[W]e all believed that wars were over, that there could be no such terror," Roberta would one day recall.[4] Yet the murder of the archduke from Austria-Hungary by a Serbian nationalist was the first domino to fall in the series of events leading to war in Europe.

On July 28, Austria invaded Serbia to avenge the murder of the archduke. Germany prepared to support its Austrian ally, but cast a wary eye at mighty Russia, Serbia's ally. Russia was mobilizing its army and Germany demanded that this be stopped. It also handed France, Russia's other ally, an ultimatum – declare neutrality or face the consequences. When Russia did not respond, and France replied that it would only act in its own interests, Germany declared war on both.

The German army launched a plan to invade France in the hope of gaining a quick victory in a short sweeping war. Only neutral Belgium lay in its way. When German armies entered Belgium, the final domino fell. In a treaty made decades earlier, Britain had promised to protect Belgium's neutrality. Britain demanded that Germany withdraw from the tiny country. Germany refused to respond to the British ultimatum. At midnight on August 4, Britain officially declared war on Germany. As part of the British Empire, Canada was also suddenly at war.

A few weeks later, young men in khaki uniforms marched into the Pantages Theatre in downtown Edmonton. They were members of the Nineteenth Alberta Dragoons and 101st Regiment Edmonton Fusiliers. The soldiers were seated on the lower floor of the theatre, while members of the general public jammed the upper balconies overlooking their brothers, sons, and fathers.

Red, white, and blue bunting was draped on the walls and Union Jacks were everywhere. As the audience waited for the curtain to rise, a lone voice started to sing "O Canada." Soon the deep voices of the impromptu all-male choir took up the song. "True Patriot Love" was quickly followed by "The Maple Leaf Forever" and "Dolly Gray" and every patriotic and folksy song they could remember. Then the curtain was raised, a hush descended on the audience, and vaudeville actors performed "The Making of the Flag." The play with its gushing sentiment received only polite applause. But when it was followed by the Belle Trio singing "They're on their Way to Germany" the whole house rocked with applause, stamping feet, and encore after encore.

At the close of the performance, provincial treasurer C.R. Mitchell delivered the final send-off. "In the twinkling of an eye, a war has been brought about and England has called on you to do your part. You are going with a will to help the mother institution. You will be expected to live up to that high degree of honor which England has established for her army. You are stepping into the breach and doing the great duty for those of us who remain behind, but you must remember that if it should become necessary to raise another army those to whom you are saying parting words tonight will be ready to take your places if occasion requires," said Mitchell. "You are called to protect us. With swelling hearts we wish you God speed, knowing that as soldiers of the king, you will do your duty and do it willingly, upholding the noble traditions of the British army."[5]

Within days, Edmontonians wept and cheered as the first group of soldiers filled troop trains destined for the hastily constructed military training camp at Valcartier, Quebec. Soon they would be on their way to England to train again on the Salisbury Plain.

The doors of recruiting stations swung open across Alberta.
Unknown.

Roberta, who had been enjoying her summer vacation with her
parents in Sarnia, returned to a changed Alberta. From the windows in the sewing room at Victoria High School, she heard the
crack of rifle fire and the sound of teenage cadets marching back and
forth under the barking orders of veterans from the South African
war.[6] While military cadets had long been a tradition at Edmonton
schools, this year their training was more than just an exercise in
earnest patriotism. Many of these boys were counting the days until
they were old enough to join up.

"The possibilities for slaughter stagger the imagination and
leave the mental machinery limp with the attempt to grapple with
the ghastly presage," wrote Bill MacAdams in the *Edmonton Daily
Capitol*. But his dissenting voice was drowned out by the swinging open of recruiting station doors across Alberta. Over the next
year, some towns across Alberta saw almost their entire population
of young males gradually disappear.[7] Homesteading ground to a

slow crawl as signs saying "Gone to War" appeared on the doors of empty cabins. Some men joined the army out of patriotic duty. Others wanted to experience the romance of war so vividly portrayed in "Boys Own Annuals" and the stories of Rudyard Kipling. After the disastrous droughts and high unemployment preceding the war, many others just wanted a paying job. In 1915, Alberta led the country in recruitment – over fourteen thousand men joined up, nearly 4 per cent of the province's population.[8]

As they waited for orders to proceed to Valcartier, new recruits marched, fought "to the death" in mock battles, and demonstrated their marksmanship. Some built well-constructed demonstration trenches in Edmonton's parks and practised going "over the top" as admiring teenage girls watched and local politicians made patriotic speeches.

When these prairie ditch diggers eventually reached France, they found themselves wallowing in unstable, frost-covered trenches that were as spongy and damp as the sloughs where they once shot ducks and beaver. Only a year after the war started, the line of trenches and fortifications that many Canadians would call "home" extended from the coast of Belgium to the border of Switzerland. Within its muddy confines, the myths of heroic, charging battles fought by chivalrous men were quickly sucked away by harsh, ugly realities.

In April 1915, the German army used poisonous chlorine gas against Canadian troops at Ypres, the last piece of Belgium in Allied hands. Despite the choking, burning fumes, the Canadians managed to hold their position. Then the Germans attacked them again at nearby St. Julien, in an effort to break through Allied lines. Over six thousand Canadians died or were wounded during these battles.

〰 〰 〰

In June 1915, Roberta left Edmonton to take an advanced course in domestic science at the University of Chicago. She was unable to finish it when word arrived that her mother was seriously ill. Roberta forfeited her own plans and rushed to Sarnia to care for her. Catherine recovered and Roberta spent the remainder of the summer in the town of her birth.

The clouds of war now hovered over her family. Johnston MacAdams had spent the previous eight years dutifully shepherding the *Sarnia Canadian* with his brother Leslie. In his spare time he had joined the local militia. Although he was now thirty-seven years old and could easily have claimed that his age prohibited him from serving, he joined the 34th Battalion and began training in Guelph. In October, he would be sent overseas with the Canadian Expeditionary Force (CEF). By November he would be working as a musketry instructor at Britain's Shorncliffe Military Camp.[9] Johnston wasn't the only family member rushing to enlist. Young Neil Hanna had registered at the Royal Military College in Kingston in spring 1915 and was training as a gunner. In September, he planned to attend a military aviation course at Hendon, England. Neil expected to join the Royal Flying Corps, a goal his parents secretly hoped would not be fulfilled. Both preferred that their reckless son would join the artillery and keep his feet firmly on the ground. Meanwhile, Jack Hanna was busy with the war effort, finalizing plans for a provincially-funded military hospital in Orpington, England and giving impassioned speeches at packed recruitment rallies in Toronto.

After being assured that her mother had recovered from her illness, Roberta returned to Edmonton in September 1915. It promised to be a busy school year. Nearly five thousand domestic science lessons were now being taught each month in Edmonton schools. The war was had now become part of Roberta's curriculum. She taught her students to sew and roll miles of bandages for the men overseas.[10]

Sometime in the fall, Roberta began to quietly make formal inquiries about volunteering for overseas service. She wasn't alone. At a time when refugee women and their ragged children were clogging the roads leading out of Belgium, thousands of North American and European women were fighting to get as near to the front as they could.[11] Some were galvanized by the same things men were – a hunger for adventure, desire to serve the Empire, and opportunities to gain social status through military service. Some were overwhelmed by sympathy for the victims of Germany's invasion of Belgium. The stories of innocent villagers slaughtered in the early months of the war incensed many women and propelled them into action.

The desire to escape was also a powerful motivator. In the first decades of the twentieth century, a sure sign of a man's wealth was his daughter's exemption from physical or intellectual work.[12] Upon graduation from respectable boarding schools, many single middle- and upper-class young women were expected to ornament their fathers' drawing rooms, sipping tea, making light conversation, and playing the piano. For many, it was a life of unrelenting boredom.

The establishment of Voluntary Aid Detachments provided them with a socially acceptable opportunity to shake the dust from their heels. British Voluntary Aid Detachments were groups of twenty-three untrained, unpaid nurses who were sent wherever their services were needed. While the initials "VAD" initially stood for individual detachments, they soon came to refer to each individual member of the group. The organization was established in Britain in 1910 and was managed by the British Red Cross Society and the St. John's Ambulance and Brigade Associations.[13] With the advent of the Great War, women flooded into the service. By 1916, eight thousand young, single, middle- and upper-class women from across the Empire had joined British Voluntary Aid Detachments.[14]

Many of the women in the British VADs were Canadians. Although the Canadian branch of this program had been established in 1914, Canadian VADs were not called to overseas service until the summer of 1916.[15] Impatient with waiting, many women withdrew their applications, financed their own trips overseas, and applied directly to the British program. Many "Macdonald girls" became VADs, and would later come home and share their experiences with a new generation of students at the Institute.

Hands that were more experienced in sewing fine seams or tinkling the ivories were now expected to sterilize needles, change bloodied dressings, and massage the feet of men suffering from trench foot and frostbite.[16] Some VADs also found themselves doing the greasy work of maintaining and driving ambulances and staff cars. Only the affluent had been able to purchase automobiles before the war. For this reason, VADs were among the few women who knew how to drive, making them excellent chauffeurs for the military.

While some privileged women found roles as volunteers, others sought professional, paid opportunities for service. A growing number of women from progressive families had nursing training or attended universities and colleges in the first decade of the twentieth century. When war broke out, those who were qualified as nurses eagerly applied to the various military nursing organizations. By the end of the conflict, nearly thirteen thousand paid professional nurses would be working in Britain's Queen Alexandra's Imperial Military Nursing Service (QAIMNS) and the Territorial Force Nursing Service.[17] In Canada, 3,141 nurses had joined the Canadian Army Medical Corps (CAMC). Twenty-five hundred of these women would eventually serve overseas.

Uneducated, and without any "services" to offer, poor and working-class women were initially excluded from war-front occupations. That would change in 1917, when the girls from London and Liverpool's back streets would be actively recruited to work in newly formed military auxiliaries. These capable women would do the same kinds of tasks they had done before the war – rolling up their sleeves and cooking, cleaning, laundering, and serving food at military and hospital camps. Eventually they would be made responsible for baking the thousands of loaves of white bread that were sent up the line to the men in the trenches.

While a limited number of women were able to participate in British or warfront services, most women did what they had always done in wartime – supported families and filled the social and economic gaps left behind by the thousands of men who were soldiering. It wasn't easy. Soldiers' wives would support families on budgets cut precariously close to the bone. In Canada, most would live on about $60 per month.[18] This seemed like a lot of money to poor families at the beginning of the war. However, as

ABSENT (2).

And sometimes, in the twilight gloom apart,
The tall trees whisper, whisper heart to heart;
From my fond lips the eager answers fall,
Thinking I hear thee, thinking I hear thee call.

BAMFORTH (COPYRIGHT). WORDS BY THE KIND PERMISSION OF MESSRS. BOOSEY & CO., LONDON.

Postcards summed up the feelings of loss and
longing experienced by many women during the war.
Author's Collection.

the years would pass, rocketing inflation would make their income vastly inadequate.

Unmarried women from poor and working-class families also had to fight to survive. Life in the parlour was not an option for them. Their main career choice in 1914 was domestic service. Even this low-waged, "unskilled" work was insecure. The economic recession that had plagued Canadians in the years leading up to the war had caused many wealthy families to economize. They dismissed servants, forcing many domestic workers onto the streets and into poverty.

By 1915, all this changed. War industries and a growing call for Canadian agricultural goods increased demand for women workers while driving some salaries higher. Women now filled vacant spots on assembly lines left by men rushing off to war. Before the conflict was over, more than thirty-five thousand women would work in Canada's munitions factories.[19] (Millions of British women would work in their country's industries.)

War work wasn't limited to cities and towns. Canada was still a farming nation. Crops needed to be seeded and harvested, whether or not there was a shortage of male farm hands. Women had always farmed, but their labours were usually restricted to gardening, dairy, and poultry production while men worked in the fields. During the war, this gender-based division of labour was temporarily abandoned. For the first time in the history of the West, female farm workers were transported by special trains from Ontario to Alberta to help bring in the harvest. In the evenings they were joined by women who had spent their daylight hours working as teachers, store clerks, and secretaries.[20]

Women also knit scarves, rolled bandages, and filled jars full of sticky peaches and ropey string beans for the soldiers overseas. While the image of women's groups packing crates full of two-quart sealers and hand-knit socks may seem poignant now, the parcels that they prepared were a vital contribution to the war effort, particularly in the latter years. The Ontario Women's Institutes alone sent the $1.65 million worth of cash and goods overseas, roughly equivalent to $26.7 million in 2006.[21]

There is no record of why Roberta MacAdams wanted to serve but it seems likely that she did not want to sit patiently at home while her brother, nephew, and friends risked their lives. By serving her country overseas, Roberta could place herself physically closer to those she loved.

There was stiff competition for the limited number of positions for women in military hospitals overseas. Roberta was not a nurse and no dietitians had yet been "taken on strength" by the Canadian Army Medical Corps. Shortly before Christmas she received a "don't call us, we'll call you" letter from a government official, informing her that "just as soon as we are able to give you any more definite information on the question of your appointment, I will be glad to see that you are advised."[22]Frustrated with government inertia, Roberta may have made an appeal to her brother-in-law Jack Hanna. He had already pulled a few government strings to get a commission for his son Neil. It was more than likely that he was also prepared to do so for Roberta.[23] The hospital that he had helped establish in England was becoming a reality and the CAMC was looking for people willing to staff it.

While Roberta was trying to find a way to serve overseas, her friend Gladys Caverhill was facing her own wartime challenge. Caverhill was now engaged to Robert Hoyt, a soldier with the 63rd Battalion. Usually female teachers lost their jobs when they married. However, in a January letter to William Carpenter (now School Superintendent), Roberta asked that Gladys be allowed to "continue in her present position under the Edmonton Board" after her marriage. Carpenter agreed, saying that her employment after marriage was "a war measure and as such would be considered an exception."[24]

On January 22, Roberta sat at her desk in the three-room apartment she had recently rented in the fashionable new Buena Vista Apartments. The room was warm from the glowing gas fireplace. Through the tall windows of her third-floor suite she could see the snow-covered roofs of the wood-framed homes that had sprung up in the city's west end during the real estate boom four years before. Much had happened since she first stepped off the train into the frontier capital. Now she faced another exciting turn in the road. Writing with her usual back-slanting scrawl, she composed a short and direct letter to William Bradey.

> 17 Buena Vista Apartments
> Edmonton, January 22, 1916
>
> Mr. W. D. Bradey
> Secretary Treasurer School Board
>
> Dear Mr. Bradey,
>
> I beg to make application for an indefinite leave of absence from my position under the School Board to commence January 25th, 1916.
> In explanation allow me to state that I have this morning received official notification of my appointment as Dietitian on the staff of the Ontario Government Military Hospital, with instructions to leave as soon as transportation arrives and to report at Parliament Buildings, Toronto. I may add that I shall hold the rank of lieutenant and shall be enlisted for the duration of the war and six months afterwards.
>
> Sincerely,
> Roberta MacAdams[25]

Within a few weeks, Roberta was in Toronto, wearing the crisp blue and white uniform of a nursing sister.

CHAPTER 7

ORPINGTON

CANADA'S WAR CAKE

Boil together 5 minutes:
1 packet raisins
2 cups brown sugar
2 cups boiling water
1 teaspoon salt
1 teaspoon cinnamon
½ teaspoon cloves
½ teaspoon ginger
½ teaspoon nutmeg
2 tablespoons shortening

When cold, add:
3 cups flour
1 teaspoon soda

Bake in a slow oven, ¾ hour.

(Favorite Recipes of Phebie Hallock, **Florence B. Hallock, 1922***)*

It was half past seven on a grey February morning in 1916. It was quieter than usual at the slippery parade grounds at Toronto's Exhibition Camp.[1] The railway siding on the edge of the field was empty. There were no crowds of teary women and stoic pensioners waving to trains filled with crowds of cheering soldiers. Instead, the only sound was the muffled tramping of high-top leather boots on powdery snow. A group of blue-uniformed women were doing their morning drill. A wide-shouldered policeman, black gloved hands clasped behind his back, stood at the corner of the field and smiled as he watched the women march disjointedly back and forth, hopelessly attempting to step in time with one another.[2] One tall slender woman was particularly noticeable – her hair kept slipping out from under her felt hat and her scarlet-lined cape was flying into the air, just like a magic carpet trying to take off for a warmer climate.

The tall woman was Roberta MacAdams. She had arrived in January to take her place with the eighty nurses who had been detailed for the Ontario Military Hospital in Orpington, Kent. Although the 1,040-bed hospital was officially open, its wards were still under construction. Until it was complete and ready to accept patients, the women would spend their time in Canada, drilling and preparing themselves for the heavy responsibilities that awaited them. Each afternoon, they gathered at the Ontario Parliament Buildings to hear lectures on proper military procedures and wartime medical techniques. One of their teachers was Dr. Helen MacMurchy. The founder and editor of *Canadian Nurse Magazine*, MacMurchy was a staunch advocate for women in all branches of medicine. She soon became a mentor to many of the women preparing to serve at the hospital in Orpington.

Roberta stood out among the sea of nurses scribbling copious notes as MacMurchy lectured. At thirty-five years old, she was one of the oldest women training in Toronto (thirty-eight was the cut-off age for nurses in the Canadian Army Medical Corps[3]). Roberta was also preparing herself for a unique role. She was the only dietitian ever accepted into the CAMC. The fact that her enlistment papers

Lt. Roberta MacAdams in her dress uniform.
Spaulding Collection.

described her as a "nursing sister" underlined the fact that there were few other jobs available to women in the military.

The eighty nurses with whom Roberta was serving were also a rare breed. When the war began, there were over three thousand professional nurses in Canada. With a limited number of nursing positions available and a growing number of new graduates, there were more applicants than jobs for those who want to join the CAMC.[4] As a result, the women selected to join the corps were the cream of the nursing profession. Twenty of the nurses for the Ontario Military Hospital were former superintendents of hospitals in Canada and the United States. Since the military hospital would have a psychiatric department, another twenty had been selected because they had nursed in hospitals for the "mentally deranged."[5]

While training, Roberta stayed with Maud and Jack, who had purchased a second home in Toronto's fashionable Wychwood neighbourhood (they also continued to maintain their Sarnia house). Jack had been appointed provincial secretary and was active in armed forces recruiting drives throughout Ontario. He was also in charge of purchasing the equipment that would furnish the Ontario Military Hospital, right down to the nurse's uniforms. Soon he would leave his post with the Ontario government and be appointed Food Controller in Prime Minister Borden's unionist cabinet.

The Hanna home was full of people. Jack's nephew Harold had also come to live with them. When Leander Hanna, Jack's brother, had died a few years before, Jack promised to take an active interest in his son. From all accounts, Harold was a wild young man who spent his money freely and liked to have a good time. He was desperate to join the newly formed Royal Air Force but was not yet of legal age. It would be 1918 before he would sit in the cockpit of an Allied fighter plane. Meanwhile, Jack and Maud's eldest daughter Margaret was enrolled at the Macdonald Institute. Their youngest daughter Katherine was training as an ambulance driver.

In the guestroom of the Hanna home, with its mission oak wainscoting and wide bay windows, Roberta carefully packed her military-issue, brassbound steamer trunk. She folded four pale blue linen working dresses, twenty-four aprons, twelve white collars and cuffs, twenty-six pairs of black and tan stockings, two pairs of white silk gloves (for dress occasions), and one pair of tan kid gloves (for "everyday"). Warm flannelette and cotton nightgowns, "drawers" and slips (purchased at her own expense) were neatly folded on top of the uniforms. Tucked in the bottom of the trunk was a pair of rubber boots, a folding mirror, sweater, and waterproof apron. Already anticipating England's damp winters, Roberta had strapped her umbrella to her carry-on canvas bag, with its change of clothes, travel blanket, and raincoat. Another bag contained her camp kit with its three rough blankets, folding wash basin, waterproof sheet and telescopic folding camp cot.

In her "working uniform," with its bibbed apron and blue dress, Roberta looked more like a student dietitian at the Macdonald Institute than a member of the army medical corps. Yet her head covering suggested a different role. A square yard of snowy white muslin was folded across her brow and left to fall across the back of her head. With her soft round chin, straight nose and steady gaze, she looked like a military Madonna, a woman to be treated with respect.

There was another sign that Roberta and the nurses with whom she was training were to be taken seriously. On their shoulders they wore two brass lieutenants' stars. Canadian women were the only nurses in the British Empire assigned military rank. Their dress uniforms underlined the point — each woman wore a navy blue serge uniform with scarlet collar and cuffs, great coat, short cape, and a dark blue felt hat. The stars were repeated on their coats, as though to ensure there would not be any doubt as to the women's rank.

As Roberta waited for her orders to arrive, there was bad news from Ottawa. On the evening of February 3, 1916, as Members of Parliament debated a bill in the House of Commons, the doors to the legislative chamber burst open. A parliamentary staff member shouted, "The building is on fire! Get out as quickly as possible!" By morning, the flames had reduced most of the building to rubble. Only the parliamentary library was saved. While all the Members of Parliament escaped, seven staff members did not.[6] When he heard the news, Jack Hanna told all who would listen that the fire was the work of saboteurs. "We all have our opinion as to the origin of the fire though we may be unable to prove it. It will take very direct and conclusive proof indeed to convince me that it was not the work of the enemy."[7] The war suddenly seemed much closer to home.

Another month would pass before Roberta received word that she and her colleagues were to proceed overseas. Construction on the hospital was finally complete. Sixty-nine orderlies and a small group of officers had already been transferred to the hospital and were preparing for the Ontario-based staff to arrive. On Wednesday, March 29, Roberta, eighty nurses and thirty-six doctors took the train to Halifax, arriving in the port city on Saturday, April 1. There they and eight thousand Canadian troops boarded His Majesty's Troop Ship *Olympic*,[8] sister ship of the ill-fated Titanic. At thirty-five years old, Roberta was about to reverse the journey that William and Mary McAdams had made more than seventy years before.

Despite the excitement of being so close to the final leg of their journey overseas, there was grumbling among some of Roberta's colleagues when they discovered that although the ship would be in port until the following Wednesday, no one would be granted leave. "My one sorrow was not being able to see my sister before sailing, especially as she had not been very well this winter and had so set her heart on seeing me," wrote Nurse Isobel Draffin to Dr. MacMurchy. "I (thought I) might have been allowed at least 36 hours leave of absence – but one had to submit to discipline, I expect."[9]

At least Draffin was able to cool her heels in a ship that had a fascinating history. When the *Olympic* was first launched by the White Star Line in early 1911, its first-class passengers enjoyed unparalleled comfort. Their cabins were spacious, with private sitting rooms, bathrooms, and decks. In the evening, men in formal evening suits and women in filmy Paris gowns walked down the elegant grand staircase to the dining saloon where they were served seven-course dinners by attentive waiters. Second-class accommodations were scaled-down versions of first class, with large staterooms, a library and smoking room. Even in third class or

The Olympic, sister ship of the Titanic.
Maritime Museum of the Atlantic; MP 18-142-2.

"steerage," passengers enjoyed a large dining saloon, lounge, and oak-panelled smoking room.

In September 1915, the British Admiralty drafted the high-speed *Olympic* into war service. When Roberta and her colleagues stepped on board in the spring of 1916, the trappings of luxury had been removed. So too were many of the distinctions in accommodation. The *Olympic* was originally designed to accommodate 3,295 passengers (including a crew of 860).[10] Now, with eight thousand troops on board, space was at a premium.[11] Soldiers slept in hammocks that were so close together they have to crawl under them to get to their own berths. Those men who entered the ship last were assigned to "F" deck. It was the worst billet, located in the bowels of the ship, where the air was stale and fetid.[12] Officers and nurses were better off, although they, too, had little privacy. A stateroom that once held one or two people in first class now accommodated Roberta and three nurses.

On Wednesday morning, April 5, the ship finally set sail for Liverpool. Flat grey paint covered its once gleaming black hull.[13] Six anti-submarine guns had been added to the ship, a reminder of the two German submarine attacks the ship had successfully survived a few months earlier. With its decks filled with uniformed nurses and men in khaki, it bore little resemblance to the five-star floating hotel it had once been.

A bugler trumpeted everyone awake each morning. Soldiers drilled and paraded on deck all day long while doctors and nurses got their first taste of military medicine. One hundred soldiers visited the ship's clinic each day to be treated for fevers, cuts, and bruises. Fifty men became seriously ill en route to England. Several suffered from pneumonia. Their hacking coughs and hollow cheeks reflected the fact that early in the war, a large portion of Canadian soldiers arrived in Britain unfit for military service. Many had lived in poverty before the war, victims of the economic recession that had until recently been gripping their young nation. As Roberta would later tell the Alberta legislature, "before the war [these men] have walked the streets because there was something wrong in our social system and we could not rightfully and safely direct them."[14]

Despite bouts of seasickness and the limitations imposed by military regulation, the spirit on board was high. Soldiers and medical workers alike were excited by the prospect of meaningful work and, for some, high drama and adventure. Many of the recruits were young men who had eagerly waited their turn to fight the hated "Boche." Few had any understanding of what war really meant. The Great War was the first major conflict to engulf Canadians since the days when the South African War had provided limited military service to over eight thousand equally eager recruits.[15]

The six-day journey passed quickly for Roberta, with spare moments taken up with letter writing, walks on the deck, lifeboat drills, and even the occasional concert. Between four and six each afternoon, she and the other women wrapped their travel rugs around their legs and stretched out on curving wooden steamer chairs on the main deck. They drank tea and made conversation while the ocean waves rose and fell. In the evenings, a military band played while a formal dinner was served in what had once been the elegant first-class dining saloon. According to Nurse Grace McPherson, "the blue and scarlet dress uniforms look so pretty in with all the khaki."[16] After the meal was over, an officer stood and proposed a solemn toast to the King.

On April 10, the *Olympic* docked in Liverpool. As they stepped onto shore, many of the women declared they would not have missed the crossing for anything.[17] They soon took the train to Orpington, arriving in the middle of the night on April 12.[18]

⬠ ⬠ ⬠

The plane was packed for the eight-hour flight to London's Heathrow Airport. In the row ahead of me, an elderly British woman was shoving a large striped plastic bag filled with souvenirs and other "essentials" into the tiny space under the seat in front of her. The air smelled like lavender and that wonderful bookish smell that in my childhood accompanied parcels from England filled with soft toffees, knitted doll clothes, and Enid Blyton story books.

My journey in Roberta's footsteps was taking me to Britain, home to my own ancestors and hers. I planned to visit the places where Roberta once lived and worked — the hospital at Orpington, the London hotel where she celebrated her election victory, and the coastal village where she visited with one of Punch Magazine's most famous artists. In endless searches through archives across Canada, I had gathered every scrap of paper I could find, documenting her words and actions. It was still precious little. By going overseas as she did, I hoped to excavate her experience far from home.

While thoughts of the Roberta and the Great War ran through my head, the in-flight movie began to play. I ignored it at first, hoping to sleep through most of the trip. Then I was fumbling for my headphones, eyes focused on the screen where a dazed young soldier, his bayonet drawn, climbed over the top of a crowded trench. He ran like a football player, dodging exploding shells and ripping his skin on barbed wire, while his friends dropped into the oozing green mud beside him. After the battle ended he walked through a fog of spent ammunition, a lone survivor in a field of bodies.

The movie was the "Legend of Bagger Vance," an American film that traces the impact of World War I on one young man. But the images were too real and my mind filled in any blanks. I might have been in a silver steel tube flying thirty-five thousand feet in the air, but the ghosts of the Great War were flying with me, flickering on a tiny screen above my head.

❧❧❧

On a chilly late April afternoon in 1916, Roberta was walking through an empty ward of the Ontario Military Hospital, her heels clicking on the eight-foot-wide strip of linoleum laid in the centre aisle. Beside her was Georgina Villiers,[19] a journalist for *The Nursing Times*. Villiers had come to tour the hospital and record her impressions of "the princely gift of the Province" to the care of the Empire's soldiers.[20] Captain Fox, the hospital's quartermaster – his bushy moustache waxed and curled for the occasion – walked ahead of the women, providing a running commentary on the hospital's innovations.

"All I knew about Orpington was that it was where the fowls came from," MacAdams whispered to Villiers, as Fox began a lengthy dissertation on local history.[21] As the two women listened, they leaned against a pile of wooden crates – one of the many that now blocked the aisles of the hospital. Forty-one boxcars of equipment – everything from scalpels to beds – had been purchased in Ontario under the direction of Jack Hanna. It had been shipped overseas in February, but was still in crates when the medical team arrived.

The three spent the rest of the morning touring the hospital. There were twenty fifty-two-bed wards – long narrow huts with light green asbestos walls, white ceilings, and brown polished floors. The wards were arranged horizontally on a hillside like wings in a giant biplane. Two sets of covered gangways connected the wings together in the middle, allowing nurses to travel from ward to ward without having to brave the damp English weather. At the entrance to this complex, a building that looked like a cross between a school and a church stood ready to admit the wounded. Above its wide front doors was a clock tower with a curving roof. On each side of the cupola were two stained-glass windows, lit from the inside, each bearing the international symbol of the Red Cross.

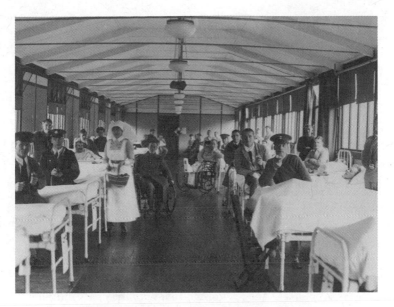

One of the wards at the Ontario Military Hospital.
Provincial Archives of Ontario; C224-0-0-57.

Roberta hugged her navy blue sweater closely around her shoulders as she stepped outside with Villiers and Fox. The sky was steel wool grey and the gravel pathway was dark and wet. The damp English chill made many western Canadians long for the dry cold of a prairie spring. As the group slipped along the path, they stopped now and then to step into the many buildings that stood at angles to the wards.

There was much to see. The hospital was one of the most modern in Great Britain. There was an X-ray department, pathology laboratory, and a psychiatric building. The dental clinic was filled with state–of–the–art drills, special chairs, and gleaming silver tools encased in glass-fronted cabinets. In this place, jaws torn apart by shells and bayonets would be rebuilt and infectious diseases like trench mouth would be brought under control. There were operating theatres, administration offices, a mortuary, theatre, recreation hut, butcher's shop, wash and bathrooms, dining rooms, sitting rooms, and a chapel. All the buildings were steam heated (a novelty in Britain) and electrified, with simple white glass lamps hanging from the ceilings at regular intervals. Every ward had its own diet kitchen, pantry, medicine room, bath and wash rooms, and nursing sister's "chart room." Even telephones, an expensive luxury in wartime, were allocated to each ward.

The final stop on the tour was the staff quarters. The "boundary house," the rambling brick mansion that once overlooked empty fields dotted with buttercups, had been conscripted as the new home of the hospital's commanding officer, Lt. Col. McPherson, his wife, and a small group of high-ranking officers. The remainder of the staff was housed in the south end of the hospital complex in buildings similar to the wards. There were five dormitories for day nurses and three smaller buildings for those who worked the night shift. The nurses also had their own dining and sitting room, a wide building that separated their quarters from the men's. Male officers lived in a U-shaped compound, with the men's dining hall and recreation rooms in the centre of the "U."

Matron Margaret Smith invited the group into her private sitting room, its walls hung with pictures of nurses standing in front of bell tents, hospitals at Le Treport and Shorncliffe, as well as a photograph of a "lonely and dignified" duck, a hospital mascot. Villiers had already discovered that most of the nurses had developed a deep affection for Smith. According to one nurse, she had a "kind face and an agreeable manner, and seems take a personal interest in the sisters."[22]

Smith's esprit de corps was the product of an earlier stint with military nursing. She was one of the few nurses to join with Canadian soldiers for service in South Africa in the Boer War. During that conflict, most British military hospitals had fewer than twenty nurses to care for hundreds of men. Smith arrived in South Africa in 1902 with the third group of Canadian nurses sent overseas. They were assigned to the British hospital in Harrismith, where the greatest challenge was the weather – bitterly cold nights and ferociously hot days.[23]

When war with Germany was declared in 1914, Smith enlisted with the CAMC. She traveled overseas with the First Canadian Contingent and was immediately assigned to nurse at the Canadian military hospital in Le Treport, France. She was later transferred to hospitals in Britain, eventually accepting the post of matron at the Ontario Military Hospital. As Villiers listened to the short stocky nurse, she quickly gained the impression that Smith preferred life "under canvas" in the theatre of war, rather than the relative comfort of the Orpington hospital.[24]

Villiers' tour ended at the women's dining hall, seated at the linen-covered head table with the Assistant Matron, Home Sister, and Roberta. "There was a camaraderie about the Canadian hospital that was difficult to describe," Villiers would write. It was a camaraderie that would be put to the test as the first wounded men arrived.

———

While the staff of the Ontario Military Hospital were preparing to serve at Orpington, back at home the women of Alberta were experiencing some changes of their own – changes that would eventually have a huge impact on the life of Roberta MacAdams. On the afternoon of March 1, 1916, the Alberta legislature finally extended voting rights to women. On that special day, two hundred women filled the steps of the Alberta legislature, ready to have their photograph taken. They were members of the Alberta Women's Institutes (AWI), in Edmonton for the group's annual convention. The organization that Roberta had helped establish had grown from two official branches in 1912 to 145 in 1916.[25]

The photographer adjusted his camera and motioned to the crowd in front of him to stand absolutely still while their picture was taken. There was still a winter chill in the air – the women's hands were buried in thick fur muffs, their heads weighed down by hats heavy with decorative piles of velvet, fur, and ostrich feathers. There were a few men in the party, too. Roberta's old friend Duncan Marshall stood front row centre, right next to Nellie McClung and Emily Murphy – the two women who had faced Premier Sifton on those very steps in 1913.

As she posed for her picture, McClung was triumphant, although she well knew that Premier Sifton had been motivated not by some great spiritual conversion to the women's cause, but by pure, old-fashioned politics. He was looking ahead to a provincial election in which he believed women's votes would play a key role in keeping his party in power.[26]

After their photograph was taken, the women of the AWI walked proudly through the heavy oak doors of the legislature, their long winter coats sweeping the floor of the grand marble entranceway and up the grand red-carpeted stairway to the spectator's gallery. There were "white-haired women, women with little children by the hand, women with babies in their arms, smartly dressed women, alert, tailor-made business women; quiet dignified and earnest; they were all there," wrote Nellie McClung. "When the Premier (Liberal A.L. Sifton) rose to move the second reading of the bill, the silence of the legislative chamber was tense, and the great mass of humanity in the galleries did not appear to breathe. The Premier outlined the reasons for the granting of the franchise; he did not speak of it as a favor, a boon, a gift, or a privilege, but a right, and declared that the extension of the franchise was an act of justice; he did not once refer to us as the 'fair sex'."[27] The leader of the Conservative party, Edward Michener, seconded the motion. The motion was carried, with only one member opposing.

⁓⁓⁓

Back in Britain, the staff of the Ontario Military Hospital had only a few convalescent patients to care for. For the few months before the first trainloads of wounded would arrive, doctors and nurses levered crates apart, prepared sterilisers, unpacked dental chairs, and smoothed crisp white sheets on empty beds. Most of the nurses wore wool stockings and two petticoats under their uniforms. Spring had still not yet brought a reprieve from the frigid weather. A hot water bottle was issued to each staff member.

Across the English Channel in the boggy trenches of France and Belgium there were no such comforts. Sleet, snow, and rain were the constant companions of the men, some of whom would soon fill the hospital beds at Orpington. Troops bored by inactivity and spurred on by directions from Sir Douglas Haig's headquarters, played risky games of "capture the flag" with the Germans. They raided each other's trenches, capturing prisoners or sniping at careless soldiers. In the first six months of 1916, eighty-three thousand British soldiers were killed and wounded in what was called the "normal wastage" of trench warfare.[28]

In April and May, Canadian troops were fighting desperately around a town in Belgium called St. Eloi. They fought in a sea of muddy water-filled craters, tripping over broken bodies mired in mud, shells bursting all around them. But worse was yet to come. On June 2, explosions rocked the ground in and around nearby Mount Sorrel. Four mines exploded under that hill itself, and many more destroyed trenches, sending dirt, men, and guns into the air.[29] The Germans blanketed the Canadians with shells, and followed up with waves of infantry. The Canadians pushed back and regained lost ground, but at a huge cost. Between June 2 and June 13, eight thousand Canadians were killed in the battles. The German army suffered too, losing 5,765 men from shells, rifle fire and exploding mines.[30]

Some of the men who survived the battle were likely among the 127 wounded Canadians, Australians, New Zealanders, and British who arrived in Orpington by train at 10:30 pm on June 8. Orderlies and nurses quickly drew men out on stretchers and lined them up on the station platform like so many loaves of bread disgorged from an oven. Nine ambulances, each with a red cross and "Canada" emblazoned on its sides, delivered the men to the hospital within forty-five minutes, their tires protesting as they rumbled down the sloping road from the station to the hospital. The next evening, another ninety wounded arrived. Some still wore the bandages applied by front-line hospitals in France. Their clothes were torn and stained with blood, their boots streaked with dried mud. The surgical ward was filled with muttering men suffering from arm, shoulder, and leg wounds. One of the most seriously injured had a bullet pass right through his body, entering through his back and coming out in front of his stomach.[31]

Hospital trains continued to arrive at all hours of the day or night. Four more convoys of patients arrived in June, adding 445 patients. Another eight convoys reached Orpington in July with 983 wounded men. Extra beds were added, but the hospital had reached its capacity. Some of the wounded were sent on to seven VAD hospitals in Oakley, Southwood, and Farnborough.[32] Plans were made to double the size of the Canadian hospital.

In the main kitchen on the west side of the complex, Roberta supervised the production of roughly thirty-five hundred meals each day. One side of the kitchen was lined with forty-four bake ovens arranged in four deep tiers. Six free-standing steel soup kettles the size of bushel baskets stood sentinel along the other wall. Their heavy lids were raised through a system of pulleys and ropes attached to the walls behind them. Four heavy iron ranges and five steam ovens stood next to the kettles, ready to cook mountains of potatoes and roast the chickens raised in pens by hospital staff.

Sometimes the heavy smells pouring out of the deep pots forced Roberta outside to breathe in the clean, earthy air of late spring in Kent. One warm afternoon, she could hear what sounded like a giant carpet being beaten somewhere in the heavens. It was actually the sound of individual machine gun bursts and the explosion of shells coming from Flanders – about 120 miles away.[33] Usually listeners could only hear a dull thud, thud, growing more intense, then slowing down, then booming again. But on that day, there must have been an especially fierce battle, since the sounds were so loud and distinct they made the windows rattle in the nearby wards.[34]

The battle sounds were a reminder that her nephew Neil was now in France, serving with the British army. He had not been able to realize his dream of joining the air force, and instead had accepted a commission in the Royal Field Artillery. Soon he would be transferred to the cavalry. His safety was a gnawing preoccupation – Neil was more kid brother than nephew for Roberta. She had kept a close contact with him since her arrival in Britain. Roberta knew that for Maude and Jack, the sun rose and set on the twenty-one-year-old. They wrote to him a few times a week, sending copies of his replies to Roberta. They were proud that he was serving but constantly worried about the dangers that he was facing.

There was one saving grace – Roberta's brother Johnston was not yet in France. Although he had joined the 34th Battalion as a Captain in October 1915, he had not yet been sent to the front since the Canadian forces had more officers than they could use in the field. Johnston was assigned to work as a musketry instructor at the famous Shorncliffe military camp. Even there, accidents could happen. In the summer of 1916, he was thrown from his horse and broke several ribs.

Despite his injury, Johnston's relative safety reassured Roberta and made it easier for her to focus on the challenges of her new job. Life at Orpington made her former work in Edmonton look simple. She planned menus and directed kitchen staff under the supervision of Captain McIntosh, assistant quartermaster. A strict process was followed each day to keep meals flowing punctually to patients. At 10 a.m. every morning, doctors completed the menu chart hanging at the foot of each patient's bed. The nurse in charge collected the charts and wrote a report listing the food requirements for her ward. She sent the report to McIntosh, who checked the totals and compared them with the rations available from the Quartermaster's stores. When McIntosh was satisfied that everything was in order, the menu charts were forwarded to Roberta. She sat at her desk, head bent over piles of paper, and developed meal plans that fit the kinds of diets requested and the rations McIntosh was willing to release.

Roberta was no longer dealing in the trifling amounts of food that she had once ordered for domestic science classes in Edmonton. In an average month, patients and staff at the military hospital consumed 10.5 tons of meat, 2.5 tons of bacon, 14.5 tons of bread, 4 tons of sugar, 0.75 tons of tea, 2 tons of butter, 33,000 eggs, 5,518 gallons of milk, and 300 chickens.[35] Every egg and potato in this mountain of food had to be accounted for. Food costs rose by 65 per cent between 1914 and 1916. Shortages grew and prices escalated.[36] Across Britain, queues for food and coal were common. Hundreds, sometimes thousands, of women lined up at butcher shops at five in the morning and waited hours for a few sausages. Even in middle-class and wealthy families, a full coal scuttle was rare. Basic commodities such as sugar, tea, butter, margarine, lard, rice, and raisins were in especially short supply. In this time of scarcity, the amount of money allotted to the feeding of troops was calculated to the last pence – 16.4 pence per day to be precise, for each man in hospital, 14.14 pence for those on active duty.[37]

Such scrimping for injured men seemed deeply unfair to Roberta. On a trip home during the war, she would be struck by the "comparative cheapness of good food and by the serving of white finger rolls, cream in coffee and iced desserts, things that had long ago disappeared from England." It seemed to her that while soldiers, nurses, and volunteers overseas were putting their lives on the line to give Canada a "leading place in the roll of nations," Canadians themselves were making little, if any, sacrifice.[38]

❦ ❦ ❦

More than eighty years after Roberta first came to Orpington, I arrived to see what remained of the community and the hospital in which she once served. I soon learned that what was once a rural farming village is now just another suburb of the all-encompassing urban sprawl that was "greater London." Roughly thirty thousand people live within a mile of the centre of the former village, largely the families of white-collar workers, stockbrokers, and middle managers.[39]

It was pouring rain when I stepped out of the Orpington train station and banged on the window of a black cab whose driver was more engrossed in the Daily Mail than in potential customers. I asked him if he knew of the Ontario Military Hospital. I was surprised to learn that it was still a familiar landmark and that he was willing to take me there. As he drove the cab down the village's high street, I saw fish and chip shops sandwiched between Tandoori takeaways and Pizza Huts. Yet the earlier community – the one that Roberta knew – had not completely disappeared. "1912" was etched onto the brick and plaster facades above many of the stores and restaurants and a monument to the Great

GIVE YOUR OTHER VOTE TO THE SISTER

War dead stood in the centre of a busy roundabout. A turreted church nearby hinted at an even greater antiquity.

I had purchased a copy of the booklet "Orpington from Saxon Times to the Present," and flipped through it as we drove towards the hospital. I learned that up until war was declared, Orpington was a quiet country village of about four thousand. That changed on the evening of August 4, 1914. That night, and for many nights following the announcement of war, express trains thundered through the village's train station carrying soldiers to the coast. A year later, the sound of building construction began to fill the air. In 1915, the government of Ontario decided that it had a patriotic duty to build and equip a military hospital that would minister not only to the Canadian forces but also to soldiers from across the Empire. Government representatives searched Britain for an appropriate site, and settled on the "Boundary Estate," a 160-acre parcel on the edge of Orpington. The land was chosen for its location (only one mile from the train station), pristine water, and good sewage system. It was also vacant. The cost of the hospital — roughly $2 million (approximately $34 million in 2006 dollars) — was covered through a special tax levied on Ontario's citizens.[40]

Although the land was leased in July, construction did not begin until October because building materials were scarce and skilled workers even harder to find. Eventually the dogged persistence of politicians, military leaders, and businessmen overcame the obstacles. Where billows of starlings once skimmed the tall grass, an enormous complex of timber, brick, and asbestos sheeting gradually emerged. It would become one of the largest and most up-to-date hospitals in the world. By war's end, 26,278 men from all over the British Empire would be treated there. The lion's share of the wounded would be British and Canadian — 12,156 British and 12,483 Canadian.[41]

Unbelievably, I would still be able to see an echo of that huge Great War hospital. My cab drew up to the front doors of Orpington Hospital, a modern boxy beige building surrounded by a mass of well-kept, upscale brick bungalows. I sloshed up the steps into its warm entry hall. Shaking off the rain, I found myself facing a display of framed yellowing photographs on a pillar in the centre of the hall. They were pictures of the military hospital at the end of the war, as well as later shots of its wards being demolished. A photo of the clock tower being lifted down by a crane made me feel strangely sad.

I later learned that in 1917 the Ontario government, burdened by the high cost of maintaining the hospital, transferred its ownership to the Canadian government. It was renamed No. 16 Canadian General and expanded to 2,040

All that remains of the Ontario Military Hospital
is this clock tower, carefully preserved.
Author's Collection.

beds. After the war, it was sold to the British Ministry of Pensions for £80,000. The buildings were used for the care of convalescent and disabled soldiers. As the years passed, the hospital underwent many incarnations: home for the elderly, casualty centre (during World War II), tuberculosis hospital, and male nurse training school. In 1977, the old wards were torn down and replaced by the present hospital building.

Walking down the hospital hallway, I spotted a row of windows overlooking a small outdoor courtyard where patients could sit on warm summer days. In the centre of the courtyard sat the old clock tower that once loomed above the building where wounded men were admitted to the hospital. The hands that once marked off the minutes of the war had been permanently set at 3:18 and the stained glass windows with their simple red crosses remained intact.

The tower and the handful of photographs seemed to be the only physical reminders of the hospital's Great War origins. However, near the exit, was one last remnant. The hospital's directory pointed to the "Canada Wing" and "Ontario" ward. The military hospital may have been gone, but its Canadian origins were not entirely forgotten.

❦ ❦ ❦

The experiences of women serving overseas seldom found their way into the poignant poetry that poured out of the trenches during and after the Great War. Yet women were intimate witnesses to the day-to-day concerns of men recovering from the trauma of the battlefields. They treated terrible wounds, bore witness to the suffering and dying, wrote letters to anguished parents, and worked non-stop eighteen-hour days when trainloads of patients arrived. Many worked near the front lines, facing the same risk of death as the men they were treating. Much has been written about what the stress of the trenches did to the minds and hearts of many of the men who served in battle. Little has been said about what witnessing their suffering did to an army of women.

In diaries of nurses and other female volunteers, women often transformed their experience into actions on behalf of the men. They used their own salaries to buy them books and magazines, chocolates and other comforts. Although Roberta was not a nurse, she also used her role as dietitian to champion the needs of the men lying in the wards at Orpington. Every soldier is "hungry for all the physical comfort, even indulgence, he can secure," she said. For Roberta, food was the one way she could help heal the wrecked bodies that filled the hundreds of beds at the hospital. The war had swept away everything from these men but the memory of the smells and tastes of home. On the front lines, meals were prepared by cooks whose only qualifications were that they couldn't march and thus were allowed to travel behind the troops on the back of baggage carts.[42] The culinary nightmares they served were legendary – muddy tea and a greasy stew made from lumps of fat, skin, gristle, and corned beef, all "nicely browned with a dose of cook's snuff."[43] This stomach-turning diet was only broken by the occasional arrival of fresh loaves of bread made in field ovens and sent forward. When stew couldn't be made and bread didn't reach them, troops lived on rock-hard biscuits and one-pound cans of the soupy "bully beef," all carried in their packs.

One morning, a nurse told Roberta that a patient in Ward 10 adamantly refused to eat anything but tomato soup. Tomato soup had not been requested by any of the other wards and she knew that McIntosh would not release an eleven-pound can just to tempt one man's failing appetite. In her travels across Alberta, Roberta had learned that tomato soup was a kind of prairie ambrosia that could be enjoyed at any time in the year. A farm wife would empty two-quart jars of chopped tomatoes and a handful of sugar into a blue and white granite kettle on top of a hot wood stove. Then she would stir in pinches of soda, salt, and pepper. On a separate burner, a pot of milk with a thick slice of onion floating on top would be brought to a boil. While everything was bubbling away, the woman would mix a small amount of flour and butter in a crockery bowl and stir this into the milk mixture. Then she would combine the contents of the two pots and the kitchen would be filled with the heady smell of resurrected tomatoes.[44]

With some exceptions, convalescence was one of the few chances for soldiers to eat decent food, well-prepared. It was a chance that few were willing to miss. "One man who had several pieces of shrapnel removed from his shoulder in France, still thought there was another piece left in, so an operation was ordered for him," wrote Orpington Nurse Catharine Lawrence in a letter home. "When he was asked whether he would rather go without breakfast and have chloroform or have breakfast and cocaine injected, [he] chose the latter method in no uncertain tone. He did not want to miss his breakfast. At one meal hour, I happened to remark that he could have all the water he wanted, it was cheap enough. He said there were times in France when it was not very cheap."[45]

If a wounded man wanted a tinned copy of the tomato soup his mother once prepared with her own hands in a distant farm kitchen, then Roberta was determined to see that he got it. She spent the next hour going from bed to bed, persuading any man whose stomach was fit to receive it, that tomato soup was the one item of food for which they had an overwhelming yen. Nearly every soldier she asked succumbed to her smile, persuasive wit, and graceful good looks. With the nurses' support, she readjusted the diet cards and the solitary soldier got his wish.[46]

CHAPTER 8

BELOVED AND
HONOURED SONS

From little towns in a far land we came,
To save our honour and a world aflame.
By little towns in a far land we sleep;
And trust that world we won for you to keep.

(From "Two Canadian Memorials," in Epitaphs of War, Rud-
yard Kipling)

In July 1916, Roberta and Captain Fox organized a dinner dance
for the nurses and officers. Starched white cloths and bowls of fresh
roses were placed on the tables of the nurse's mess. The conversation
hummed while orderlies served a dinner of poached fish, roast potatoes, and peas. The women wore their navy blue dress uniforms, their
hair drawn up into fashionable chignons. The men's khaki uniforms
were pressed and clean, their brass buttons gleaming in the light of
the single bulbs hanging from the ceiling of the long hut. After the
meal was over, the dishes were cleared away and tables pushed back.
A piano was rolled in and a band of convalescent soldiers dressed in
blue hospital uniforms tuned their instruments.[1]

It had been more than five years since Roberta had attended that
other dance in Stony Plain. Time for a whole world to change and
shift, for the lives of men and women to alter in ways unimagined

when their shadows waltzed on the white walls of the ballroom in Hardwick and Rossell's store. Thousands had died and thousands of others had been asked to do unthinkable things in the name of God, king, and country. But as the band struck up a slow, lilting tune, soldiers and nurses became men and women again. They danced and laughed and flirted. The world could have been ending but, for the moment, the suffering and dying were forgotten.

There were other diversions that summer. On days when the warm air was heavy from the scent of roses and freshly cut grass, Mrs. MacPherson – wife of the hospital's NCO – hosted teas for patients and staff in the garden of the Boundary House. Those who could walk and swing a mallet played croquet on the lawn while others stretched out on striped canvas lawn chairs as nurses and Red Cross workers served them hot tea in bone china cups.

Sports were encouraged at the hospital. A stranger walking its narrow paths on a clear day might have been surprised to see nurses playing tennis or hear the groans of soldiers tackled to the ground in rough games of football. There was something for everyone. Those who couldn't manage strenuous pursuits could join the daily procession to the local Soldier's Club. Each afternoon, men on crutches, in wheelchairs or leaning on the arms of healthier men, walked from the hospital to the club, ready for a game of chess or a good smoke. In the cool summer evenings, Spencer May, the owner of the Orpington Picture Palace, showed films free of charge in the hospital's theatre. There were live performances, too. "Artistes" from London traveled down regularly to perform comedies and dramas for men bored by bed rest and hungry for diversion.[2]

But the beauty of summer could not shut out the ugly reality of war for Roberta. In early August, she received the kind of news everyone dreaded. Neil had been wounded in action in late July and was recuperating in an officer's hospital in London. Roberta asked Col. MacPherson for a few days' leave. On August 4, the second anniversary of the beginning of war, she took the train to the capital.

London's streets were filled with men in khaki and women in strange uniforms – from the peaked hats and narrow skirts of

Neil Hanna. Spaulding Collection.

subway ticket-collectors to the puffy overalls of yellow-skinned munitions workers. Posters were glued to every available wall, inviting readers to "Spend Less, Save More," and "Buy Only War Savings Certificates."[3] When Roberta reached Queen Alexandra's Hospital, she was ushered into Neil's room. She found him propped up in bed, smoking a cigarette. His hair seemed redder than usual against his pale white face. Neil had a cracked rib and a fracture of the crest ileum – a pelvic injury that would send him back to Toronto in October and keep him out of the front lines for three months after that.[4]

Between slow drags on his cigarette, Neil explained what happened. Apparently, he was one of the lucky survivors of one of the worst battles of the war thus far. It began along a winding twenty-five-mile stretch of trenches north of the River Somme in the heart of Picardy. British and French troops planned to mount a blazing infantry attack against the German trenches, opening the way for cavalry to ride through to victory. But the reality was much less romantic. The first day was the war's bloodiest. It began early on the morning of July 1. Nearly 250,000 shells were fired at German forces, followed closely by the explosion of ten mines that had been silently planted beneath German trenches by Allied tunnellers. With mud still flying and machine gun fire rattling through the air, British troops emerged from their trenches and began their slow, lumbering movement toward enemy trenches. They were each loaded down with sixty-six pounds of equipment, creating conveniently bulky targets for the well-fortified German machine guns that had somehow survived the massive shell fire.

A barrage of bullets made short work of thousands of British and French soldiers. Despite the carnage, two villages – Mametz and Montauban – were taken, as was the Leipzig Redoubt, an important German fortification. The cost was high. At the end of the first day of the battle, twenty-one thousand men from France and the British Empire were dead, their limbs strewn like flower petals blown apart in a violent summer storm. Another twenty-five thousand were wounded, and the carnage was only beginning. In the days that followed, the opposing forces played a lethal game of see-saw, gaining ground one day, losing it the next.

On July 12, the British took Mametz Wood, just north of the Village of Montauban. A few days later, a British pilot was ordered to fly across German lines and radio back: "Enemy second line of defence had been captured on a front of 6,000 yards. British cavalry is now passing through in pursuit." It was believed that the Germans would intercept this message and be demoralised by the news of Allied gains.[5]

The British cavalry did indeed pass through, and it was somewhere around the battle-scarred remains of Mametz Wood that the war nearly ended for Neil Hanna. Despite the obvious incompatibility of machine guns, shellfire, and horses, British General Haig still believed that cavalry could play an effective role in modern warfare. Amid machine gun bursts and exploding shells, it was little surprise that Neil's horse stampeded and fell, throwing him to the ground where he was run over by a gun carriage. By the time he regained consciousness, Neil found himself in No. 13 Field Ambulance. Later he was transferred to No. 2 Stationary Hospital at Abbeville and from there, sent on to England. Now he – along with Robert Graves, a more famous survivor of the battle[6] – was a patient in Queen Alexandra's Hospital, Highgate.

As Roberta listened to Neil's story, she was joined by Colonel Bruce, an old friend of Jack Hanna's. Bruce wasn't just any colonel – he was the Inspector of Medical Services for the CAMC. He had received a cable from Hanna earlier that afternoon asking him to track Neil down and find out if his injuries were severe. Bruce examined Neil. Reassured that her nephew was in good hands, Roberta excused herself and promised to call on him the next day.[7]

The visit with her nephew likely made Roberta long for some human connection to Canada and the comfort of home. The next morning, she stopped in at the Alberta Agent General's Office perhaps to see if she could get some news from home and write a letter to Maud and Jack in the office's writing room. She crossed Trafalgar Square with its faded recruitment posters and pigeons disconsolately pecking on barren pavement. Then Roberta dodged buses, hansom cabs, horse drawn carts, and even a few motor cars on Charing Cross Road and ducked into the stairwell of a flatiron building. When she reached the Agent General's fourth floor office, it was empty except for an auburn-haired woman busily tapping away at a typewriter. There was a sweet smell of lavender water hanging in the air. The woman looked up and Roberta found herself looking into the mischievous blue eyes of Beatrice Nasmyth, Agent General Reid's publicity secretary. Roberta introduced herself and the two women shook hands, not knowing that at that moment they were forging a relationship that would eventually make history.

⊱⊰⊱

Neil had survived a terrible battle. Many soldiers were not so fortunate. During my visit to Orpington, I went to the cemetery of All Saints Anglican Church. Any of the men who died at the Ontario Military Hospital were buried there. It was easy to find their resting-places. On one side of the cemetery, English ivy tumbled over tilting eight-hundred-year-old headstones, filled cracks in the broken stone pathway, and climbed up the sides of a broad-leaved lime tree. Beneath its wide boughs, pale mauve bluebells on slender stalks and bouquets of yellow crocuses filled the cracks in a stone tomb like a giant gothic window box. Mingled in the ground below was the dust of Celts and Romans, Saxons, Normans, and English, their individual life stories long forgotten.

The Great War section of the cemetery was noticeably different from the rest. Compared to the sculpted, moss-covered stones that ornamented the older part of the graveyard, the Great War section was austere. A low hedge surrounded a rain-drenched square of green lawn, the grass clipped as close as a soldier's haircut. A tall, slender "cross of sacrifice" overlooked 182 graves. This small, protected area was known locally as the "Canadian Corner." The men in this corner were buried facing west, looking to Canada.[8]

I walked among rows of identical headstones, most with maple leaves carved onto their hard white surfaces. Reading their epitaphs was like walking back through some of the war's worst battles.

The "Canadian Corner" of the Orpington Cemetery.
Author's Collection.

Six of the Canadians buried there had died from wounds received at Vimy Ridge. Their journey to this quiet graveyard began in a wet, muddy trench facing a low, seven-mile hump-backed ridge in Flanders. This slippery escarpment had been filled with German troops since October 1914. But on Easter morning, 1917, that situation changed. As dawn broke, one thousand Canadian guns opened fire on the German defences. As snow and sleet swept into their faces, eight thousand Canadians climbed out of their trenches and marched forward across the no man's land that once divided their ditches from those of their enemies.[9]

The battle continued until April 12, by which time the Canadians had decisive control of the ridge. It was a victory that was sorely needed after nearly three years of a war in which both sides seemed to be locked in a vicious stalemate. But the cost of the battle was huge, and for many Canadian families, beyond accounting. The first day of the battle was the last day of the war for Private John Alexander of the 16th Battalion, Canadian Scottish. Badly wounded, he remained alive long enough to make it across the Channel to Orpington. Despite the best efforts of the surgeons and nurses, he died "a dearly beloved and honoured son," one of 3,598 Canadians killed to gain a pock-marked slice of Flanders.[10]

Each "Private Alexander" who lay in the Orpington cemetery filled an important space in the lives of his family and community. We will never know what contributions they or their children might have made to a young nation, and how the lives of those they left behind were altered by their deaths.

Yet what was also striking was how few soldiers were in that small sad cemetery. Over twenty-six thousand men were admitted to the Ontario Military Hospital during the Great War. Only 182 never made it home again.[11] This was part testament to the skill of the medical staff, partly due to the fact that the most serious cases never survived to make their way across the Channel. This meant that much of the work of the Ontario Military Hospital was about helping men recover and return – either to the front lines or to lives radically altered by physical or mental disability.

In every hospital, nurses were front-line workers in the battle to reclaim lives. They sterilized surgical tools, prepared men for operations, and assisted during surgery. Each day they bent over the beds of men whose crackling, gangrenous wounds smelled like swamp water. They changed blood-soaked dressings and helped feed men who were too weak or unable to lift a spoon to their lips. In quiet moments, they stirred together buckets of the disinfecting liquids that were their chief weapons in the fight against infection and death

– "one pound (of lime) to one gallon of cold water; salicylic acid 46 grams, bicarbonate of soda 30 grams, water one quart."[12]

The women at the Ontario Military Hospital also worked on the invisible wounds of war. They resocialized men and helped them re-enter a nearly forgotten world. For Roberta, this meant providing comfort through freshly baked bread, cottage puddings, and any kind of comfort food she could cobble together from limited rations.

For many soldiers, the nurses, VADs, and other female staff represented those they'd left behind – wives and lovers, homes and families. The comfort that the women gave could be as simple as the soft touch of a cool hand on a hot forehead. Many soldiers would recall these small kindnesses long after the war was over. In his book **The First Day on the Somme**, author Martin Middlebrooke describes one soldier's memory of a nurse at Orpington. According to Middlebrooke, six days after his leg was spattered with shrapnel at the Battle of the Somme, Private Allsop was taken into surgery at the Ontario Military Hospital. When he woke up, a doctor and nurse were standing beside his bed with broad smiles on their faces. "It's missed the bone by a hair's breadth, laddie," said the doctor. The nurse bent down and kissed his cheek.[13]

About ten thousand Canadian soldiers and at least twenty-five thousand British troops were treated for shell shock or "neurasthenia" during the war.[14] Some of these cases ended up at Orpington, where they were assigned to a ward set aside for shell shock victims. The nurses assigned to this ward had been recruited from mental hospitals across Canada. As part of their work, they prepared continuous baths for men suffering from shell shock, "often with fine results."[15]

Mental breakdown was an extreme outcome of the nightmares that soldiers were forced to live. Many bore emotional scars that didn't lead to institutionalization. Discouragement, despair, and apathy were often the lot of those who were slowly returning to health. For these men, comfort often came in the form of a visitor or sympathetic nurse. On Mondays and Fridays, Red Cross workers walked through the wards of the Military Hospital, carrying baskets of glossy apples wrapped in tissue paper. String bags filled with cigarettes, candy, and books hung from their arms. Some of the women would stop and sit quietly beside beds, writing letters home for men who were too tired or unable to write.

In one of a handful of photographs of the hospital that survives, beds line both sides of a long narrow ward. One man sat quietly near a window, one arm resting on a night table. His other arm was gone, an empty sleeve neatly pinned to his jacket. In the centre of the room, a one-legged teenager sat on

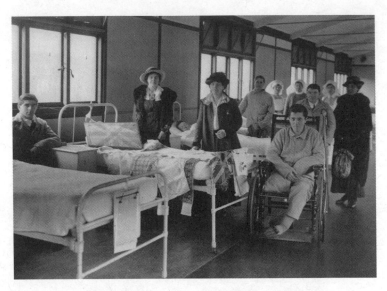

Soldier "rehabilitation" during the Great War.
Provincial Archives of Ontario; C 224-0-0-57.

a wheelchair near a group of women. The women's mouths were drawn into tight lines, like the fine needlework displayed on the bed in front of them. They were members of the "Ladies' Work Association."

Princess Patricia, the same woman who had lent her name to the Princess Patricia's Canadian Light Infantry (PPCLI), founded and actively participated in the Association. Each week, the group visited the hospital to teach sewing to wounded men as part of their "ward occupations." According to **Orpington from Saxon Times to the Great War***, the "industries taught were embroidery, lace, wood carving, bead work, basket work (Indian and other sorts), old English embroidery, knitting, sewing, painting, and stencilling; and net bags for the blind men."[16] Broken men, repairing their lives by doing what had once been "women's work."*

Such activities were crude attempts at soldier rehabilitation. They mirrored an international concern: how could disabled soldiers be retrained for civilian life? Back home in Canada, blind veterans were being taught to weave baskets; men with artificial limbs were shown how to use lathes.[17] An article in the *Windsor Magazine*, a popular British publication, declared that "Large numbers of men who have lost limbs were being trained as makers of artificial limbs. Thus was served the double object of providing a profitable occupation for these men and largely increasing the output of limbs."[18]

Yet such efforts were ultimately inadequate to the needs of disabled men, and disclosed the limited range of ideas open to helping men when they returned – healthy or disabled. Women tried to fill the gap as best they could. On their shoulders would rest the day-to-day support that such men would need in order to survive and take a role in society after the war. Allied governments ultimately abandoned the men who had sacrificed their bodies and health for their country; the soldier's wives and lovers could not.

In the older part of the All Saints cemetery, many of the marble slates have been wiped clean; the names of those resting beneath them erased by rain and the passage of time. Roberta's life was like those headstones – her life, once famous, now nearly forgotten, along with the lives and contributions of so many Canadian women who served during the Great War.

≈ ≋ ≈

Neil returned home to Sarnia in October 1916 to be watched over by his anxious parents. He seldom complained, but it was clear to Maud and Jack that he was often in great pain. They insisted that their son visit a specialist in bone fractures. The doctor reported that Neil's "left iliac bone of the pelvis is very much crushed and fractured, the upper fragment is markedly displaced downwards and impinges somewhat upon the hip joint interfering with its freedom of action. In addition to this one of the processes of the lumbar spine is fractured."[19] He noted that if Neil returned to the trenches, he risked permanent disability.

It must have been a hard sentence for Neil to receive. He had always been, in the words of his father, a "strong, healthy, rugged boy with lots of work in him and able to do it."[20] Jack Hanna had also actively promoted the war, and his much-loved son was well aware of his father's views.

"Can all the might of Great Britain be said to be in the field, if the Dominion of Canada does not do her share?" Jack had asked in one of his many recruiting speeches. "And was there a man who would not be sorry to have to admit that when all the might of Great Britain had been thrown into the scale, he was not there?"[21] Neil did not want to someday admit he had not "been there" when Great Britain needed him. But it was clear that in his disabled condition, he would be a liability to his unit. He would have to find some other way to serve. In February, Neil returned to London to take a desk job at Canadian headquarters. He would not remain there for long.

While Neil was struggling to return to active service, Roberta was immersed in the daily routine of providing meals for hungry men and hospital staff. She couldn't have known that back in Alberta, political changes were brewing that would alter the course of her life.

∾ ∾ ∾

On a cool Alberta afternoon in May 1917, Arthur Sifton took a well-earned break from his legislative workload. He rocked back in his swivel chair and rested his feet on his oak desk, sucking on his cheap cigar and blowing out perfect circles of smoke. It was good in the legislature today. He'd really annoyed the Conservatives when he dropped the writ. But what were they going to do about it? With only seventeen members in grumpy opposition, the only thing they could do was pound their desks with their fists. So what, if none of Alberta's labour, farm, or women's groups were lobbying for an early election? He wanted one now – and he was the only one with the power to make that decision.

Besides, there were lots of good reasons to call an election. Alberta's economy was the best it had been for a long time. The recession had been over for years. The farm economy was booming, the product of good crops and wartime food shortages in Europe. The powerful farm lobby group, the United Farmers of Alberta, could be relied upon to throw its weight behind the Liberals. And women, who were voting for the first time, would repay his belated support of the franchise with their votes.

The only group that could have caused trouble for him was the thirty-eight thousand Alberta soldiers and nurses now serving overseas. Soldiers were notorious for voting Conservative. Even here, Sifton had hedged his bets. In April, he introduced legislation separating the soldiers and nurses into their own constituency with two members-at-large to represent them. The "Alberta Military Representation Act" meant that soldiers couldn't vote in their own home ridings, effectively preventing them from swaying the vote in any way that would be detrimental to his reigning Liberals.

On June 7, 1917, in dry and dusty community centres and newly minted town halls across Alberta, women lined up for their first opportunity to cast a ballot. They bumped to the ballot box in democrat buggies behind tired old nags or drove on corduroy roads in Model-T Fords, babies and young children packed into the back seats. Some walked down wooden boardwalks on crowded city avenues, taking time to savour the experience of deciding where they would print their X on the slip of paper that had once been the sole property of their husbands, sons, and fathers.

When the votes were finally tallied, the Liberals — as expected — had won a landslide victory. However, the election did yield one stunning surprise. Forty-nine-year-old schoolteacher Louise McKinney was elected to the Alberta house as the non-partisan member for Claresholm. She was the first woman to be elected to a legislature in the British Empire. McKinney, a well-known temperance campaigner, was the former president of the Alberta and Saskatchewan chapter of the Women's Christian Temperance Union (WCTU).

McKinney never craved a life in politics, believing that it was a dirty game in which the interests of the voter were frequently sacrificed on the altar of party loyalty and personal ambition. "When Alberta women were enfranchised I was delighted, of course; but never dreamed that I would sit in the Legislature — indeed, I had no special ambition in that direction, and declined to unite with either political party," she told one interviewer.[22] So when members of the Non-Partisan League — a group that claimed no affiliation with traditional parties — approached her to run in the election, she turned them down flat. Fortunately, they did not abandon their quest, arguing that by running for office McKinney could elevate the cause of women's suffrage, temperance, and a broad spectrum of farm issues. She finally agreed to let her name stand, embarking on an intensive two-week campaign.[23]

On June 7, no one was more astonished than Louise McKinney when it was announced that she had won her seat, becoming the first woman elected to a legislature in the British Empire. That would not be the only surprise in an otherwise predictable election. The soldier's vote, to be held overseas in August, would also produce another landmark in the struggle for women's rights.

≈ ≈ ≈

Normally, Roberta wasn't the superstitious type. But it *was* Friday, July 13 and an orderly was telling her that a long distance telephone call had just come to the hospital. Could she come and take the call in Col. McPherson's office? Roberta's thoughts almost certainly flew to her family. Perhaps her mother was ill again or something had happened to Neil or Johnston. In November 1916, her brother had reverted to the rank of lieutenant so that he could be sent overseas. He had been "taken on strength" by the 14th (Royal Montreal Regiment) Battalion and now was fighting "somewhere in France."

Roberta rushed, heart pounding, across the green lawn and into the Boundary House. When she picked up the phone there was a strangely familiar female voice on the other end of the line. "You want me to stand as a soldier's candidate to the Alberta legislature? I can't imagine… I have no intention…" Exclamations followed by long silences. Then, "I'll have to think it over. We'll meet tomorrow at five o'clock at the hospital." Roberta slowly put the phone down and sank into a chair. What was she to do?

CHAPTER 9

SOLDIER'S CHOICE

"Three times I have seen women in fights at the polls and as many times I have seen them ignominiously fail. Women in public life will never prove satisfactory. I have devoted the best of my energies for the best part of my life to the cause, but now I confess I was wrong, and advise all young women to marry and try to become good housekeepers."

(Suffragist Phoebe Couzins, quoted in **Saturday Night Magazine**, May 15, 1897)

Beatrice Nasmyth's voile blouse stuck to her skin as she sat on the edge of the stiff velvet seat in the humid first-class carriage. She pulled the thin fabric away from her back and a gust of air slipped under her collar and skimmed down her spine like a sled down a snow-covered slope. Then the heat sucked away the orphaned breeze and the damp cloth glued itself to her skin again. Seated directly across from her, looking frustratingly cool and unflustered, was her cousin Nell Dennis.

The pair were travelling to Orpington to convince Roberta MacAdams that she was the ideal candidate to run in the forthcoming "soldier's poll" to the Alberta legislature. They planned to argue that not only was MacAdams eminently well-qualified, she also had an obligation to represent Alberta soldiers serving overseas. Yet, there was another, more basic reason for wanting Roberta to run. Less than forty-eight hours remained in which to nominate candidates for the election and Beatrice had exhausted all other

Beatrice Nasmyth, Roberta's campaign manager.
Monica Newton Collection.

possibilities. Roberta wasn't only the best choice – she was their last chance.

The train swayed past bottle-green fields, sheep, and the occasional thatched-roofed cottage. Suddenly it was slowing down. A flush of steam surged past their window as the train pulled into Orpington. The two women soon emerged from the station, eyes blinking in the late afternoon sunshine. There were no cabs, so Beatrice and Nell walked down the village high street to the hospital past prosperous brick shops like E.J. Elton's Butcher (with "home killed English and Scotch meat") and A.J. Turner's Dry Cleaners (where soldiers could have "service uniforms cleaned and tailor pressed at special reduced prices").[1] Some of those same soldiers were strolling along the pavement in hospital uniforms, looking as though they belonged to some exclusive men's club that favoured blue flannel blazers.

It was five o'clock when the two women finally walked up the gravel drive to the hospital. An orderly directed them to the building that housed the nurse's sitting room. Roberta, still in her pale blue working uniform, quietly greeted them at the door and motioned them inside. The room was as reserved as their hostess. There was a straight-backed piano at the far end, a collection of stiff, thinly upholstered chairs, and a vase of roses on top of a cluttered bookcase, overlooked by a picture of the king.[2]

Roberta placed a tray on the table in front of them, set with a pot of scented tea and a few biscuits she'd scrounged from the kitchen. She didn't see any harm in making the women comfortable, even though she was not planning to let her name stand for election. Roberta had an intimate knowledge of the ups and downs of political campaigning, having witnessed Jack Hanna's early failed attempts at public office. And she remembered her father's uphill struggle against the Liberals of Lambton County. Politics held little allure for the daughter of the embattled Conservative.

A product of the late Victorian era, Roberta was also uninterested in the women's rights movement and didn't see herself as its torch bearer. She had always seen women's and men's spheres as somewhat separate. Although the war had begun to shake that perception,

Roberta was at heart a domestic crusader like Adelaide Hoodless, more committed to improving the domestic lives of women than to overturning their traditional role in society. Besides, she had come overseas to serve her country against an aggressor she believed responsible for the appearance of so many friends on the casualty lists published daily in the *Edmonton Journal*. It was not easy to see how running for election would help her comrades-in-arms.

Roberta had not reckoned on the persuasive powers of Beatrice Nasmyth, a woman who was to become her lifelong friend and greatest champion. Beatrice was a sophisticated, hard-headed fighter with the gift of the gab. The thirty-two-year-old had spent the four years before the war as a reporter for the women's page of the *Vancouver Province*. When war was declared in 1914, she jumped at the chance to travel to London to cover something a little more exciting than the changing length of women's skirts. She arrived before Britons celebrated their first wartime Christmas.

Since the *Province* paid Beatrice by the article, she needed a stable job to supplement her income, preferably one where she could conveniently observe wartime activities and report on them. Her first was a brief stint with the estates branch of Canadian Pay and Records, the London-based office charged with compiling war statistics, registering the location of graves, and processing the estates of dead soldiers.[3]

The long days and low salary at the Records Office soon made Beatrice desperate to find another job. "The trouble is that I have no time for chasing copy now as when I stop work everyone else has stopped too and there is no one to see or interview and I am much too tired to go looking for further trouble," she wrote to her father.[4] Just when things seemed to be going from bad to worse, the position of publicity secretary at the Alberta Agent General's Office became vacant. Beatrice applied and was quickly accepted. Not only did she have the journalistic qualifications for the position, her influential family connections probably eased her way in. Beatrice's middle name was Sifton. Her second cousin was Alberta premier Arthur Sifton.

The function of the Agent General's office was to promote Alberta's industry and opportunities for settlement, so the new publicity secretary was expected to be an encyclopaedia of all things Albertan. "It would take a century to learn all that I am expected to know in this office," Beatrice wrote to her father from her fourth-floor office overlooking Trafalgar Square. "A man rings up one morning to know where Bottle Ridge is and all about it. I spend the morning finding out from various maps what sort of country it is in, what the taxes are, the class of people who have settled there, the amount of rainfall, the condition of the land... and think I am all ready for any similar questions and take it easy till the next one comes. But the next man wants to know the name and address of the official dog catcher in Bog Gulch."[5]

Beatrice's suffragist enthusiasms, born during her years covering the women's beat in Vancouver, remained intact in her new job. In June 1917, she was ecstatic when she heard the news that Louise McKinney had been elected to the Alberta legislature. Beatrice immediately hoped and expected that an overseas nurse would follow McKinney's example and run in the soldier's special poll, to be held in early August. But as the weeks passed, none of the seventy-five Alberta nurses serving overseas stepped forward to run for one of the two seats.

On July 13th, with less than three days until nominations closed, Beatrice began the journey that would eventually lead her to Roberta MacAdams. "I thought that to be really worthy of the name suffragette I ought to have a woman candidate in the field for our overseas election," wrote Beatrice to her father. "We went to the office of the Director of Medical Services first and interviewed numerous colonels and majors and even a captain or two to try to get a line on someone who would be suitable and eligible and would consent to stand for election. We wasted a lot of time this way and got nothing."[6]

Frustrated and hungry, they decided to have dinner at a nearby cafe. Beatrice pushed her food impatiently around her plate. It was warm inside the restaurant, just like that day about a year ago when... then she was recalling the tall blue-uniformed woman

who had stopped by her office the previous August. Roberta Mac-
Adams... Perhaps she would stand for election! As they waited for
their bill, Beatrice explained her idea to Nell Dennis. They rushed
back to the Agent General's office and placed a long-distance call
to the Ontario Military Hospital.

❦❦❦

Once ensconced with Roberta in the nurses' sitting room at Orpington, Beatrice launched her arguments. For the next five hours,
the quiet of the cosy retreat was broken by the noise of women
arguing back and forth. "But I have no time, and no money – why,
I haven't even a photograph!" Roberta protested.[7] She knew how
costly and risky electoral campaigns could be. Although her brother-in-law Jack had been able to draw on his extensive financial
resources to run his election campaigns, he had never been able to
forget what it was like to lose his deposit after his first failed attempt
at a parliamentary seat. Roberta only had her modest military salary
– far too little to finance a full-fledged political campaign. Besides,
she argued, wouldn't a soldier be a more appropriate representative
for the fighting men?

Beatrice systematically knocked down every argument, point-
ing out that photographs were easily taken, strict rules about campaigning would limit costs, and Beatrice – with her vast knowledge
of Alberta – would be her campaign manager. Besides, Roberta
had a patriotic duty to the soldiers and to the women back home
who had already sacrificed much to the war effort.

It was this last argument that finally broke Roberta's resolve
to stay out of the contest. She had spent the past eighteen months
helping to meet the needs of the broken men who filled the hospital
beds at Orpington. Roberta felt a keen loyalty to those soldiers
– and also to their wives, daughters, and sisters. Her early working life had centred around the needs and wants of women, from
steam-faced girls bending over bubbling pots of soup in domestic
science classrooms to the women who struggled to keep their families clean in sod houses. It became clear to Roberta that what she

could offer her potential constituents was rooted in the experience of these prairie and mountain women, whose hardships had been compounded by the absence of soldier husbands, sons, and brothers. If she were elected to the legislature, she would not only work for the interests of soldiers, but for their wives and dependents. "Is this an opportunity for good that I ought to seize?" she wondered. Her answer was a resounding "Yes."[8]

Ten signatures were needed for Roberta's nomination papers.[9] A Calgary captain stationed at Orpington promised to get the names and send them to Beatrice's London apartment. If everything went smoothly, the signatures would arrive by 2:00 the next day (Sunday). Nominations officially closed at noon on Monday, at which time all documents had to have been received at the Agent General's Office. Beatrice and Nell said a hurried goodbye to Roberta and caught the late train, reaching London at midnight.

Beatrice spent Sunday in worried anticipation. At five o'clock in the afternoon, a telegram arrived at her London flat. She ripped it open, only to learn that the signatures would now be delivered early on Monday morning. The next day, Beatrice left for work at the Agent General's office, leaving Nell stationed at the apartment to wait for the courier to bring them the completed nomination papers.

"An hour before closing time they had not appeared. Imagine our anguish!" Beatrice wrote to her father. "I spent the entire morning on the long distance and in phoning Mrs. D. [Nell] and finally a very leisurely messenger turned up and Mrs. D. rushed the papers to the office just with twenty minutes to the good. It was thrilling to say the least. However, they were all in good order and we felt very much gratified."[10] The campaign was on.

❧ ❧ ❧

The nomination was only the first hurdle in a short and intense election campaign. Roberta took two weeks' leave and arrived at Beatrice's apartment, suitcase in hand. The two women laid out their battle plan. Their first move was to court the attention of the press and harness its considerable influence in the service of their campaign. Beatrice got on the trail of press baron Lord Beaverbrook, one of Canada's most famous exports to Britain.

Beaverbook, formerly Max Aitken, was a controversial Canadian millionaire and financier. In 1910, he had weathered a storm of controversy following his involvement in the promotion and merger of thirteen cement companies. Aitken had been accused (possibly unfairly) of raising the price of cement and making an excessive profit for himself in the process. Whether to avoid the controversy or to pursue business interests abroad, Aitken and his wife left for England. His ambitious nature did not evaporate in the ocean crossing. In the general election of 1910 he won a seat in the British parliament and in 1911, he was knighted.

After the Great War began, Aitken returned to Canada, where he became a popular speaker on the recruiting rally circuit. He met with Prime Minister Robert Borden and Sam Hughes, the minister of militia. They quickly decided that Aitken could be of great use to them as a promoter of Canada's contribution to the war effort. He returned to England, acquired the military rank of lieutenant colonel, and embraced a new role as "Canadian Eye Witness." Aitken wrote books about Canada's war contribution and founded the Canadian War Records Office – an invaluable archive of photographs and print records related to the war. He also jumped into the newspaper business, establishing a daily newspaper for Canadian troops called *The Canadian Daily Record*, and purchasing the British newspaper, *The Daily Express*. Early in 1917, he was made a peer, taking the title "Beaverbrook."[11]

Beatrice finally located the millionaire at his office in one of the many financial institutions in which he had an interest. Beaverbrook was more than accommodating. Known more for his interest in beautiful women than in their suffrage, he was happy to use his influence on behalf of the lovely Roberta and vivacious Beatrice. He personally accompanied the two women to the offices of *The Daily Express* and introduced them to the newspaper's editor. "Luckily I was ready with all biographical details of the candidate and our campaign was soon launched," Beatrice wrote to her father.[12]

Next, a promotional flyer had to be made. This was a vital piece in the campaign package, since, under military law, soldiers could not attend political meetings. Campaigning would be limited to one-on-one visits in hospitals and camps and the distribution of circulars. Beatrice decided that a photograph of Roberta was needed to grace the centre of her promotional flyer. But not just any photograph. She hustled her candidate to the fashionable Cromwell Place studio of celebrated portraitist Emil Hoppé. The thirty-nine-year-old Hoppé was a brilliant theatre and fashion photographer who was quickly becoming famous for his portraits of the rich and notorious, from Virginia Woolf to George Bernard Shaw. One of his most compelling portraits was of Robert Ross, the former lover of Oscar Wilde and the literary patron of such Great War poets as Siegfried Sassoon and Wilfred Owen. Since Hoppé's fees reflected his growing acclaim, the two women probably pooled their savings to pay for a session with the famous photographer.

Although Hoppé's house – the former home of painter Sir John Millais – was elaborately decorated, his attached studio was simple and plain. It reflected a portrait style in which, as Hoppé said, "character rather than flattery (was) the dominant note."[13] This was exactly the right approach to apply to Roberta, who had grown up in a home where principle and duty were placed on a platform above human desire. Hoppé placed her against a softly swirling dark backdrop. Roberta wore her pale blue working uniform, her white veil framing her soft face like a Madonna's halo. Her lips were pressed together with the whisper of a smile. She sat at an angle to the camera, her head turned towards the photographer, her gaze steady and direct.

The striking photograph was quickly reproduced in the centre of a single sheet campaign flyer. It read:

SOLDIERS AND NURSES FROM ALBERTA!!

You will have **TWO VOTES** *at the forthcoming
Election under the Alberta Military Representation Act.*

GIVE ONE VOTE TO THE MAN OF YOUR CHOICE AND
THE OTHER TO THE SISTER*.*

*SHE WILL WORK NOT ONLY FOR YOUR BEST INTERESTS BUT FOR THOSE
OF YOUR WIVES, MOTHERS, SWEETHEARTS, SISTERS AND CHILDREN AFTER
THE WAR.*

*Remember those who have helped you so nobly
through the fight.*

"The other to the sister" was an inspired campaign slogan that built
on the admiration (and desire) felt by many soldiers for the women
who had left comfortable homes to tend them and their wounded
comrades. Seven thousand copies of the circular were distributed
to men in camps and hospitals in England and France. Overnight,
Roberta became a virginal pin-up girl for Alberta soldiers.

The reaction from the other candidates was understandably
mixed. Those who had carefully organized and launched their
campaigns had "the wind taken out of their sails completely by the
nomination of a woman at the eleventh hour," according to Beatrice.[14] And despite Beatrice's attempts to give her own involvement
in the campaign a low profile, it soon became known that a Sifton
relative was behind Roberta's candidacy. This inspired outrage and
open accusations of partisanship. In the words of Harold McGill,
medical officer with the 31st (Calgary) Battalion, Roberta was "pal-
pably the candidate of the Alberta government and I am strongly of
the opinion that the interests nearer her heart will not be those of
the soldiers but those of A.J. Sifton. In every way I think her a most
unsuitable candidate."[15]

Roberta was also running against twenty men, many of whom
were experienced soldiers who had spent the previous few years en-
during the bullets and bayonets of the trenches. Among them were

SOLDIERS AND NURSES FROM ALBERTA!!

You will have TWO VOTES at the forthcoming Election under the Alberta Military Representation Act.

GIVE ONE VOTE TO THE MAN OF YOUR CHOICE AND
THE OTHER TO THE SISTER.

LOOK
FOR
No. 14
ON YOUR
BALLOT PAPER!

LOOK
FOR
No. 14
ON YOUR
BALLOT PAPER!

Miss ROBERTA CATHERINE MacADAMS,
Lieut. C.A.M.C. Ontario Military Hospital,
Orpington, Kent.

SHE WILL WORK NOT ONLY FOR YOUR BEST INTERESTS BUT FOR THOSE OF YOUR WIVES, MOTHERS, SWEETHEARTS, SISTERS AND CHILDREN AFTER THE WAR.

Remember those who have helped you so nobly through the fight.

The famous election flyer.
Monica Newton Collection.

some of Alberta's most respected and colourful characters. One was "Peace River Jim" Cornwall,[16] now a lieutenant colonel. The well-known sailor, trapper, and trader already had political experience. He had represented the Peace River district in the Alberta legislature between 1908 and 1912. Other opponents included Col. Hewgill of the 31st (Calgary) Battalion,[17] Sgt. George Harper and Rev. Capt. Bob Pearson, both of the 49th (Edmonton) Battalion. Like Roberta's nephew Neil, Pearson had seen duty on the Somme.[18]

While Roberta faced strong challengers, she also had her advocates. She and Beatrice met with Lady Astor at the Bond Street Gallery. The former Nancy Langhorne of Virginia, now married to British millionaire Waldorf Astor, introduced the two women to some "important people," according to Beatrice.[19] Lady Astor was extremely supportive of the women who volunteered for service during the war. She would eventually run for office herself, becoming the first woman elected to the British House of Commons on November 28, 1919.

Lord Beaverbrook, as promised, ensured that Roberta received ample coverage in his newspapers, including an article and photograph in the July 21 issue of the *Canadian Daily Record*. (Forty thousand copies of the *Record* went to Canadian troops each day.) And Roberta probably didn't realize that she was receiving support from some unexpected quarters. In early August, Major Margaret MacDonald, the matron-in-chief in charge of all Canadian military nurses overseas, received a letter from her friend Captain Mary Plummer (CAMC). Plummer was campaigning for one of the male candidates and wanted MacDonald to give her the names of the units where there were "likely to be Nursing Sisters from Alberta."

Plummer soon learned that MacDonald favoured the only female contender in the race and was unwilling to assist any of the other candidates. "[I]t is regretted that we are unable to furnish you with a list of the Alberta Sisters in the CAMC showing the Units to which they have been posted," responded MacDonald. "I am quite confident that Nursing Sister MacAdams will be duly elected. She quite deserves the confidence of the voters."[20]

Roberta MacAdams fought her election campaign against the backdrop of the costly struggle of British women to gain the vote. Trafalgar Square was the site where that struggle was frequently played out. The plinth under Nelson's Column, flanked by four great stone lions, had once been the personal podium for suffragists Emmeline Pankhurst and her daughters Christabel and Sylvia.

Nearly ninety years after Roberta's election, I too stood in the shadow of Nelson's Column. I tried to imagine what it must have been like before traffic constantly flowed around the square and tourists with digital cameras snapped pictures of the National Gallery and the Church of St. Martin-in-the-Fields. I knew that Roberta had once crossed this square to get to Beatrice Nasmyth's office in a wedge-shaped office building on Charing Cross Road. I also knew that from her fourth-floor office windows Beatrice often watched suffragists promoting the war effort.

Among those demonstrators might have been the Pankhursts. In 1903, Emmeline Pankhurst had established the "Women's Social and Political Union" (WSPU), an organization committed to championing the vote for women. For a time, the WSPU made polite presentations to sympathetic members of parliament. But after yet another women's suffrage bill died a slow death on the floor of the British legislature, the organization took radical action. When a general election was called in 1905, they made the franchise a campaign issue. During a debate between Sir Edward Grey and Winston Churchill, the Pankhursts and fellow activist Annie Kenney called on the men to say whether they would support women's suffrage. The candidates refused to answer and the women were dragged from the hall by police and charged with obstruction. The women's suffrage issue was now front-page news and a new tactic – imprisonment – had been used for the first time.

For the next eight years, the WSPU would grow to become one of the largest women's suffrage organizations in the country. Key figures would include Scottish-born Flora Drummond. The short, stocky Drummond organized mass demonstrations and became known as the "General" because of her quasi-military dress and her role as an organizer.[21] She and other leading members of the WSPU would take its most radical actions – burning the homes of politicians, smashing windows, breaking into public buildings and (when imprisoned) launching hunger strikes.

Instead of trying to understand the women's demands – as politicians were doing in Canada – British MPs reacted with fear and outrage, calling for harsher sentences for suffragists. Police began to abuse and sometimes sexually assault protesters, a fact that went unreported. In prison, female hunger-strikers were violently force-fed.

This battle between government and women came to an abrupt end in 1914, when Britain declared war on Germany. "For the present at least our arms are grounded, for directly the threat of foreign war descended on our nation we declared a complete truce from militancy," announced Emmeline Pankhurst.[22] The WSPU abandoned its protests and threw its energies into promoting enlistment and conscription, encouraging women to work in munitions factories and in fields previously closed to them by virtue of their gender. As men flooded out to the war zone, women took their jobs and kept the economic and social machinery of Britain turning. Women's rights advocates hoped (rightly as it would turn out) that by committing their movement to the national interest no one would be able to deny women the vote when the war was over.[23]

But the decision of the WSPU to support the war effort caused a schism among the ranks, a division that extended right into the Pankhurst household. Many supporters of the WSPU – including Sylvia Pankhurst – believed that poor women and their dependent children would be harmed by war and governments and businessmen would exploit women workers. They were right. The poorest of the poor were harmed the most when food prices rose and there were shortages of flour and coal. Women workers were consistently paid less than men and often worked in appalling and dangerous conditions.

Demands for change were often met with violence. When Sylvia Pankhurst mounted a protest calling for equal pay, peace, and women's suffrage at Trafalgar Square – the same place where the WSPU held its first large public demonstration – they were met by a mob. Soldiers ripped their banners to shreds and wads of paper dipped in paint were hurled at the protesters. Emmeline Pankhurst, touring the United States to promote its entry into the war, cabled a letter home condemning Sylvia's "foolish and unpatriotic conduct."[24]

⁘ ⁘ ⁘

Given the profound support that the pro-war suffragists received during the first years of the conflict, it was little wonder that the election campaign of a Canadian woman wearing a military uniform would be received warmly by the British press. On July 16, 1917, Roberta was invited to speak to a group of journalists at the Lyceum Club – a two-thousand-member organization that provided women with opportunities to discuss art, science, literature, education, and philanthropy. Forty women and two men sat at linen-covered tables and chatted as a skimpy (war rations) luncheon was served. Beatrice came along for moral support and found herself seated between the only two male reporters in attendance – one representing *The Pall Mall Gazette*, the other, *The Morning Post*. Their constant stream of questions made her feel as though her neck was going to give way under the strain of answering first one, then the other. Eventually she was given a break when Roberta was introduced and invited to the podium.

In her navy blue dress uniform, Roberta made a distinguished figure. "I don't think a woman could be electioneering in a more effective garb than a nursing sister," noted the representative of *The Daily Sketch*.[25] Roberta had never shrunk from public speaking in her work for the Alberta Department of Agriculture or in her years as head of domestic science at Edmonton's schools. Reporters didn't intimidate her either – after all, she was the daughter of a veteran newspaper publisher. Standing gracefully at the slender wooden podium, she hammered down the planks in her political platform: post-war reconstruction, soldier rehabilitation, and meeting the challenges that the war had created for women.

After the short speech, the journalists peppered Roberta with questions. Her answers incorporated the concerns of the soldiers who filled the beds at the Ontario Military Hospital within a legislative agenda as rooted in Alberta as the foxtail barley that hugged the railroad tracks connecting Edmonton and Calgary. "I shall work for the pension scheme for our soldiers, and I shall put my best efforts into plans for placing soldiers on the land when they return to Canada," she told a journalist from the *British Journal of Nursing*. "Occupation must be found for our fighting forces and suitable training provided for them. The organisation of hospitals will be a very great part of my interest. The setting up of a standard of living for people who settle on the land will be an important item in the parliamentary programme. Right social aims will have to be established, good schools provided, and, in my opinion, in order to secure the right type of citizen, we must make it possible for our settlers to keep in touch with the world at large."[26]

Hospitals, schools, and a decent standard of living were goals that Roberta shared in common with western Canadian suffragettes. They were also the chief concerns of the prairie women she had met in her criss-crossing tours of Alberta. Her continued embrace of these ideals made it clear that her essential optimism had not been clouded by the war. She believed in a province and country that would not only survive the current hardships but also continue to prosper and develop, thanks to the efforts of men and women intent on planning a better future for themselves. But a new layer had been added to her thinking, the product of Roberta's wartime exposure to people from across the Empire: "we must make it possible for our settlers to keep in touch with the world at large." The better future that she envisioned depended not just on the pioneering spirit of Canada's people, but also on their interaction with the wider world.

This was a theme that Roberta would return to many times over the next few years. In her view, Canada could no longer be just a satellite of the mother country but an independent nation in its own right, ready to negotiate its own place in a complex world. Its entry fee into the ranks of nationhood was the hundreds of thousands of Canadians who had committed themselves to the defence of Britain and her allies.

Those Canadians who had served must be rehabilitated and plans for reconstruction must be made now, argued Roberta. Settling soldiers on the land was a popular idea, and she promoted it with some reservations. She knew from first-hand observation that not everyone was a born farmer. As she would later argue, "the usual homestead undertaking cannot be expected to meet the needs of a great many of the returning men who have been unfitted for isolation and the hard experiences of homesteading by the strain of war."[27] Retraining and rehabilitation for the disabled worked well when only a few were returning home. What would happen when thousands flooded back, hoping to re-establish normal working lives?

Well-established politicians might have perceived Roberta's platform as overly optimistic and naïve. In 1917, few were expending much energy planning for life after the war. "What had we to do with peace," Winston Churchill would write during the Paris Peace Conference in 1919, "while we did not know whether we should not be destroyed? Who could think of reconstruction while the whole world was being hammered to pieces, or of demobilisation when the sole aim was to hurl every man and every shell into battle?"[28]

Yet hope for the future was one of the few things that buoyed up the spirits of the men serving in the trenches. The welfare of one of those men was often on Roberta's mind. It would have been difficult if not impossible for her to wage her campaign from the comparative safety of London, had she realized that soon her brother Johnston would be fighting for his life near a bluff in France known as Hill 70.

✧✧✧

In late November 1916, Johnston had been "taken on strength" by the 14th (Royal Montreal Regiment) Battalion. From April 9 to early July 1917 (with a brief break in May for rest and reorganization), the 14th was involved in the battle to claim and hold Vimy Ridge. Then, in mid-July, the Battalion withdrew, eventually marching to Braquemont, where the men spent five days doing bayonet drill and practising the use of their gas helmets and the formations used in attack. After five days, the unit was on the march again, this time for Houchin, a small village about five kilometres north of Bethune. There they bathed in "great vats of hot water and received clean underclothing and socks."[29] Then it was back to drilling again, with more rifle grenade practice, bombing, wiring instruction, and gas helmet drills. Johnston, now Brigade Grenade Officer, directed some of that training.

It was clear that all this preparation was leading up to a major battle. On July 25, soldiers were told what they could expect.

British commander Sir Douglas Haig had recently appointed Canadian-born Sir Arthur Currie, the former commander of the 1st Canadian Division, as the new head of the Canadian Corps. Haig wanted Currie to marshal his forces to regain Lens, a place that historians Desmond Morton and Jack Granatstein describe as a "ruined coal-mining town that had defied them since the Battle of Loos in 1915."[30] Currie thought Haig's plan was a bad idea. He argued it would be tactically wiser to take one of the two hills overlooking Lens, preferably Hill 70 to the north of the town, forcing the Germans to waste men in an effort to take it back. Haig gave Currie the go-ahead. Now the 14th Battalion was being asked to play its part in the coming battle.

Johnston had lived a charmed life during the war. His closest brush with death had been a month or so earlier when, according to Roberta, "his little basement office was shelled out, happily while he was up the line."[31] However, before the Battle of Hill 70 was even to begin, he faced a much closer encounter with disaster.

On July 27, the members of his battalion marched to the village of Aix Noulette to carry out battle practice with other battalions of the 3rd Canadian Infantry Brigade. An area representing Hill 70 had been prepared, with German trenches taped out. Soldiers rehearsed for battle daily until August 3, when the 14th Battalion was marched to Mazingarbe. There they were again called into the front lines, this time to relieve the 16th Battalion. On August 7, officers of the 14th telephoned 3rd Brigade headquarters to say that they were experiencing heavy shelling – including a "certain number of gas shells" – in their front line trenches.[32]

On August 9, the 14th again experienced heavy shelling by "guns of heavy calibre."[33] Sometime during this bombardment, Johnston almost ended his wartime service permanently. The torn casualty records in his military file simply note that he was "sick" with PUO and taken to a French hospital where he would spend the next eleven days. "PUO" was the short form for "pyrexia of unknown origin" or "trench fever," a painful and debilitating condition brought about by lice in the trenches. PUO was a kind of catch-all illness that military doctors, harassed by floods of casualties, assigned to patients who were simply too ill to be in the lines. But in Johnston's case, it was a convenient mask covering a much more controversial illness. He would later tell Beatrice Nasmyth about the real reason for his sudden withdrawal from the lines of combat.

"Captain MacAdams has recently come out of a French hospital after having been gassed and is still looking rather seedy," Beatrice wrote to her father. "He led the hundred men under him to safety – he himself being the only one who got the gas. And as he didn't have on his gas helmet at the time (keeping it off purposely in order to detect the gas and do the best for the men under him) he is equally liable for a court martial (for self-inflicted wounds) or for a DSO. He is hoping one will counterbalance the other and he'll get nothing at all!"

The shells that had hit the line during the heavy bombardment of August 9 probably contained a high proportion of gas shells.[34] Fortunately for Johnston, the doctor who treated him was either careless or sympathetic and labelled his illness PUO. Johnston's immediate superiors however, did not forget his actions. Shortly after returning to his unit, Sir Douglas Haig mentioned Johnston "in despatches,"[35] the regularly published list of soldiers who had acted above the call of duty.

<hr/>

Back in London, Roberta was marshalling her forces for a very different kind of battle. In a quiet corner of the writing room at the Agent General's office, she established her headquarters. She and Beatrice asked officer friends to provide them with lists of soldiers who might support the campaign. Each morning they wrote dozens of letters and stuffed them into envelopes along with copies of the precious flyer.

Roberta received an avalanche of letters from enthusiastic supporters. She consigned most to the wastebasket as soon as she answered them. "[A]n unerring instinct of orderliness leads her to deal with her letters from day to day, and to keep her mind as free

Harvey Price re-entered Roberta's life in 1917.
Robert Price Collection.

from congestion as her desk," wrote Beatrice in the *Vancouver Province*.[36] That sense of orderliness reflected the fact that, to Roberta, it was the work that mattered, not the person. She was not in the race to promote herself but to promote the needs of the soldiers and their families. Roberta's self-deprecation would prove maddening years later, when I would begin to scan the thin file of archival records that she left behind. Unlike well-known female leaders such as Emily Murphy or Nellie McClung, Roberta did not leave behind overflowing scrapbooks and semi-autobiographical novels. Only the personal records of her friends and scattered family records ensured that her story would not be lost forever.

Between bouts of letter writing, Roberta and her "campaign manager" toured hospitals and visited military camps. The personal approach often garnered votes, as Beatrice discovered when she received a letter from an Alberta man that she had visited in hospital.

Dear Miss Nasmyth,

I have voted as you wished me to and also got Pte. Huestis of Calgary to vote for Miss MacAdams. I am shure I do not approve of Lady Members in the House of Parliament and the trueth is that I am very bitter against it and perhaps you may have noticed when here that I did not like the idea, but as you were looking forward to some future for yourself so I decided to vote for her. I am like the Scotchman who said – "I would do it for you but not for any ither body."

Pte. Allen
St. Thomas Hospital[37]

One morning, as Roberta was hunched over yet another letter, she heard a familiar voice in the outer office. It brought back a rush of memories, a sense of a faraway time. When she looked up, it was to see the face of Harvey Price, the awkward hunting guide she had met in Jack Hanna's law office. He had heard about Roberta's campaign and decided to visit and wish her luck.

A lot had happened to Harvey in the seven years since they had last seen one another. He was now thirty-two. His hair had thinned, but his face still had the dark rich tan of the outdoors. Roberta was surprised to learn that he – like Roberta – had moved west in 1911. That year, Harvey had graduated from law school and articled at the Calgary office of R.B. Bennett and J.A. Lougheed. He later left the firm and opened his own office in the Town of Grouard, in Alberta's Peace River region.[38] Unfortunately, the war altered his career plans, as they did for so many of his contemporaries. In November 1915, he joined the 9th Battery of the Canadian Forestry Battalion. In September of the following year he was transferred to the 238th Forestry Battalion, given the rank of major, and sent overseas to build airdromes in England and France.[39]

Harvey would visit Roberta again and again during the war. One night when London was suffering through one of its many air raids, the pair carried chairs up the steps to the roof of the building in which the Agent General's office was housed. They sat and watched as British airplanes attacked a zeppelin that had somehow managed to find its way through the country's aerial defences. Despite the threat of being bombed, Roberta and Harvey – like so many other Londoners – stayed and watched as the zeppelin caught fire and slowly twisted to the earth.[40]

Roberta wasn't the only one embarking on a wartime romance. Lively, vivacious Beatrice found herself constantly warding off suitors – from a privileged English gentleman to a Canadian soldier. But one of the most persistent was a tall dark-haired Englishman whom she had met en route to England in August 1914. Guy Mackenzie Furniss was an officer with the Argyll and Sutherland Highlanders. "He has an immense sense of humour – which I am only beginning to understand a little bit, a love of books and art, and the good taste to find my companionship absorbing – not having had much of it," Beatrice later wrote home.[41] Perhaps the strongest feature he had in his favour at this stage, however, was persistence. Each time he had a few days' leave, Guy

Soldiers voting during the Alberta election, 1917.
National Archives of Canada; PA-1633.

would magically appear at the Alberta Agent General's Office and carry Beatrice off from her ever-busy typewriter.

When her two weeks of leave ended, Roberta returned to her work at Orpington. She remained blasé about the looming election results, as Beatrice noted in a letter home to her father: "(She) is not at all excited over the results. She is a very level-headed person."[42] Beatrice was much more nervous about the outcome of their campaign. "Lord Beaverbrook told us the other day he had his money on Miss M but of course no one could really tell how things would go."[43] When Alberta Premier Arthur Sifton arrived in London to observe the election results, she informed him that if Roberta were returned he would have the finest member the entire overseas forces could offer – if she lost it would be because their campaign had been too honest and unfinanced.[44]

Back on duty, Roberta continued to receive phone calls and letters about the election. "My dear Silent Partner," she wrote to

Beatrice. "My brother [Johnston] writes 'Send me the figures of you and the other member by wire.' He will be over in about ten days now, Glory be… I am still getting letters and messages from resurrected friends – some of them I do not even remember – some Guelph dentist worked for me in a Forestry Corps in France and sent me messages by their M.O. over on leave. I have absolutely no recollection of the man. Capt. Carson – an M.O. who used to be here sent me word that he had got me sixty votes.… A Victoria girl whom I had not seen for seven years came to see me a few days ago, had been a VAD in a hosp. in Leicester and is going to Egypt. She said she got me the only vote in their hospital."[45]

Not all of Roberta's supporters were as confident as Johnston about the campaign's outcome. An old friend of Roberta's, now living in London, had been following the election with a keen eye. Gladys Hoyt had taken over Roberta's job as domestic science superintendent when the latter joined the CAMC. In July 1916 she resigned her position. Her officer husband Robert had received a permanent transfer to Headquarters Staff in London and Gladys decided to join him there.

"Saw Berta many times while in London but not since the 'Great Idea' seized her to be an MP," wrote Gladys in a letter to William Bradey. "Bob says he's afraid her chances are slim as the Canadian nursing sisters are unpopular among the men. However she was a fine girl to let her name be used and I hope she gets a good vote."[46] Nursing sisters were more popular than Robert Hoyt believed, as events would soon prove.

☙❧

On September 18, 1917, the results of the election were announced. The slogan "Give One Vote to the Man of Your Choice and the Other to the Sister" turned out to be prophetic. Captain Robert Pearson and Roberta MacAdams were elected as "representatives at large for Alberta" for the soldiers overseas. Pearson, an officer with the 49th Edmonton Battalion, was the first-place winner with 4,286 votes. The "sister" won her second-place seat with four thousand votes, defeating her nearest rival by seven hundred.

Roberta was swamped with congratulatory letters and telegrams. In an October article in the *Vancouver Province*, Beatrice described the reaction of women's rights advocates to her victory. "When the results were first made known she was inundated by a wave of congratulation and good wishes – a wave which swept her into half of the illustrated papers and proclaimed her a wonderful 'boost' to the women's cause in England. 'The first woman to be elected to Parliament on British soil,' said the despatches that flashed over the island."[47]

The news of Roberta's victory was featured in the pages of the London *Times*, Boston's *Woman Citizen* and the Toronto *Globe*. One British newspaper declared: "In Alberta, manifestly, women have established their claim to share the burdens and responsibilities of citizenship, and men do not regard this claim as unreasonable or as the assertion of a novel right which has to be limited and safeguarded by all sorts of checks and balances. To those who have watched the slow progress of the women's cause in this country, this straightforward and very matter-of-fact recognition of woman's citizenship is refreshing. By contrast, our timid and half-hearted 'concession' of a truncated franchise for women looks ridiculous – and the bitter struggle that the women of this country have had to wage to get even this small measure of justice can be seen in its true light as a tragic waste of energy."[48]

Friends back in Canada celebrated her victory. "We are indeed proud of Miss McAdams for the splendid position she has won in the regard of those with whom she is serving," wrote William Carpenter in a letter to Gladys Hoyt. "[W]hen she left, although it was a leave of absence, I must confess that I did not expect that she would return for the simple reason that her excellency would be so proved in the broader field to which she was called, that what there was to offer here would be comparatively insignificant. But now that she has been honored in the way in which she has, she will no doubt return to Edmonton in order to take her place in the Legislative Assembly at its sessions."

The lobby of the Grovesnor Hotel, site of Roberta's victory celebration.
Author's Collection

For Roberta, there was a sudden and sober realization of the responsibility she had accepted. "What can I do to justify the confidence that had been placed in me – how can I be of the greatest service to the men who trust me?" she wondered.[49]

Roberta was granted a short leave and returned to London. The wave of victory had brought numerous invitations to open fairs and buildings, address women's groups, and meet with reporters.[50] In one of her first statements to the press after her election, her words reflected again her own ambivalence about the role that gender played in her election. "The fighting men and nursing sisters of Alberta did not elect me because I was a woman, but because I was a human being whom they could trust to look after their interests in Parliament... The soldiers and the sisters chose me as their representative exactly as they selected Captain Pearson who headed the poll. They did not think they were doing anything very startling in voting for a woman. Why should they think so? If they thought about it at all, they probably thought it was quite as natural for a woman to be a member of Parliament as a member of a nursing corps. I regard the result of the election chiefly as a tribute to my uniform and to the corps to which I am attached."[51]

On September 27, Roberta and Beatrice took time to celebrate and savour their victory. A small group of Roberta's most avid supporters were invited to an intimate gathering in the dining room of Beatrice's favourite hotel – the Grovesnor on Buckingham Palace Road. Among the guests were well-known Alberta officers such as General Griesbach (the former mayor of Edmonton). One soldier with whom Roberta would have especially enjoyed sharing her victory was missing, however. Harvey Stinson Price had been sent to France. Fortunately, there were many other friends who would help her forget his absence, at least for a short while.

Stepping through the arched doorway into the stately hotel's marbled foyer Roberta could smell a vague odour of tea, soap, and mystery. The Grovesnor had once been home to the "Metaphysical Society" – a group that included Liberal statesman (and misogynist) William Gladstone, writer John Ruskin, and poet Alfred Tennyson. In the hotel's private parlour, they had once debated everything from the divine (prayer and miracles) to the ridiculous (whether or not frogs had souls).[52] Ruskin, Gladstone, and Tennyson had been dead for over a decade, however, and this evening the election results were more likely to be the topic on everyone's lips.

Beatrice had not yet arrived, but someone else was waiting for Roberta. A solitary soldier was standing with his back towards her, amid the straight-backed armchairs and slender potted palms in the hotel's great hall. Johnston's skin was tinged with yellow and his uniform hung loosely on his six-foot frame. Roberta ran over to her brother and slipped her arm through his. Together they made their way down the long hall towards the dining room and the celebration dinner that awaited them.

CHAPTER 10

SOMEWHERE IN FRANCE

"This then was war, this grim and prolonged suffering, this crying of strong men at night."

(Mary Rogers Rinehart)

On a hot day in May, I stopped at a busy fish market on the dock in Boulogne. Fishermen poured buckets of gleaming plaice, cod, and black-shelled mussels onto white shelves in wooden stalls while their wives chatted and kept watchful eyes open for customers. A market had been there for hundreds of years. Photographs from the late nineteenth century showed pipe-smoking men standing next to cartloads of fish while wide-hipped women in long skirts look for the best price. Their calm, friendly expressions revealed little of the tumultuous history of that place.[1]

Situated not far from where the cold North Sea and English Channel meet, Boulogne had been more than an ideal location for fishing. It had been a launching pad for war. Julius Caesar dreamed of invading England as he walked the sandy beaches of this ancient port city. In 1803, Napoleon I matched Caesar's dreams with some of his own. On the hills overlooking the Liane River, he established his Grande Armée – a force of 185,000 men and 2,000 ships ready to challenge Britain's supremacy on the high seas.[2] The tide would eventually turn and over one hundred years later enemies became friends on the cobbled streets of Boulogne. In 1914, English and French soldiers gathered there, ready to share a common misery in the trenches of World War I.

On the day of my visit, the only troops that poured into Boulogne were the thousands of English tourists who crossed the Channel each year for a cheap holiday in France. I was a tourist, too. But I wasn't there for the seafood or the taste of good French wine. I was there to pick up Roberta MacAdams' trail. In mid-December 1917, MacAdams travelled to the "lines of communication" in France to observe the conditions in the lives of the soldiers and nursing sisters she had been elected to represent.[3] The tour had a lasting impact on her view of the war and the policies she promoted during her short political career. It made the "soldier's representative" an impassioned advocate for the Red Cross and an impatient champion of soldiers' rights.

Four Canadian women journalists accompanied Roberta. They included Mary MacLeod Moore, a London columnist with Toronto's **Saturday Night** and the **Montreal Star**. She had first come to public attention with her fashionable coverage of the coronation of King George V.[4] Elizabeth Montizambert was a correspondent for the **Montreal Gazette**, writing under the pseudonym "Antoinette."[5] She lived in Paris and would meet the women when they crossed into France. Roberta's friend and campaign manager Beatrice Nasmyth represented Vancouver's **Daily Province** and the Alberta Agent General's office. Florence MacPhedran was a reporter for the **Toronto Daily Star**.[6] Together the five women would travel along the coast of France, and visited Paris and the Village of Arques, a few miles from the front. Their journey began in the port of Boulogne.

It wasn't easy to get into Boulogne in December 1917. The only people allowed to cross into France were combatants, medical staff, and others approved through a complex process woven with red tape. As Mary MacLeod Moore wrote, it was easier for "a camel to go through the eye of a needle than for any unauthorized person to go to France during war-time."[7] This was especially true for journalists. At the beginning of World War I, the British government had virtually outlawed their presence in France. Any writers found near the troops without military permission could be arrested. Reports from the front came in the form of dispatches by generals such as Field Marshall Haig and Sir John French.

As the war ground on, the public in Britain and across the Empire grew tired of sketchy or sanitized reports that didn't reflect lengthening casualty lists. Some had also received the news of terrible battles and conditions from sons, husbands, and fathers serving in France. Under intense public pressure, the British government began slowly allowing a few accredited male reporters access to the front, provided their reports promoted the interests of the Empire. By 1917, parties of journalists were allowed to make special tours of the war zone, if they had been cleared by military headquarters in France and were accompanied by a military escort.[8]

Female writers faced even greater barriers than their male colleagues in covering the war. Popular opinion and government policy officially excluded them from the terrors of the conflict simply because they were considered too emotionally and physically fragile to withstand its effects. This masked the reality that women were already on the front lines. French and Belgian women, medical staff, the new women's military auxiliaries, women whose soldier relatives were seriously wounded in hospital, influential upper-class women with military connections, and even female soldiers (such as Irish Sergeant-Major Flora Sandes) were facing the bullets, bombs, and mud of the battlefields.

Despite this reality, most female journalists found it nearly impossible to report on the story first hand. The sole party of female journalists from the British Empire to precede the Canadians was a group led by Mary Augusta Ward, a prolific biographer of upper class England and a staunch anti-suffragist. Ward believed women could never decide questions of "foreign or colonial policy or grave constitutional change." A fierce supporter of the Allies, her 1916 book **England's Effort** painted a picture of a heroic Great Britain, bearing up under the onslaught of barbarians.

In contrast to Ward's group, Roberta and the Canadian journalists represented the "new women" of the twentieth century. Roberta had already broken down a major barrier to women's participation in electoral politics. In doing so, she had become an important symbol in the ongoing struggle for women's rights internationally. Those who accompanied her were equally committed to that struggle, often using their newspaper columns to raise women's issues.

The Canadian journalists intended to profile the work of women behind the lines. In particular, they wanted to describe the contribution of women in Canadian hospitals and for the Canadian Red Cross. The International Red Cross had just won the Nobel Peace Prize for its work since the beginning of the war. It seemed particularly appropriate that a group of female journalists should write about an organization that was largely staffed and supplied by women.[9]

The journalists also wanted to give families back home some windows into the experience of their sons, brothers, and husbands. "For [Canadian women] the war is a dark impenetrable curtain which envelops her soldier, letting through no glimpse of his later life on which she can rely," wrote Beatrice Nasmyth. "So, if I can bring to those at home just a few of the human pictures in which I saw their men in France, if I can make the war curtain just a little less impenetrable, I shall be glad."[10] Beatrice didn't mention, of course, that it would give both her and the other women a chance to see the conditions in which the men they cared about were also living. Both Guy Furniss and Harvey Price were now in France — Harvey doing construction work for the troops and Guy fighting with the Argyll and Sutherland Highlanders.

Given the unorthodox nature of the group, it is unclear how Roberta managed to get the military permission needed to get into France. However, both she and Beatrice were politically well-connected — Roberta as the sister-in-law of Jack Hanna, and Beatrice as the second cousin of Arthur Sifton (soon to become a member of Borden's coalition cabinet).

Roberta may have also pulled one other string. Lord Beaverbrook — the millionaire publisher who had supported her campaign — was on the verge of becoming Britain's first "Minister of Information." In his role as "Canadian Eyewitness" he had accompanied politicians and male journalists to France early in the war, and may have seen this as another opportunity to promote Canada's participation in the conflict. Such connections were probably more than enough to open the door to France — a possibility borne out by Elizabeth Montizambert's later comment, that the trip had been "kindly arranged by the Canadian authorities."[11]

There may have been other reasons that the women were allowed to tour France. In 1917, the Canadian government needed to feed the fires of propaganda for its own ends. In December, Robert Borden's Conservative government was waging a federal election focusing on his advocacy of conscription. Forced military service, introduced in August that year, had been a highly unpopular measure in some parts of Canada, particularly Quebec. The December election was a test of the new policy. Borden used every method at his disposal to get the votes he needed. Men in hospital wards in France — barely able to lift their heads from the pillows — were given ballots so that they could mark their choices.[12]

Just as the Sifton government in Alberta had passed legislation so that votes could be concentrated in the best interests of the governing party, Borden likewise introduced legislation that would ensure his own victory. According to the Wartime Elections Act of 1917 men and women in uniform could vote in the constituency of their choice. Female relatives of soldiers would also be allowed to vote in the federal election. This was a calculated move. The government hoped that women whose husbands and sons were facing the horrors of war would be happy to vote for a government that was forcing "slackers" to join up. Immigrants from Germany, and central and eastern Europe, lost their votes.[13]

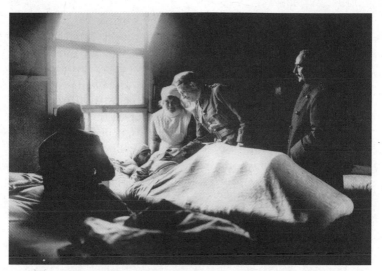

A wounded Canadian soldier voting in the federal election, December 1917.
National Archives of Canada; PA–003314.

Conscription wasn't the only albatross hanging around Borden's neck. Following the loss of nearly sixteen thousand Canadians at Passchendaele during October and November,[14] his government needed more than ever to inspire renewed support for the war effort. Officials in the Canadian War Records Office may well have hoped that a leading female politician and a group of Canadian women journalists – arriving on December 17, the date of the federal election – would provide yet another spin on the now familiar images of the courageous Johnny Canuck and the valiant nursing sister. Their reports would also underline the rightness of the government's decision to allow women to vote – after all, women were earning the franchise by their heroic contribution overseas.

As I was to learn during my journey to France, what the female reporters would actually experience and reveal would be much more complex than the limited expectations of propagandists and politicians.

Roberta, Beatrice, Mary, and Florence were given two days' notice to report to authorities at the port of Folkestone for the Channel crossing. On December 17, 1917, they travelled on a steamer packed with men returning to France from leave in Britain. The trip took place at night because of the presence of enemy submarines. The women were assigned a cabin below deck for the short voyage. The men were packed on board by the hundreds, crammed together in the ship's hold or on deck. No lights were allowed, all portholes were shut. In the claustrophobic conditions and with the lurching of the ship, even the seasoned travellers were sick.[15]

As the ship crossed the Channel, the murmur of soldiers' voices on board grew quieter. Most had made the crossing before and weren't looking forward to returning to the trenches. These were not the fresh-faced farm boys and shop clerks who had enthusiastically crossed into France during the first years of the war. They were the bloodied survivors of Ypres and St. Eloi, Mount Sorrel and Sanctuary Wood. Yet there were a few fresh "troops" on board. They were the members of the Women's Army Auxiliary Corps (WAACs), working-class women from London's back streets. The unthinkable had happened. British women were taking on pseudo-military roles in the theatre of war.

It was not a victory of feminism but of warfare. The hard truth was that half of all soldiers who had enlisted were killed or wounded, a figure that would rise to 60 per cent for those who served on the Western Front. By 1917, Allied governments were desperate for men to fill the gaps left by those who had been lost in over two years of fighting. The British government established paramilitary organizations for women such as the WAACs. Men who were doing military tasks behind the lines could now be sent to join their comrades on the killing fields. Women would do their jobs, working as drivers, clerks, cooks, typists, telephone operators, mechanics, and waitresses. Recruiting for the women's corps began in the spring.

The WAACs who were crossing to France with Roberta and her party of journalists were likely some of the first members of the Corps to be sent abroad. To Roberta, the brown-uniformed women symbolized the sea change in gender roles she had experienced in her work at Orpington. She had overseen male bakers, cleaners, and kitchen staff. She had seen female factory workers, drivers, and ticket collectors. "I don't know what is the work of women and what is the work of men," Roberta would tell one interviewer. "I don't think we'll ever be able to straighten it out again."

Always acutely conscious of social position, Mary Macleod Moore saw the WAACs as valiant girls extending themselves for the sake of the men while maintaining their femininity. Yet tough-minded Beatrice may have had the most realistic view. She wondered if she could stomach the conditions that the women would serve under. In a column a few months later she wrote, "Supposing I had to stay in France for six months with one uniform, to sleep rolled in blankets, to live under military discipline, to do whatever I'm told to do, be it congenial or otherwise!"[16]

During the journey across the Channel, most of the WAACs tried as best they could to weather the waves of seasickness. Some lay flat on their backs with packs for pillows and their soft hats over their faces. Others clung to the pillars in the cabin and laughed as their luggage slid back and forth across the floor. As the ship at last entered the harbour, their commanding officer organized the women for roll call.

Roberta and the Canadian journalists went up on deck to peer through the darkness for a first glimpse of Boulogne. As the ship docked, a light rain began to fall. The women struggled through crowds of damp serge to the lower deck where their passports were inspected before they could leave the ship.

As the soldiers and women swayed down the gangplank, they had only a limited idea of the stage that the war had reached. Christmas 1917 would turn out to be a quiet one for those stationed on the Western Front. One quarter of France was now in German hands. Soldiers on both sides of the trenches had dug in – the white snow in Flanders equivalent to a spotlight on any troop movements. It would be the last uneasy respite between the brutality of Passchendaele and the sweeping German offensive of March 1918.

Met on the dock by a representative of the Red Cross, the Canadian women were bundled into a waiting car. As they drew away from the ship's side, the car's headlamps gleamed on the helmets of the khaki ghosts who marched in slow procession into the darkness. The echo of "Take Me Back to Dear Old Blighty" faded as they passed through cobbled streets lined with shuttered houses. An ambulance moved slowly past them in the opposite direction, a lantern swaying above the four men lying inside.[17]

❧ ❧ ❧

Driving through the streets of Boulogne, Roberta must have felt like one of the many pilgrims who wore down the cobblestones on the steep hill to the city's famous cathedral of Notre Dame. Beginning in the thirteenth century, kings and peasants, priests and prostitutes made their way to the ancient domed church that held a simple wooden statue of the Virgin. The first stop on Roberta's pilgrimage (after a good night's sleep) would be the Hotel Christol, the headquarters of the Canadian Red Cross.

During the Great War, the Red Cross provided a distribution channel for the goods that women produced for the soldiers serving overseas. Women in homesteads on the bald-headed prairie and matrons of stone mansions in Toronto's fashionable neighbourhoods worked in common to provide comforts – a pair of knitted socks, a roll of bandages, a jar of preserves – for "their boys overseas."

Initially, these gifts were likely seen as "extras" that would give the men a taste of home while they fought in foreign lands. However, after two and a half years of war, this was no longer the case. The coffers of Allied governments were depleting. In England, food was rationed and often difficult to get. Those who could not stand in line for long hours suffered terribly. Soldiers in the trenches were worse off. When food reached them (and it often didn't), it was barely adequate. In hospitals in England and France, medical supplies and clothing were desperately needed. What were once "extras" were now "essentials."

Roberta knew about the impact of the Red Cross from first-hand experience. As a dietitian in a major military hospital, she had to requisition ingredients for every meal prepared at the hospital.

Canadian soldiers marching "somewhere in France"
during the bitter winter of 1917-18.
National Archives of Canada; PA-2306.

The average cost of rations issued to Canadian troops in England in 1917 was 14.14 pence per day. The amount allowed for patients in hospital was 16.14 pence. At a time when food was rationed in Britain and grocery prices had reached well beyond pre-war highs, the preserves, fresh fruit, and chocolate provided by the Red Cross were important supplements to the meagre menu the hospitals were forced to offer.[18]

In 1917 alone, nearly four million dollars worth of goods were packed in crates and shipped overseas to the Red Cross from Canada, and an additional seven million dollars was donated for the work in France.[19] The money funded hospitals, ambulance units, and medical supplies, including portable electrical generators for surgical units. These supplies often made the difference between life and death, as the women would observe when they toured hospitals closer to the front. "The stock of dressings and of clothing dwindled rapidly. Yet always they had behind them the Red Cross

Society with its fresh supplies, and even as they worked the lorries were rushing up from the base laden with all that was needed by the men and women fighting death," wrote MacLeod Moore.[20]

After a short visit at Canadian Red Cross headquarters, the women toured the warehouses where donated materials were housed before they were sent out to hospitals throughout the country. There was frost on the ground and the women's long dresses stiffened as they toured the cavernous buildings. Inside they found pianos, billiard tables, and gramophones next to ceiling-high piles of crates containing cigarettes, chewing gum, crutches, lemons, lamps, generators, pyjamas, and sweaters. "Christmas was near and there was a Chrismassy look and smell about the boxes that were being opened," remembered Beatrice. "One great row of them contained nothing but Christmas stockings stuffed with gifts and sweets. Every Canadian in a hospital in France received a stocking and a special gift on Christmas."[21]

<hr>

High on the hill overlooking Boulogne's harbour was a monument to Napoleon. A sprawling complex of iron, wood and asbestos huts stood in its shadow. This was Number 3 Canadian General Hospital, built among the ruins of an old Jesuit College and staffed by doctors, nurses, and medical students from McGill University in Montreal. It was also the second stop on the women's tour.

The hospital was an important hub in the network of British, American, and Canadian hospitals that were strung like pearls along the lines of communication. The human cargo disgorged from the ambulance trains in Boulogne were transported via a main road to that large hospital. "Many of the wounded are in a frightful state. Some are wounded in the head, or the face, and are swathed in bloody bandages," wrote Alfred Pearson, a Red Cross orderly who transported some of the wounded. "Worst of all were those who'd been gassed. I saw on one occasion a line of gas victims, one behind the other, with their hands on the shoulders of the man in front, and it looked like a procession – of animals almost – most distressing. They were all blind."[22]

Roberta and her friends lunched with Matron MacLatchy, the head of nursing who had been with the hospital since it was formed in Montreal in the spring of 1915. Then Colonel John Elder, the officer in charge of surgery, led the group through the hospital. They toured the admitting room through which patients passed at a rate of two a minute for several hours during "big pushes." A stable had been converted into an operating room of glittering white, with "the most modern of appliances," according to Beatrice.[23] There were offices and a pathology laboratory. Sunlight poured in through high blue-stained windows as the Canadian women journalists entered the old lecture hall in what remained of the Jesuit College. Standing on the stage at one end of the hall, they looked down on hundreds of exhausted men lying on army cots, bathed in the blue light from the high windows.[24]

Number 3 was also home to a physician known more for his work as a poet than as a surgeon. Colonel John McCrae, now famous for his poem "In Flanders Fields," was on staff. During the summer of 1917, his brother Thomas McCrae had served as Senior Officer in charge of medicine at the Ontario Military Hospital. While no record exists of such an encounter, Roberta may well have taken time to say a word to his brother John. In less than two months, John McCrae would be dead of pneumonia and meningitis, another casualty of the conditions of war.[25]

The hospital McCrae served had a capacity of twenty-four hundred – and it needed every bed, particularly in the months following the autumn battles. In 1917 alone, 48,465 patients were admitted there. Three hundred nurses ministered to the men's needs. The women made beds, stocked ward kitchens, prepared and changed dressings, washed wounds, fed soldiers, checked pulses and temperatures and assisted doctors in surgery. Sometimes they were even called on to perform the role of anaesthetist – another barrier broken in what was formerly a "man's job."[26]

On the evening of their visit to the hospital, Roberta and the other women took a cold moonlit walk on Boulogne's cobbled streets. They encountered a group of cheerful Canadian soldiers who quizzed them about the results of the Canadian election. "We gloried together that the loyalty and strength of Canada were proved for all men to realize," wrote MacLeod Moore.[27] The women took time to visit a Canadian Salvation Army recreation hut that was being decorated for a fundraising event. When asked what charity the show would benefit, they were told that the men were raising money for the victims of the Halifax explosion.[28]

⧖⧖⧖

The next day the Canadian women left Boulogne to begin their tour of the lines of communication. The "lines" were a vast network of hospitals, ambulance convoys, convalescent homes, roads, supply depots, veterinary hospitals, training grounds, repair shops, laundries, prisoner of war camps, postal services, and cemeteries. Arranged along the northwest coast of France, these vital services were linked by railways, roads, canals, and rivers. Half a million horses and mules, twenty thousand trucks, and 250 trains per day serviced this network. A quarter of a million men sorted, stored, and transported food, sandbags, uniforms, and all the other items needed by the men at the front. Another three hundred thousand were engaged in labour of various kinds. Two hundred thousand of these men were low-paid West Indian, Egyptian, East Indian, African, and Chinese workers. Of these, only the West Indians had military status. They were infantrymen who were expected to carry out non-combatant work.[29]

Soldiers were also transported back and forth along the lines of communication. New recruits would arrive in Calais, Le Havre, or Boulogne and proceed to training centres along the coast. From there they would travel to the trenches. Those who were wounded and who survived the tortuous ride back to safety would be moved to hospitals and convalescent camps along the coast. If they received a wound serious enough to free them from military service, a ship would take them back across the Channel on a one-way ticket.

As the Canadian women drove eastward, a thick powder of snow covered the roads and fields. It was one of the coldest winters in memory. There was only one other vehicle on the road, a truck filled with Chinese workers dressed in thick hooded coats. These workers made up the largest group within the labour corps. They were there as part of an agreement between the British and Chinese governments made in December 1916. The first group appeared in France in April 1917. Unlike members of the military, these Asian workers were kept behind barbed-wire in compounds and only allowed out for work. Their customs and dress made good copy for the *London Illustrated News*, where photographs of their traditional celebrations were displayed for a fascinated public.[30]

Soon after the truck passed their car, the women saw barbed wire, sparkling with hoarfrost, surrounding a compound for German prisoners of war. Hundreds of men stared as the women passed, some smiling, others with blank faces. They wore corduroy suits with numbers on them, front and back. "We had read of German prisoners' camps but we looked for the first time on hundreds of these captives inside their barbed wire entanglements and watched them working in gangs. There were many types amongst the Germans we saw, from the low-browed, stolid, grouse-nursing and doubtless homesick kind to the blue-eyed, open-faced, happily grinning ones who waved (at) us as we passed," wrote Beatrice.[31]

The roads were lined with chestnut trees, their branches encrusted with snow. Strangely shaped mounds began to appear in the fields. Soon the travellers saw that some were weapons, camouflaged to hide their true identity from German planes. Above, a line of dark birds made a black billowy line against a blue sky. They were about thirty miles from the trenches.[32]

Finally their driver turned the car up a rough road near a collection of tents and huts sheltered within the remains of a ruined mill. This was Number 7 Canadian Stationary Hospital, a medical unit established by Dalhousie University early in the war. A nearby stone chateau – the "miller's lordly seat" according to Beatrice – housed the medical staff. The hospital was located within hearing distance of the roar of battle. Blood-stained Ypres was just north of Arques, while Armentières was slightly south.[33]

Stationary hospitals were often the third or fourth stop for a wounded man coming "down the line." His journey usually began with a precarious ride on a stretcher, between two bearers who slipped and slid on wooden duckboards, dodged shells and tried not to get sucked into the slimy yellow mud. If the wounded man survived this ordeal, he was examined at a first aid post. From there, a motorized or horse-drawn ambulance drove him over bumpy and barely passable roads to a "casualty clearing station."

There were a number of such stations in the area around St. Omer and Arques, and the Canadian women passed through at least one of these warfront surgical clinics. "At the casualty clearing stations the ambulances rolled up in a steady stream and for hours the tramp of the stretcher bearers might be heard as they moved the wounded to the wards to which they were assigned," wrote Mary Macleod Moore. "Many of the men were gassed and choking for breath; others fearfully wounded, their faces ghastly and their clothes dirty and blood-stained."[34]

Ten or twelve nurses and a handful of doctors provided initial care and surgery in these small tent hospitals. If a soldier's wounds were considered too severe for recovery, he would likely be allowed to die at the station. However, if there was hope of survival, he might have been operated on or sent by ambulance train to a larger stationary hospital. It was this type of hospital that the women visited at Arques.

According to Beatrice, Number 7 Canadian Stationary Hospital had several hundred beds. "Being but a few miles back of the lines, it is sometimes bombed and then the nursing sisters are ordered to their dugouts," she wrote.[35] Here, still within the sounds of the guns, more complex surgery was performed. Wounded men were readied for a final trip to a larger general hospital along the coast or, more happily, straight back to "Blighty."

I took the train to St. Omer, a village within walking distance of Arques. I was hoping to find the remains of the mill that the women toured. In what marked the beginning of a series of coincidences, I arrived on May 14, the anniversary of the day that Number 7 Stationary was established at Arques in 1917. Leaving the train station, I crossed an old stone bridge and walked along the quiet canal that connected the two villages together. It was overcast, with a soft spring breeze rustling the branches of the heavy chestnut trees that hung over the water. The only people I met were fishermen sitting quietly along the edge of the water, their lines taut.

When I finally reached the old stone buildings that lined the main road of Arques, it had begun to pour with rain. I huddled under a narrow awning, eating sweet, custardy "mille feuilles" purchased in a tiny patisserie. Most of the buildings appeared to predate the war, and I imagined Roberta, Beatrice, Mary and the others, their skirts swishing on the mud and snow, their curious faces scanning the aged buildings. But this time, Roberta remained elusive. I did not find the mill that she and her friends toured, and the only chateau worthy of the name belonged to the owner of Cristal d'Arques – a local maker of fine leaded crystal. The tall tan building stood near a busy intersection, across from a cemetery that contained both the simple headstones of the Great War and the garish angels of earlier times.

The next day, I took a bus from Boulogne to Etaples, another of the stops on the women's tour. Grey stone cottages framed with purple lilac bushes, their windows hung with Flanders lace, lined the curving roads leading to the village. On one side of the highway were the railroad tracks that were once a vital artery in the lines of communication. On the other, an expanse of scrub bush and sand dunes swept down to the Canche River. There were no signs that a temporary city of about one hundred thousand people once occupied both sides of this road. That city was the base camp of Etaples.

⟡ ⟡ ⟡

As the Canadian women drove along, scenes of wartime life passed their car windows like slides in a magic lantern show. They saw French women carrying heavy loads of firewood on their backs. Two West Indian soldiers bought chocolate from a woman standing in the shadow of a squat farmhouse. Uniforms were everywhere – khaki hanging on French clotheslines and on the backs of

Following Roberta's footsteps near Arques, France.
Author's Collection.

marching soldiers – the "quaint" uniforms of the French poilus in black and white photographs in roadside shrines, propped against stiff crucifixes. Then their car stopped with a jolt at a railway crossing while an ambulance train with twenty-one cars pulled slowly by. Soldiers waved from the windows. As the train receded into the distance, a French woman opened the gate and they again drove into a cold winter landscape.

"Here's the convoy," announced their driver as the car swooped suddenly under a railway arch and then up through a wide gate and between two long rows of motor ambulances.[36] They had reached the Canadian Red Cross Motor Ambulance Convoy at the base camp at Etaples.

In 1915, the British established four military hospitals, an infantry base depot, and new railway sidings near the small coastal village of Etaples. By 1917, this camp had become the largest complex of military hospitals any country has ever built abroad. There were nearly twenty hospitals, able to accommodate more than twenty thousand patients at one time. Most were general hospitals, but some specialized in certain kinds of illnesses or special needs. There were separate hospitals for officers, German prisoners, women, and men suffering from venereal diseases. Laundries, kitchens, bakeries, quarters for soldiers and nurses provided for the needs of the living, while a mortuary and growing cemetery formed the final stop for those who would never see their homelands again.[37]

Etaples wasn't only a medical base, and this may explain why it was sometimes the subject of aerial bombardment by the Germans. It was also a training ground for new recruits from Britain. Here the men were drilled in the infamous "bull ring" by swaggering, foul-mouthed non-commissioned officers who many of the men secretly believed were afraid of being returned to the front themselves.[38]

It is hard to estimate the number of people living in the Etaples base, since soldiers were constantly entering and leaving. Of the roughly one hundred thousand people who were living in the camp at any one time, twenty-five hundred were women – nurses, WAACs and VADs. The working-class WAACs laboured in bakeries and kitchens, worked as clerks, telephone operators, typists and

Drivers running to their ambulances at Etaples.
IWM; Q2452.

driver–mechanics. The VADs worked as ambulance drivers, chauffeurs, nurse's aids, and staff for the recreation huts for convalescing men.[39]

As the Canadians stepped from their car, they saw young women dressed in leather skirts, khaki great coats, and heavy gauntlets. Like soldiers, they wore heavy boots and puttees – long strips of wool cloth wound around their legs. The women were painting wheels, oiling machinery, filling radiators, or washing and sweeping out the interiors of the ambulances. Pillows and blankets were lying flat on the ground to air. "Their hands were not lily white but they looked extremely efficient as they plunged in and out of pails of water or polished some shiny surface," wrote Beatrice a few months later. "Their faces glowed ruddily in the frosty air. Their whole appearance suggested sturdiness and pluck."[40]

One young woman ran off to find an officer to greet the visitors. While they waited, the women wandered among the ambulances. The cars were labelled with the names of the donors who had financed them – "Women and Girls of Peel County," "WCTU of Toronto," "Women's Institute, Grey County," "Women of Montreal." There were sixty-five ambulances and in one year alone they would carry 180,745 patients. They would also transport the dead to cemeteries for burial.[41]

Eleven months before the Canadian women arrived in France, women replaced the men who operated these ambulances for the Red Cross. Most of the new ambulance drivers at Etaples were VADs. Roberta would later tell a Toronto *Globe* reporter that she believed that the VADs had made an even greater sacrifice than the nursing sisters serving overseas. All their work was done with a "serene good humour and wonderful patience." This favourable view of the VADs may have reflected the fact that they were volunteers, while nurses were paid workers. For the middle-class Roberta, the commitment of privileged women to work for no return seemed to embody a higher moral virtue than the contribution of those who had to earn their living.

Yet, there were many good reasons to respect those privileged volunteer drivers. While some may have become VADs to break the boredom of a drawing-room existence, many were there because they wanted to offer comfort and help to the wounded and dying. Some had lost brothers, fathers, and lovers. As VADs, they worked in twelve-hour day and night shifts from eight to eight – longer when a major battle was underway. They were allowed only half a day off per week, with one full day off per month. They unloaded and loaded ambulance trains, and transported supplies and wounded men between hospitals in the midst of bombs and severe weather. When ambulances broke down, they spent frozen nights alone on empty roads.[42]

Roberta and the journalists were introduced to the six Canadian VADs in the convoy. One of these was Grace MacPherson. In a photograph of the twenty-three-year-old Vancouver woman taken around the time of the Canadian visit, her dirty jacket sleeve was drawn up to her elbow and she was pouring water into her car's radiator from a large white metal jug. There was a broad smile on

The only photograph taken of some of the women journalists who toured France in 1917. Beatrice and Roberta stand in the back row. Florence MacPhedran stands front row, second from the left. Monica Newton Collection.

her face that didn't hint at the fact that MacPherson's brother was already a casualty of war, killed in the Dardanelles.[43] Like Roberta and Beatrice, many of the women serving overseas hid their own fears and losses behind veils of smiles and hard work.

The visitors spent the remainder of the morning touring the convoy's ambulances, mess tent, and recreation hut with Miss Mellor, the unit's second in command. "Do come back for tea," begged Phyllis Baker, a Canadian VAD from Montreal. The visitors agreed and later enjoyed large cups of steaming tea in china bowls amidst the chintz pillows and eiderdowns of the VAD sitting room. But for now, they toured the base that the ambulance convoy served.[44]

As they walked the streets of the sprawling hospital complex, Mary MacLeod Moore mused that Etaples was a great "White City of Healing." In reality, it was also a tinderbox that on more than one occasion had threatened to explode into violence and despair. Only a few months before the Canadian women's visit, soldiers rebelled at the inhuman conditions inside the "bull ring." On September 9, a New Zealand artilleryman was arrested by camp police for overstaying his leave in town. Over the next few days, the event became a catalyst for riots and mob scenes, with soldiers storming out of the camp and into town. New troops were brought in to quell the thousands of soldiers who could no longer be controlled. Eventually fifty-four men were court-martialled for their part in the uprising, and one man was executed for insulting an officer.[45]

While no women stationed at Etaples were hurt during the revolt, they were threatened. On the day that the riot began, the WAACs were recalled to their camp. Hundreds of women were locked into a recreation hut by their superiors and ordered to sing hymns. A mob of soldiers soon surrounded the camp and demanded that the WAACs come out. A Red Cross nurse and a WAAC officer courageously spoke to the men and persuaded them to leave the women alone.[46]

Even if the Canadian women knew about this incident, it was unlikely that they would have reported it. Throughout the many articles Mary and Beatrice wrote during the war, they portrayed soldiers as chivalrous white knights and nurses and women in military uniform as feminine creatures providing maternal care far from the bullets and bayonets. To portray them as anything else would have fuelled public anxiety and increased demands for women to be recalled from the dangerous theatre of war. So it was likely self-censorship rather than ignorance that prevented the women from describing the difficulties of women's work near the front.

Roberta and the journalists visited the two general hospitals funded and staffed by the Canadian government — Numbers 7 and 1. Like their British counterparts, these hospitals were collections of long narrow corrugated iron huts lined with asbestos and rough wood paneling. Metal cots filled with wounded men were

The interior of one of two Canadian hospitals at Etaples.
National Archives of Canada; C-80026.

arranged in an orderly row along each wall, with a narrow passage between. Many were covered with bright red blankets – the gift of the Canadian Red Cross. Here and there, a wooden frame was raised above a bed with a canvas hammock hanging from the upper beam. Within these hammocks, fractured limbs rested and healed. Hollow-eyed nurses, working twelve-hour shifts, moved from bed to bed, changing dressings and administering medicines.[47]

Mary MacLeod Moore observed the arrival of a group of wounded. "The wounded men arrive from the Casualty Clearing Stations by ambulance train and in ambulances in various stages of helplessness, and suffering all the pain of having been lately wounded. They were carried to the admission hut, and here the details of each case were entered and each man is assigned to a ward. Next they were bathed and fed and put into the first bed most of them have occupied for many months. Henceforth they receive the most tender and constant care until they were sent to Blighty – the ambition of every wounded man – or to a 'Con. (Convalescent) Camp' if the injury is not severe."[48]

The Canadian women talked with patients and nurses as they walked through the wards of Number 7. The air was hazy. Since painkillers were only available to the most seriously hurt, nearly all the men smoked in an effort to deal with the pain of injuries exposed to air and doused in the "Carrel–Dakin" solution or "Hypochlorous Acid 1/4 % solution." Years later, nurses would still be able to smell the pungent lime-like smell of the cleansing liquid that was used extensively in the irrigation of wounds.[49] Despite the cold, a few windows were left open to let out the smell of the solution, along with the odours of smoke, gas gangrene (gas created by bacteria in wounds), and bodily fluids.

Here, as in other hospitals, the Canadian women were given the opportunity to visit the kitchen facilities. Keenly aware of shortages and interested in the day-to-day concerns of common soldiers, they were often preoccupied with food during their tour in France. During one brief stop earlier in their tour, they had visited the largest field bakery in France, from which a quarter million two-pound loaves were baked each day and sent on trucks to soldiers in the trenches. At Etaples, there was a special diet kitchen where according to Mary MacLeod Moore "any dish asked for a by a sick man is prepared by a Home Sister, skilled in invalid cookery."[50]

Before they left, Roberta and the other women poked their heads into a room where a cluster of Canadian nurses were looking through a pile of mail, searching for something from home. As they chatted with the women, excited voices suddenly called them outside. They emerged into the cold air and looked up to see white puffs of smoke and a group of planes locked in combat. Despite warnings, they stayed outside, mesmerized by the conflict. They didn't know that within a few months, planes would rain death on the very ground on which they now stood.

The stone marking Canadian Nursing Sister Margaret Lowe's grave in Etaples. Author's Collection.

A simple stone cross stood sentry at the Etaples Military Cemetery. From the concrete platform behind it, I looked down on a vast, rolling green hill, banked with railroad tracks that once transported soldiers and supplies. Nearly twelve thousand identically shaped white headstones were arranged in neat rows like the hospitals that once tried to save the men now buried here. In one of the stone monuments overlooking the graves, I discovered a compartment with a copper door. Inside I found books with the names of the dead and directions to where their graves could be found, including the location of the graves of three Canadian nurses who were mortally wounded on a warm May evening in 1918. That night, fifteen German planes attacked Etaples. During a hellish two hours, 116 bombs were dropped over the hospital complex. Alice McKinnon, a British nurse at Number 24 General (next door to Number 7) recalled the raid:

> One night the German bombers came and bombed the hospital. We didn't know that, earlier in the evening, some horses had evidently been tethered outside our huts and one of the bombs which I suppose was meant for us, hit these horses instead. The noise was something terrible. I never knew a horse could scream, scream all over.... I thought in my own mind that it was very important that I didn't show any fear, to try and help the men, to keep them all calm, because some had only just come out of the trenches and could not bear the thought of something happening now they were out.[51]

Number 7 Canadian General, also hit in the raid, lost many staff and patients, although none of their nurses were killed. The scene was different at Number 1 Canadian General. A bomb made a direct hit on the nurses' quarters, scattering debris and setting it on fire. Canadian Nurse Katharine MacDonald died instantly. Nurses Gladys Wake and Margaret Lowe were terribly injured. Lowe was one of the original eighty nurses who had trained with Roberta in Toronto and served with her at the Ontario Military Hospital in Orpington. Later she was transferred to Etaples, where she faced a grim fate. She died on May 28 of injuries sustained in the raid.

As flames crackled around her, Wake, recognizing that she was unlikely to survive, begged black-faced stretcher-bearers to leave her and save themselves. Despite her protests, they pulled her from the burning hut. Above them, German planes flew low, sending a spray of machine gun fire among the rescuers. Throughout the raid, nursing sisters like Canadian Marguerite Carr-Harris

The base camp at Etaples has been replaced by a modern military cemetery.
Author's Collection.

tended the wounded, rigging up makeshift operating theatres.[52] Some assisted with surgery, taking the place of orderlies who had been killed.

While most patients and nurses were instructed to lay beneath their beds for protection from flying glass, the three hundred men in Number 1 Canadian General who were anchored to their beds with fractured femurs had to remain where they were. Many nurses chose to stay nearby, calming their fears. As morning dawned, sixty people were dead or dying, and seventy-three were wounded.[53]

The May raids marked the beginning of the end for Number 1 Canadian General. Three more raids followed the May 19 bombing. One almost destroyed the hospital. Several patients were injured – one fatally. Nearby, the St. John Ambulance Hospital was also destroyed. The two hospitals were shut down, their staffs reassigned and patients sent to other hospitals in France and England.[54]

It was difficult for me to imagine how the women working here were affected by the death and suffering they witnessed each day. There are a few accounts that suggest that some were overwhelmed by what they experienced as they worked tirelessly through hellish situations. One Canadian nurse, Nettie Shearer, worked straight through the raids.[55]

Clare Gass nursed at Number 1 Canadian General at Etaples in 1915. In her diary, she was reserved and matter-of-fact about her work. But now and then, the devastation and suffering became intolerable. "Some of these new patients have dreadful wounds. One young boy with part of his face shot away both arms gone and great wounds in both legs. Surely Death were merciful," wrote Gass. "These are the horrors of war. But they are too horrible. Can it be God's will or only man's devilishness. It is too awful. Our boy with both his arms gone is only 20-years-old."[56]

The Canadian journalists whose path I was following wrote about passing a rest home for nurses en route to Etaples. Early in the war, it became apparent that these "ministering angels" didn't have endless reservoirs of compassion from which to draw through all the horrors that they witnessed. Now and again, nurses needed to withdraw, to strengthen themselves to care for the broken bodies of literally thousands of men. Standing among the white stones with the names of three Canadian nurses printed on them, I wondered how Roberta and the journalists felt as they observed the women who tried to heal the wounds of war.

Mary Macleod Moore recorded her impressions of the Etaples cemetery – a burial place that has now become one of the few memorials to the life and death struggles that occurred here: "Near this White City of Healing, through *which have passed so many wounded men in the war years which seem so long, there are other men. They lie at rest with a cross to tell the name of each. Near them are other graves and other crosses bearing German names, for friends and enemies are as one when the time comes to make the last long journey Home."[57]*

≈≈≈

While Roberta was touring France, her brother Johnston was immersed in intelligence work for the Canadian military. Sometime around December 23, he received instructions to report at once to General Currie's headquarters. No explanation was given and he was curious to know what new assignment he might be receiving. As he waited to be called into the General's office, he carelessly glanced at some newspapers lying open on the hall table. His sister's photograph stared back at him from the pages of both the New York Times and the "L'Illustracion" from Paris.[58] When he looked up, Roberta was standing in front of him, with General Currie smiling over her shoulder.

The visit with Currie capped the women's journey into France. "It was a proud moment for the first Canadian women writers who visited France when they were presented to the Canadian Corps Commander, General Sir Arthur Currie, and thought of Vimy Ridge and Passchendaele," wrote Mary MacLeod Moore.[59] The four journalists returned to England, and each began to write a series of articles about their experiences. Roberta, however, managed to stay on in France a few days longer than her friends. In the *Edmonton Journal* of February 7, 1918, an anonymous reporter provided a tantalizing clue to what she did during those extra days. "Lieutenant MacAdams was granted a few extra days' furlough and an extra privilege, in that she was permitted to go as near the firing line as any British woman has been allowed to go," said the report. "This, of course, did not include a visit to the front trenches, but to the soldiers quarters where she saw the men going on duty and returning, and witnessed the various war activities directly behind the lines."[60]

As my train travelled through the French countryside, I thought about some of the gaps in my knowledge of the women's journey to France. In a photograph at the Glenbow Archives, Roberta, Beatrice, Mary and Florence pose with some of the staff of Number 8 General Hospital in St. Cloud, near Paris. The hospital, which served many French soldiers, was never mentioned in the women's newspaper accounts. This lonely photograph was one of only two pieces of evidence that suggested that the women were in the vicinity of Paris. The other was an article about Beatrice, written late in the war. The anonymous writer wrote that "[Beatrice] was one of the members of the Canadian women's press party who under Government sanction and chaperonage recently toured the lines of communication in France and 'did' the Christmas leave clubs in Paris."[61] As my train drew into Paris, I wondered what those "leave clubs" might have been like during that last December of the war.

CHAPTER 11

LADIES IN THE LEGISLATURE

"The soldiers and the sisters chose me as their representative exactly as they selected Captain Pearson, who headed the poll. They did not think they were doing anything very startling in voting for a woman. Why should they think so? If they thought about it at all, they probably thought it was quite as natural for a woman to be a member of Parliament as a member of a nursing corps."
(Roberta MacAdams, quoted in **The Globe**, Friday, September 21, 1917)

It was sixteen degrees Fahrenheit outside the Alberta legislature. Although hard, glistening snow was piled high beside its granite steps, it could have been summer inside the legislature's great marble rotunda. The air was hot from people in heavy winter coats who had crowded inside to witness a historic moment in Canadian politics – the first time women would takes their seats as elected members of a parliament anywhere in the British Empire.

Upstairs, inside the legislative chamber, many MLAs were gathering to receive their seat assignments. Most wore the high collars still popular during the war, while others were dressed in military uniforms. A rainbow of coloured light from the stained glass windows in the dome above their heads cascaded down onto their dark wool suits and khaki jackets. As they stood talking, some puffed on thick cigars, filling the air with the smell of cognac-dipped tobacco leaves. Then a gush of cool air washed into the room as the Assembly's heavy oak doors swung open. Roberta MacAdams stepped inside, escorted by a smiling Robert Pearson. Louise McKinney slipped in behind them, her back straight and eyes glowing behind round spectacles. According to an eyewitness, "Miss MacAdams was immediately surrounded by an admiring knot of spectators, who eagerly shook her by the hands and congratulated her on her safe return after her war-time experiences...."[1]

Louise McKinney was invited to step forward and sign the legislative roll – officially becoming the first female legislator in the British Empire. Although she and Roberta had been elected in the same provincial election, their polls had been months apart. Like the twin sister who had been born first, Louise was to be forever remembered as the first woman elected. As she signed the document with her careful flourish, John Cowell, Clerk of the House, began to tactfully encourage members to take their seats.

The dark polished desks in the chamber had been arranged in a U-shape, with Conservative members on one side, Liberals on the other, and non-partisan and independent members – including McKinney and MacAdams – sitting in two short rows at the bottom of the "U." As the two women sat down, the room was noisy with laughter and loud whispers. Above them, the spectators' gallery was packed. Men in business suits, returned soldiers in khaki and ladies in elegant three-quarter length dresses craned over the low brass balustrade to catch glimpses of the proceedings. Grace Studholme was there too, eager to witness the swearing in of her former domestic science teacher.[2]

Suddenly the room became almost silent. The only sound was the soft shuffle of shoes on plush carpet as legislators and spectators rose to their feet. Into the Assembly marched a line of Canadian soldiers, followed by Lieutenant Governor Robert Brett, dressed in a double-peaked hat and a gold-braided suit. As he took his seat on the raised throne at the south end of the chamber, John Cowell read the royal proclamation calling the legislature into session.

As the MLAs sat down, Premier Charles Stewart (Arthur Sifton had resigned as premier in order to join the union cabinet of Robert Borden) stepped forward and proposed the re-election of Charles Fisher as the Speaker of the House. After his name was seconded, the motion was quickly carried. Members applauded as the Speaker appeared in the southeast entrance. After a brief speech, he bowed to the Lieutenant Governor and promised to faithfully perform his duties and maintain freedom of speech in the legislature. Then the real business of the day began with the speech from the throne. In slow, measured tones, the Lieutenant Governor outlined the government's continued commitment to the war effort. Food production would be increased and the provincial grant to the Canadian Patriotic Fund would be met by "equitable taxation" distributed among the people of the province.[3] There were loud whispers in the gallery above – many had been wondering how the government planned to meet its wartime responsibilities. Down on the floor of the legislature, the two "soldiers' representatives" were equally interested in the new measures. Roberta and her colleague Robert Pearson would soon be hounding the government to live up to its commitments to soldiers and their dependents.

The speech from the throne was the apex of the day's proceedings. "Formal business, transacted in a few minutes and of a most routine character, followed, and on the motion of Premier Stewart the House adjourned until Friday, February 8, at 3 pm," read one newspaper account.[4]

◈ ◈ ◈

When Roberta returned to her elegant room at Edmonton's Macdonald Hotel,[5] she must have shaken her head over the few short hours that she and the other MLAs had just spent in the service of Albertans. Roberta was accustomed to twelve-hour workdays with only the occasional leave to visit friends in London. Here in Canada, it was as though the war was some far-off phenomenon that had little impact on day-to-day life – inside or outside the legislature. It wasn't the first time this thought had occurred to her. En route to Alberta for the February session, she had stopped in Toronto to visit Maud and address a luncheon meeting of the Toronto chapter of the Canadian Woman's Press Club. Although she respected the work of female journalists, Roberta was appalled by the sumptuous lunch served at the meeting. She told one member that she was "struck by the comparative cheapness of good food and by the serving of white finger rolls, cream in coffee and iced desserts, things that had long ago disappeared from England."[6] The bountiful food seemed to cheapen the sacrifices being made by men and women overseas.

Once again in the West, Roberta was determined to use her time in the legislature to improve the lives of servicemen and their families. She sat in front of her typewriter at the walnut writing desk in her quiet hotel room and mulled over the contents of her first private member's bill. Entitled an "Act to Incorporate The Great War Next-of-Kin Association," it reflected the agenda she planned to champion during the coming term. The Act gave official recognition to an organization that had been established by a group of soldier's wives in Calgary in April 1917. According to the *Alberta Club Woman's Blue Book* (a club directory) the group was "the expression of opinion of thousands of women, who feel that while they are willing to make all the necessary sacrifices that the country demands of them in her hour of need, that there is a great injustice somewhere that permits on the one hand, of the display of apparent luxury, and the piling up of immense profits through war conditions, and on the other hand that allows the dependents of those who have gone to the front to struggle on inadequate allowances with the ever-increasing cost of living."[7] The ultimate goal of the Great War Next-of-Kin Association was to secure economic justice for all soldiers and their dependents. At a time when social welfare was in its infancy, this was a radical idea. But for the next four years, Roberta MacAdams would champion just such objectives.

On Friday, Roberta stood in the Legislative Assembly and moved the first reading of "An Act to Incorporate the Great War Next-of-Kin Association." The bill was front-page news in the *Edmonton Bulletin* the next day.[8] It was not only the first bill presented during the 1918 session, it was also the first bill introduced by a woman anywhere in the British Empire. With its focus on the rights of soldiers and their families, it received little opposition from the august members of the legislature. It would eventually pass into law on April 13, 1918.

≈≈≈

Roberta and the other military members of the Alberta legislature.
Glenbow Archives; NC–6–3413.

I was in Alberta again, visiting the legislature where Roberta made her political debut. I stood under one of the faded and worn flags hanging from brass poles in the marble-lined rotunda. Some were the regimental colours of Alberta military groups that had fought in the Great War. They were decorated with golden maple leaves, Union Jacks, crowns, and battalion numbers embroidered in gold thread on purple fabric.[9]

The flags were a poignant reminder of the thirty-eight thousand Albertans whom Roberta represented in the legislature. They had left towns, cities, factories and farms to join the great adventure overseas. Few expected or received much in exchange for their service. Their wage was $1.10 a day (half the wage of an unskilled labourer) and few preparations had been made for helping them make a fresh start once they returned to civilian life.[10] At the beginning of the conflict, most people believed the war would only last a few months. There was little pressure to make arrangements for the demobilization and re-establishment of what was seen as a short-term temporary force. Instead, federal and provincial governments channelled their energies into providing the things the armed forces needed to do their work – armaments, uniforms, food, transport, and hospitals.

However, as the war ground on, the numbers of Canadian soldiers serving overseas grew into the hundreds of thousands. Soon disabled men began to return home in ever-greater numbers, looking for rehabilitation and employment. During her election campaign, Roberta had warned her listeners about the problem of soldier re-establishment. Now it finally seemed that the "soldier problem" was beginning to draw the attention of a handful of voluntary groups that lobbied the government to develop plans for reintegrating returning heroes into society. Before long, some enterprising politicians even shook out and refashioned an old political idea to address this new problem. They proclaimed that soldiers could be settled on free, undeveloped agricultural land. The Dominion would benefit because previously unsettled areas of the country would become productive and the soldiers themselves would gain a reasonable livelihood in exchange for their gallant efforts overseas.

The Soldier Settlement Act was passed by the federal government in 1917 and put into operation by the appointment of the Soldier Settlement Board in 1918. According to historian Desmond Morton: "A three-member Soldier Settlement Board could distribute an extra 160 acres of Crown land in addition to the 160 acres any homesteader could claim. The board could also loan up to $1,500 for stock, equipment, buildings, improvements, or more land, repayable at 5 per cent in twenty years. All undisposed-of government land within 15 miles of a railway would be reserved for returned men."[11] Since public lands were in limited supply, those soldiers who had to buy their own land and equipment could borrow money from the government at advantageous terms.[12]

Only six months before, Roberta had promised that she would put her best efforts into helping soldiers settle on the land. However, she also believed that options also had to be provided if soldiers were to make a smooth transition back to civilian life. On a chill February afternoon, Roberta was given the chance to promote some of her solutions to the returned soldier problem. In her first speech to the legislature, she would sketch out a new approach to the needs of veterans.

More than eighty years later, I stood in the spectator's gallery of the Alberta legislature, holding the original draft of that speech. It was carefully typed on long yellowing sheets of foolscap, the odd word crossed out and carefully changed in Roberta's neat handwriting. The speech must have been extremely *important to her. Although she kept very few mementos of her time in office, she carefully preserved this four-page document, tucked in a manila envelope with a small sheaf of press clippings and a copy of her election flyer. The pages of the speech were filled with concern for the soldiers whom she represented, her words carefully chosen to maximize their impact. As I looked at the now-empty seats in the chamber below, I imagined Roberta rising to her feet, ready to put her views on public record, knowing that every word she said would be weighed against her gender and class by the skeptical men who surrounded her.*

❦❦❦

"Mr. Speaker: As a beginning member and as one quite unversed in the manners and customs of legislators, it would be naturally my inclination to remain seated for a season at least, to sit at the feet of those of ripe experience and finished proficiency. But in this time of stress, one's inclinations go to the wall. The signal honor and the very grave responsibility which is mine to represent Alberta's overseas fighting men, seems to impose upon me the responsibility to say at least a few words on matters directly affecting them. And therefore, Mr. Speaker, I must crave your indulgence and the indulgence of the House, towards any errors or transgressions which I, in my ignorance, may commit."

There were no "errors or transgressions" in Roberta's maiden speech, only a pointed and clear analysis of the limits of soldier settlement schemes, and some suggestions for an alternative approach.

"Of the land scheme I do not wish to speak — that is a Federal matter. It may be in order to note, however, that if it is the usual characteristic homestead undertaking it cannot meet the needs of a great many of our returned men. We all know that it takes physical endurance, fortitude and a well-balanced temperament to endure the homestead experience and to make a home. The isolation of homesteading is likely to be the converse of what the returned soldier needs. The mental strain of war tends to make him unfit for the further strain of homesteading. Then our frontier agriculture is of a rather primitive type, it is the farming of rough operations, of arduous labour, often offering little of creature comfort, and the sustained discomfort of trenches and billets

is likely to have made the ex-soldiers hungry for all the physical comfort, even indulgence, he can secure."[13]

Then Roberta raised a cautionary note:

"We must be ready for these incoming throngs, or it will not be well for us to be here. The leader of the Opposition has said that every returned soldier must be welcomed. The warmth of our welcome will soon chill unless we can fit them into the scheme of mutual service. The guest, yes, even the returning prodigal soon wears out his welcome if he remains a mere parasite in the household.

There will be armies of those men coming back who even before the war worked – or walked – in armies, the men with the herd instinct strong in them, and the creative instinct in the mass, the men who have built the railways, dug the ditches, built the bridges, hewed the timbers, opened up the mining camps, the men who gathered wherever is offered a big scheme of construction – the men who before the war walked the streets of Edmonton, and of every other city in Alberta because there was something wrong with our social system and we could not safely and rightly direct their instinct. These men enlisted in hundreds and thousands early in the war. When it is over they will come back – those of them who have not made the supreme sacrifice that we might be free and prosperous and secure."[14]

Roberta reminded her audience of the role that Canadian soldiers were now playing in establishing their country as an equal among independent nations. Returning soldiers, she argued, had "performed their full share towards giving Canada a leading place in the roll of nations. They cannot, they will not return to their former status. In giving all, they have gained much. The army has brought to them self-realization; it has offered an opportunity for self-expression. As a great constructive army of peace they would be capable of even greater achievements than they have accomplished in the unnatural, the inhuman business of war. This man power, awakened, organized, trained, perfected, is coming to Alberta, and it is a power to be reckoned with."[15]

If this "great army of peace" was channelled into a civilian force it could transform Alberta into a modern industrial province, Roberta argued. After all, Alberta's natural resources, its uncut timber, asphalt beds, oil, and minerals could provide employment for thousands. "If we here in Alberta could formulate and offer some practical specific concrete scheme that would guarantee to take care of all returning men, and all incoming men, surely we might hope for a sympathetic hearing for such a proposal from the Federal House."[16] As Roberta set her speech down on her desk, the Assembly broke out into cheers and applause. To the journalists covering her speech, she had proven "that the soldiers had made no mistake in choosing her for their representative."[17] Yet Roberta knew that the proof was in the pudding – the government would have to take concrete action before soldiers really believed that their representative had successfully defended their concerns.

❦❦❦

While Roberta was defending the needs of soldiers in the Alberta legislature, overseas the tide of war was changing once again. Early on the morning of March 21, the German army launched a sweeping bombardment against the British Third and Fifth Armies; 6,608 guns, 3,534 trench mortars, and two million gas shells poured destruction on the Allies. Within moments, entire battalions were wiped out. A dense fog rolled in, allowing invading German soldiers to pour through the break in Allied defences. The Germans followed the Somme northwest to Arras, leaving destruction in their wake.[18] Territory that had been purchased at the cost of many thousands of Allied lives would soon be in German hands again. It was the beginning of the end of trench warfare and the start of a desperate conflict between the opposing forces.[19]

Civilians were experiencing the war's terrors first hand. The Germans had begun to use a new long-range weapon – a giant gun that showered Paris with shells over twenty times per day. Across the English Channel, two German aircraft dropped bombs on London, killing eleven and injuring forty-six.[20] Journalist Mary MacLeod Moore – one of the four women who had accompanied Roberta to France – described the fears of Britons during this shadowy time. "This is written during the early days of the great battle.

We are passing through perhaps the most momentous days of our history as a nation. We read, only half realizing what it means, of the tremendous number of German divisions massed against our men and we dimly understand what the conditions must be like when war is waged on so gigantic a scale. No one who has not passed through such days as a combatant, or at least as a spectator and non-combatant, can realize other than dimly what is going on. We only know that the tragedy of the war would seem to have reached some climax."[21]

The drastic reversal in the fortunes of the Allies meant that relationships between soldiers and their lovers suddenly seemed even more precarious. Guy Mackenzie Furniss, the dashing Englishman who had been pursuing Beatrice Nasmyth since the beginning of the war, finally persuaded her to marry him. On March 28, while Guy was on leave, they met at St. Martin-in-the-Fields Church for a rushed wartime wedding. There was no filmy pre-war wedding dress for Beatrice, just a simple purple gabardine suit and Georgette blouse, a bunch of English violets pinned on her lapel. Guy wore his uniform with its close-fitting jacket and kilt. A few days later, he would be back in France.[22]

For Roberta, the news of Beatrice's wedding was the only glimmer of happiness in an otherwise bleak spring. In April 1918, Jack Hanna's nephew Harold celebrated his seventeenth birthday by enlisting in the Royal Air Force and beginning flight training in England. Within a month he was dead. "Harold was making his last flight for that course and had given a perfect performance up to the time of the accident," wrote Jack Hanna in a letter to Neil. "Just what happened is not definitely known, but it would appear that coming down at a distance of 1500 feet from the ground the controllers broke or otherwise went wrong and he struck the ground at a very high speed, probably never knowing what happened."[23] Harold was buried on Salisbury Plain, the training ground of the first Canadian contingent. He was one of 1,388 Canadian pilots who died during the Great War – 449 in training accidents.[24]

Harold's death increased family fears for the welfare of Neil Hanna. In February, after his long convalescence, Neil had returned to England. Although he could have been transferred to a comfortable office job, he had chosen to return to his unit in France. By May, he was in a "quiet part of the line" and despite Harold's death, lobbying military authorities to transfer him to the Royal Air Force.[25] By the end of that month, Neil would be transferred to the RAF to begin his pilot training. He would eventually be posted to Italy, a country that had entered the war on the Allied side in 1915.

Jack Hanna naturally disapproved of Neil's actions. "I do think it would be a great mistake for you to attempt to push your way as pilot. I do not believe you are fitted for it," he wrote to his son. "However, you are into the flying now and must make the best of it. We want to see you back alive and able to carry on here and this turns to some extent at least on yourself. Please exercise the necessary care."[26]

As for Johnston MacAdams, in March 1918 he was transferred to 3rd Canadian Infantry Brigade headquarters "somewhere in France." Before long, he was assigned to the headquarters staff of the 3rd Canadian Division as an intelligence officer. Like Neil, he too found himself spending a lot of time in airplanes. Johnston's duties included checking aerial photographs and ground maps, a task that involved many flights above enemy lines.

❦ ❦ ❦

Despite the worrying war news, Roberta discovered that back home in Alberta, the conflict seemed to be the farthest thing from legislators' minds. Canadians were sick of struggling to make ends meet on incomes that didn't match the escalating cost of living. Some farmers had experienced bad harvests and food prices were rising. For the first few months of the session, the removal of agricultural tariffs and the rising price of wheat dominated the session. Roberta grew impatient with the constant focus on the needs of farmers, while the concerns of soldiers seemed to go unanswered. Although she usually was a great defender of Alberta's rural people, she suspected that greedy farmers were making money on the backs of the men overseas. According to the *Edmonton Journal*,

> [Miss MacAdams] somewhat severely censured the government for its apathy toward the returned soldiers' problem. She asserted that the attitude of the government toward the war apparently was an agricultural one, in other words, the needs of the farmers were more in the minds of the government than those of the soldiers who were fighting overseas. She pointed out very emphatically that were it not for the men holding the frontline overseas, none of the farmers or anyone else in Alberta would be in a position of advantage to themselves through the increased prices brought about by the war.... Miss MacAdams declared flatly that the entire government, and especially the department of agriculture were working in the interest of only one class – the farmer. The system was providing automobiles and delicious meals for the farmer at home, but $1.10 a day did not provide such for the men at the front who were suffering mud, privation and pain.[27]

In April, Roberta and the other soldiers' representative, Robert Pearson, successfully persuaded the provincial government to establish a department dealing with the needs of soldiers. Later that month, they also secured the passage of the Patriotic Tax Act, a measure that exempted soldiers serving overseas from taxes until one year after their discharge.[28] These were small steps, but some of the first breakthroughs in the ongoing struggle for soldiers' rights in the latter years of the Great War.

Roberta was no longer the shy Victorian young lady who had gone off to study at the Macdonald Institute. Her years as an educator and her work at Orpington had fostered a confident maturity. Despite her earlier disavowal of any interest in politics, it was clear that Roberta enjoyed her work in the Assembly. What's more, she was good at it. In April 1918, Roberta's sharp debating skills and her Irish sense of humour more than matched the arguments of a fellow legislator. Alberta was suffering from a shortage of teachers and plans were being made for the building of new teacher training facilities (known as "Normal schools.") Roberta knew that a growing number of young women were living in Alberta's two largest cities and needed ready access to these schools if they were going to pursue careers as teachers. However, when education minister George Smith rose to address the issue, he argued that "Normal schools" should be located in rural areas, since "city girls are a menace to country schools."[29]

Roberta couldn't let such a ridiculous suggestion pass without a challenge. "That brings up a grave question," she remarked to the House. "Why, I never knew there was such a danger for rural schools. I didn't think such an insidious evil existed. The only protection to the public in that case appears to be that about fifty per cent of the Normal teachers have graduated from Camrose [a small rural college]. I view with alarm the great number of teachers who have graduated from the school in Calgary."[30] As MLAs roared with laughter, Smith found himself promising Roberta that the next Normal school would be built in Edmonton. That promise would be kept. In 1930, the Provincial Normal School would open its doors on the University of Alberta campus.[31]

❧❧❧

At the Glenbow Archives there is a photograph of the Alberta legislature in session in 1918. Men sit behind desks arranged in an open square, with Louise McKinney and Roberta MacAdams seated side by side in the middle. They smile at the camera, Louise in her high-collared dress, Roberta in her working uniform, both sitting with hands clasped primly in their laps. The two women had many things in common beyond their gender. Both had grown up in Ontario and had trained as teachers. They had been important leaders in two prominent women's organizations – Roberta in the Women's Institutes, Louise with the WCTU. Both were unwilling candidates who ran for office only when persuaded that a higher moral objective was at stake; Roberta to "safeguard the soldiers' interests in matters which may come up at the local legislature,"[32] Louise to promote the rights of women and children and to eradicate the "liquor traffic."[33]

Although neither Louise nor Roberta had aspired to hold office, after their election they became powerful advocates of women's full participation in political life. Each believed that one of their most important objectives was to use their positions to improve society. "My ideal of women in political life is that she make her contribution to the general good," said Louise to the members of the Women's Political League. "What of real interest to men is not of real interest to women and vice versa? My ideal is that they shall be partners, equal partners in national affairs, together working out the destiny of the nation."[34] To Roberta, the franchise and access to political life provided women with an opportunity to address particular kinds of issues. "Social legislation [is] distinctly woman's sphere – legislation bearing upon hygiene, housing, health, education, the care of the sick and poor, factories, and all things that affected women and children," she told a group of students. "Every woman everywhere should be concerned about these things."[35]

Although they shared many common concerns, Louise and Roberta differed in important ways. Louise had grown up on a farm, while Roberta was the product of the city. Louise was a committed suffragist; Roberta a latecomer to the struggle for women's rights. Roberta had grown up in a staunchly Conservative home. Louise was a proponent of the radical "non-partisan movement." Their political and personal differences may explain why they so seldom made common cause over a particular issue or piece of legislation. The one exception seemed to have been the issue of temperance. Roberta, the daughter of a temperance advocate, was quick to come to Louise's aid when prohibition issues were raised in the legislature. One such opportunity came in March 1918. Although province-wide prohibition had been passed into law in 1916, it was unevenly enforced. Doctors still prescribed alcohol to their patients and druggists were doing an active trade in "medicinal" alcohol. On March 27, the legislature was the scene of a heated confrontation between Attorney General Boyle on the one side, and Roberta and Louise on the other. Both of the women accused Boyle of negligence, suggesting that sales of liquor had increased since he had taken office.

It is easy to forget how extraordinary it was for these two women to be challenging male legislators in a provincial parliament. In 1918, many Canadians still held the view that the political arena was no place for a woman. In Ottawa, Senator L. David moved that unmarried women under thirty should be disenfranchised because they were innocent maidens who should prepare themselves "to fulfill the duties for their noble mission."[36] Of the fifty-two votes cast, nineteen senators voted for David's motion.

Yet the times were changing. Despite attempts by traditionalists like David, the obstacles to women's participation in public life were slowly being pushed out of the way. In February, the federal government had held a national Women's War Conference. One in six Canadian women belonged to at least one national women's organization[37] and the government wanted to garner their support for the war effort at a time when Canadian enthusiasm was beginning to flag. About seventy representatives from groups such as the National Council of Women, Imperial Order of Daughters of the Empire, Women's Institutes, and Women's Christian Temperance Union shared their ideas about women and war work, the establishment of a national labour registry, food conservation, and the promotion of the war effort. The women debated and made lengthy recommendations about child labour, the vote for women, prison conditions, the lack of teachers in the West, and female unemployment. At the end of the meeting, they also released a statement urging renewed public support for the war effort: "Inspired by the bravery of our men and the fortitude of the women in the war-stricken countries, let us stand together and work steadfastly for victory."[38]

Satisfied that they had won the women's endorsement, the Borden government promptly ignored all but one of the recommendations they had made.[39] They would finally give women the vote. Yet, even here, the rights being offered were limited. Women still couldn't hold federal office and their enfranchisement was not to be truly universal. Canadians of Asian and Aboriginal ancestry – both male and female – would have to wait decades until they would be granted the right to vote.

For the remainder of Alberta's legislative session, Roberta spent much of her free time speaking to groups about women's war work overseas.[40] Before returning to England, she would also fit in a cross-Canada speaking tour promoting the Red Cross.[41] But of all the events she attended in the last few weeks of her stay in Canada, the one that brought her full circle was a special luncheon in the ballroom of the Hotel Macdonald. One hundred and seventy-five Edmonton school teachers and administrators, including Roberta's old friends Percy Page and William Carpenter, gathered to celebrate her electoral achievement and listen to her reflections on the impact of the war on Canadians overseas. "A new spirit of nationalism has been born by means of the interchange of thoughts and ideas, by the hundreds and thousands of men who meet in hospitals and other places of contact," Roberta declared. "What the outcome, or what the future holds is only a matter of conjecture, and it is our duty to breathe into the rising generation the new patriotism."[42]

That the outcome of the war was far from certain was made abundantly clear to Roberta when she returned to Britain in June. Within weeks of her arrival, a Canadian hospital ship was torpedoed off the coast of Ireland. The *Llandovery Castle* had delivered a draft of wounded soldiers home to Canada and was on its way back to Britain, carrying a group of ninety-seven Canadian doctors and nurses, and 161 soldiers and crew members. All fourteen nursing sisters on board were killed when their lifeboat was pulled under the swirling water by the suction of the sinking ship. They weren't alone. The U-boat that had sunk the ship surfaced and shelled those few lifeboats that had managed to stay afloat. By the end of that terrible day, 234 people had died.[43]

Mary McKenzie, one of the nurses who was lost on the *Llandovery Castle*, had been a member of the original group of nurses who travelled overseas with Roberta to serve at the Ontario Military Hospital. Several others had worked at the two Canadian hospitals at Etaples. For Roberta and all who served overseas, their deaths were one more reminder of the human cost of the Great War.

CHAPTER 12

PREPARING FOR PEACE

I vow to thee, my country, all earthly things above,
Entire and whole and perfect, the service of my love:
The love that asks no question, the love that stands the test,
That lays upon the altar the dearest and the best;
The love that never falters, the love that pays the price,
The love that makes undaunted the final sacrifice…

Sir Cecil Spring-Rice

The sky was threatening rain as Robert MacAdams unrolled his copy of the *Sarnia Canadian Observer*. "Big British Smash Launched at Dawn," declared the front-page headline.[1] It was August 8, 1918, and the Allies had begun to push the Germans back at the ancient cathedral city of Amiens. Within weeks, Robert and Catherine would learn that their son Johnston had been among those involved in this critical battle.

The Battle of Amiens had been planned by British General Sir Douglas Haig and spearheaded by Canadian and Australian troops. Canadian participation, however, had been no simple matter. In the months before the Battle, the Corps had been massed nearly thirty miles to the north of Amiens, and it was feared that their sudden arrival would alert the Germans to the Allies' battle plans. To avoid raising the alarm, Canadian commander Sir Arthur Currie ensured that all troop movements took place at night. Wagons, guns, and trucks travelled under cover of darkness. Buses took thousands of troops to secret forest camps. And since the attack was to be led by massed tanks, these were moved into place while Royal Air Force fighters flew above, muffling the noise made by the metal monsters.[2]

The "big British smash" began at 4:20 in the morning with a massive bombardment directed against German lines. The 3rd Canadian Division, to which Johnston had been assigned as intelligence officer, faced some of the most brutal fighting. The French Corps fought along their right flank. They had fewer tanks than the Canadians and often lagged behind, sometimes leaving the Canadians exposed. Despite such challenges, by the end of the day the Canadians had moved forward eight miles, the French five, the Australians seven, the British less than one. The German army lost twenty-seven thousand men, while the Allies lost one third that number. In one day alone, the Canadians Corps captured over five thousand prisoners and 161 guns. These gains came at a high price – roughly four thousand Canadian troops were killed, wounded, or imprisoned.[3]

The Battle of Amiens ended on August 15. Johnston wrote to his parents soon afterwards:

> *I suppose you have read about our sudden hop two or three days ago. It was Vimy over again but with the new style of fighting which consists of using tanks instead of a long bombardment. The success was wonderful. It was real "open warfare" and at the end of 24 hours our cavalry were ten kilometres into enemy's back country, and Amiens will be able to open for business once more. It looked like a relief more than a battle, the second day. One side of the roads dense with our people moving in, and the other side dense with German prisoners moving out. The weather is beautiful. We sleep in the open in light bed rolls or blankets, and a headquarters will pick up and move like a country circus.*
>
> *When I was at Amiens before, I stayed at the Hotel Belfort, the best in the city and it was as modern as Paris or New York. Last week, I rode through on horseback, and met only two people in the whole city (except soldiers). The line then ran quite close to the city and all the people had been ordered out and the place seemed very strange. The Cathedral looks as placid and majestic as ever, but is all muffled around for protection against shells.... Now the line is back where it was before and they can start the city going at any time.[4]*

Johnston, like the other Canadian survivors of Amiens, was on the move again, this time north to Arras. "We are now quartered in freshly conquered territory, and the paper on which this is written is some of the spoils of war, German stationery, which the enemy left behind in his hurried departure."[5]

❧ ❧ ❧

While Johnston was riding his horse through the silent streets of Amiens, his sister Roberta was back in London. She had resigned from her post at the Ontario Military Hospital and had taken up a new challenge, one that would place her closer to her soldier constituents. Beatrice Nasmyth described Roberta's new job for readers of the *Province*. "Feeling that the interests of her constituents could be best served by this course she obtained her discharge from the CAMC and joined the staff of the Khaki University of Canada as organizer of women's staffs, the first of its kind in this rapidly growing institution."[6]

The Khaki University was a school without ivy-covered brick walls or academic gowns. Its students were soldiers and its classes took place in army camps. The University had its origins in the voluntary night classes that had been formed in Canadian army bases in Witly, Seaford, and Bramshott during the first few years of the war. These informal study groups, run by chaplains and YMCA officers, were immensely popular. By 1917, several thousand men had registered in the programs. As demand for lectures and textbooks grew, Lt. Col. Gerald Birks, Supervisor of the YMCA Canadian Overseas Forces, decided that a less ad hoc approach to military education was needed. He asked Henry Marshall Tory, President of the University of Alberta, to survey the situation.

Tory, a stocky man with wavy gray-brown hair and a neatly trimmed moustache, had a reputation for establishing innovative educational programs. The driving force behind the development of Alberta's first university, he had also helped establish agricultural extension programs throughout that province. In July 1917, Henry toured YMCA study facilities in Canadian military camps in

England and France, frequently attending lectures along with the men in khaki. He asked the men to name the kinds of courses that they would like to attend. Many wanted agricultural, mechanical, and business programs. Others wanted to continue their university studies. At the end of his tour, Tory recommended the development of a comprehensive educational program for soldiers. Lt. Col. Birks not only agreed with Henry's ideas, but also invited him to be the first and only president of the new "Khaki University."

Between 1917 and 1919, Tory organized and oversaw a curriculum that included a high-school matriculation program, university undergraduate studies, agricultural, business, law, and engineering courses, teacher training, and continuing education for military physicians. Specially prepared libraries replaced the motley collections of books that were found piled on shelves of YMCA recreation huts, farm implements were made available for student use, and buildings in London and nearby communities were rented for use as colleges. Fortunately, Tory didn't have to lobby the government to fund this vast enterprise. The YMCA raised the money, leaving him free to focus on meeting the educational needs of soldiers.

Tory's program was shaped by his concern about the demands of a post-war Canada. He wanted to help prepare Canadian men to return to productive civilian lives and to become leaders in the "New World" that would emerge at the war's end.[7] Henry also knew that many experts predicted it would take at least a year to return all servicemen back to Canada at the end of hostilities. The "Khaki University" was designed to provide overseas soldiers with productive activities during what many believed would be a long demobilization period.[8] By the end of the war, over eight thousand soldiers had registered in its courses and between forty and fifty thousand men had attended at least one or more lectures.[9] Over three thousand illiterate men were taught to read and write.[10] The impact of the Khaki University, however, extended still farther. In addition to allowing soldiers to continue their education, it established a precedent for military education that would be followed by the armed services in Canada and many other countries.[11]

While military men were well served by the University, one group overlooked by Tory was military nurses. Physicians serving with the CAMC were given opportunities to learn about advances in medical technology that had taken place in North America while they were serving overseas. Yet similar programs were not offered for nurses. However, Henry did provide programs for one much larger group of women. Over thirty-four thousand British women married Canadian soldiers during and just after the war and the Canadian government wanted them to be well-prepared for their new lives in Canada.[12]

Unfortunately, the great majority of British "war brides" had few of the necessary skills to make a success of life in that "new and rapidly developing country" – particularly in the pioneer home-steads of western Canada. Many were urban women who had met their future husbands while the men were on leave in London. Their backgrounds varied, from middle- and upper-class women who had grown up in comfortable homes with servants, to work-ing-class munitions workers, maids, and shop girls. Yet no matter what their class, their skills were not easily transferable to life in Canada, particularly on the prairies. On western homesteads, it was practical farm experience that mattered – the ability to tend huge gardens, look after cows, pigs, and chickens, work in the fields side by side with the men, and prepare huge meals for threshing gangs in less than ideal circumstances. Most of the women from Britain's teeming industrial cities had little idea of what life had in store for them in their new country.

Tory had always been an enthusiastic backer of practical ag-ricultural education and had been a strong supporter of Duncan Marshall's extension work in Alberta. He knew that women's willing participation was often the essential ingredient for success on the farm. It was clear to him that a department needed to be established to educate British women about life in Canada. His choice of someone to head up that work was easy. When Roberta had gone on her tour of Alberta back in the winter of 1912, Tory had made an appearance in one of the towns and spoken about the need for agricultural education in Alberta. A man with a keen eye for character and ability, he probably remembered the tall young woman who was hired to teach domestic science. In late August 1918, Tory invited Roberta to join the Khaki University staff.

As in her Edmonton days, Roberta had oversight of a staff of domestic science teachers, as well as female secretaries and clerks. The courses offered under her supervision could have been copied directly from a Macdonald Institute course calendar. They included dairy production, poultry-raising, bee keeping, gardening, cooking, laundry work, dressmaking, infant care, home upholstery, and home organization. Students were also given lectures on topics such as "Settling in Canada" and the "Canada of Tomorrow."

Women's programs were offered at 49 Bedford Square in the heart of London, in local colleges scattered around the city, as well as at the Canadian base in Witley. Hundreds of women enrolled in the free courses. Although Roberta does not seem to have taken on any teaching work, she did give individual lectures.[13] Instructors were grateful for her support. "She showed great interest in our work and in fact came to one of our meetings and gave a splendid talk to the girls," wrote one teacher.[14]

Living in London at this time posed many challenges for Roberta. Walking home from an evening class was an adventure in itself. The threat of air raids meant that streetlights weren't turned on and houses and offices were shuttered. The streets were as black as coal and when one of those typically murky London fogs rolled in, Roberta found herself groping along brick walls and wrought iron gates and stumbling off curbs until she reached her destination. When she wanted to catch a taxi, she was hard pressed to find one. Heavy gas rationing and restrictions on the use of their headlights meant that many people refused to drive at night, including most taxicab drivers.

In Orpington, Roberta hadn't worried about buying groceries or preparing her own food. Living in London was an entirely different matter. Since Roberta worked long days, it was difficult to shop for food. Most stores were closed in the evenings and shopping during the day was a long, drawn-out process. With widespread rationing in force, all Londoners were forced to queue up in order to get the most basic grocery items. This had its humorous moments, as described by her friend Beatrice:

> Supposing a queue formed for butter. As long as the supply of butter lasted, it was doled out in quarter-pound packets, one person at a time being allowed to enter the shop and not being served with anything but butter. When the supply of butter ran out, the policeman would announce in a loud voice: 'You may stay in this queue for bacon.' Slowly and singly the queue would move up for bacon until this too was exhausted. Then the announcer would say: 'You may stay in this queue for cheese!' And so on until all the limited commodities would be sold out.[15]

Roberta somehow found ways to keep her pantry stocked, perhaps relying on friends to line up and cash in her ration cards. While many Canadian women serving overseas would return home malnourished, she would lose only five pounds during the war.

❦❦❦

There were some compensations for the challenges of living in London. Roberta was able to spend some of her free time with Harvey Price, who had been assigned to the headquarters of the Canadian Forestry Corps (CFC) in London. Their short idyll ended in late August when Harvey was transferred to France to oversee the building of airdromes for the Royal Air Force. There, he spent his days in the hot sun, supervising crews of soldiers and hundreds of Chinese workers while they did the tedious, back-breaking work of transforming rocky, unturned fields into serviceable runways for Allied fighters.[16]

Roberta wasn't the only member of her circle whose romance had been interrupted by the war. Guy Furniss – Beatrice's new husband – had returned to France shortly after their honeymoon to serve with the Argyll and Sutherland Highlanders. While she waited for him to come back, Beatrice continued to work for the Alberta Agent General and write for the *Daily Province*. Sometimes she and Roberta would meet and spend several of their precious ration coupons for dinner in fashionable Soho, where they would try to imagine what the future would hold for them when and if the war ever ended.[17]

It was a tense time in London. All eyes were on France, where the Allies seemed to have gained the upper hand. After years of personal sacrifice and loss, anger with Germany was at a fever pitch. Anyone who seemed to represent the hated enemy was ostracized or worse. In August, Beatrice covered "one of those huge indignation mass meetings which are so much a part of English public life, an outward expression of the impatience and resentment of the masses at what they regard as tardy negligence on the part of the government over some crying need of the nation."[18]

The event was held at London's Royal Albert Hall, a circular theatre that normally held five thousand people. On that particular evening, eight thousand crammed inside to vent their wartime frustrations against "enemy aliens." According to Beatrice, the special boxes that lined the upper walls of the hall were filled with soldiers in khaki or hospital "blues," as well as "groups of well known people. One of them bore a large card which announced that [their box] was occupied by the agent general for British Columbia."[19]

Lord Charles Beresford was the first speaker to address the crowd. Beresford was a man whom Winston Churchill once described as "one of those orators of whom it was well said, 'Before they get up, they do not know what they are going to say; when they are speaking, they do not know what they are saying; and when they sit down, they do not know what they have said.'"[20] True to form, the seventy-two-year-old former admiral called for the British government to revoke all naturalization papers belonging to enemy aliens, thus "clearing the Hun from our public and private life." The room was filled with shouts and calls for action. By the end of the meeting, the crowd had moved a resolution calling for the internment of "all persons of alien enemy blood, whether naturalized or unnaturalized."[21] As people poured out of Albert Hall, Beatrice wondered if such events were simply outlets

Hastings early in the 20th century.
Author's Collection; postcard.

for the extreme stress that so many Britons were labouring under as the war lurched on.[22]

As summer turned into fall, Beatrice invited Roberta to leave London behind and visit Beatrice's new in-laws in Hastings, a village in East Sussex. Hastings had a reputation as a welcoming community for artists and writers. It had been home to Charles Dickens, Lewis Carroll, Dante Gabriel Rossetti, Clare Sheridan, Barbara Bodichon, and James Whistler. Controversial figures also found refuge there, including suffragist Elizabeth Blackwell – Britain's first woman doctor.[23] The village had also been the cradle of a boy named Archibald Belaney, who had moved to northern Canada in 1905 to live among the Ojibwa people. After the Great War he would become famous as "Grey Owl."

This somewhat bohemian setting suited Beatrice's father-in-law, Harry Furniss. Harry was a former political cartoonist and writer for the humour magazine *Punch*. By his own account, he had drawn over twenty-six hundred illustrations during his fourteen years on staff. In 1894, Harry left *Punch* and freelanced, illustrating Lewis Carroll's book *Sylvie and Bruno* and the eighteen-volume *Charles Dickens Library*. Between 1912 and 1913 he travelled to the United States and acted in early films. On the eve of the war Harry helped produce one of the world's first animated films. (A later owner of his Hastings home found old prints of Harry's films in the attic and threw them in the trash.[24]) By 1918, he had yet another career, as a nationally famous lecturer on the work of Charles Dickens.[25]

Roberta met Harry and his wife Marion in the lofty front hall of their white Regency townhouse. The house was set on a narrow street perched high on a cliff overlooking fishermen's cottages. The Furniss's daughter Dorothy – also an artist – lived in the townhouse immediately adjoining their own. A door was cut between their two homes so that when Harry threw one of his lavish parties for fellow artists and friends, visitors could flow back and forth between the two houses.[26]

Harry was short and round, with a well-groomed white beard and moustache. Marion was a short, slender woman who seemed to be recovering from an unnamed illness that required frequent bed rest. Her condition may have been more emotional than physical. Harry was a charismatic man with a reputation as a womanizer and rumours of his infidelities may well have reached his wife. For that reason, Marion probably sighed loudly when she met the lovely Roberta and sensed Harry's immediate attraction.

Roberta was unlikely to have entered into a relationship with a man old enough to be her father, especially since she was already romantically entangled with Harvey Price. However, it was clear to her friend Beatrice that Harry found Roberta enchanting and that she found him equally charming. They shared a wry, ironic view of the world and could talk politics at length, easily Harry's favourite subject.[27] Quarrelsome and conceited, he was also a dyed-in-the-wool Irish Protestant Conservative with strong opinions about Irish nationalism – a hot-button issue at the time.[28] Roberta likely shared his anti-republican views. During her visits, the pair would set off for lengthy walks along the beach at nearby St. Leonard's. Harry

Roberta with Harry Furniss during a visit to Hastings.
Glenbow Archives; PA-913-3.

would march along in his tweed cheese-cutter cap, matching jacket and plus-fours,[29] talking a mile a minute and swinging his cane like a country squire. Roberta kept pace, her high velvet hat pinned precariously on her head and her fashionable patchwork fur coat keeping her warm.

❦❦❦

When I was following Roberta's footsteps in England, I visited the house in Hastings where Roberta and Beatrice spent some of their free weekends. It hadn't changed much since the war years. The same wrought-iron railing ran to the front door, and the back garden was still framed by an ivy-covered stone wall. The current owner, James Wheeler, took me on a tour of the house and garden. Harry's study was a square, panelled room with an oak-mantled fireplace and high windows overlooking the overgrown garden. Thick shutters – ideal for black-outs – had been sunk into the deep windowsills from which they could be drawn by a system of pulleys. I could imagine Harry bent over his desk, calmly sketching out a political caricature of Lloyd George while German zeppelins cruised the coastline near Hastings, a not infrequent occurrence during the war.

Outside the Furniss house stood an ancient fig tree, with an equally aged stone bench where Roberta and Beatrice might have sat on a warm fall afternoon. As I stood in the garden, I drew out a small pile of photographs given to me by Monica Newton, Beatrice's daughter. There were pictures of Beatrice, Roberta, and Harry's daughter Dorothy standing at the back of the house, Roberta with Marion Furniss standing near the front steps, and Roberta and Harry taking a stroll along the beach.

Using the pictures as a guide, I learned that I was standing in the same spot where Beatrice and Guy Furniss had posed to have their wedding photographs taken. Guy stood, hands on hips, smiling into the camera. Beatrice looked uncharacteristically shy, the violet corsage she had worn to her wedding still pinned to her suit. It must have been difficult for her to know that Guy had only a few days leave before he had to return to France. Their brief honeymoon was the last they would see of each other until the end of the war. The next time they would meet would be in Paris in April 1919.

At the former Furniss home in Hastings.
Author's Collection.

Roberta would face an even longer separation from Harvey Price. She would not see the young officer until after he returned to Canada in August 1919.

~~~

Despite the victory at Amiens, the end of the war still seemed distant to many people on both sides of the Atlantic. Prime Minister Robert Borden believed that it might well last until 1920. Allied military leaders held the opposite view. British General Sir Douglas Haig believed that concerted action along the Western Front would wear down the Germans and ultimately lead to the breakthrough that would win the war. With the victory at Amiens, the old days of trench warfare were over. By the middle of September, Allied forces (including American troops, who had arrived in France in June 1917) had the German army on the run. Canadian soldiers were moving through wrecked British and German trenches, en route to Cambrai. They struggled forward across hilly battlefields that echoed with the rattle of machine gun fire and noise of shells bursting all around them. There was wire to cut, German machine-gun nests to overcome and, if they were lucky, prisoners to take. An eighteen-year-old Alberta soldier named Arthur Fraser was in the midst of the fighting.

> *We marched from Amiens, on the Somme to Arras, over those terrible cobblestones and prepared to assault the old Hindenberg Line in front of Arras which the Germans had held since the start of the war. I recall vividly that morning when the heavy artillery and "whiz-bangs" opened up about 4:30 AM. They were hub to hub behind us and it was looking into hell with all of the flashes up and down the row of guns. We followed a creeping barrage about one hundred and fifty yards ahead of us. The Germans took a terrible blasting and surrendered by the thousands. The seventh brigade took about five thousand prisoners that morning, some very shell shocked. What a mess the Hindenberg Line was in, with smoking dugouts and plankwalks at all angles. We advanced without too much trouble, if one can listen to the whine of bullets going by and realize they are meant for you.*[30]

Arthur eventually found himself at the Canal du Nord. The canal was a marshy stretch of water. Behind it lay a line of German machine guns and beyond that, a system of German defences known as the "Marcoing Line." Overlooking the Line was Bourlon Woods, an oak forest that could provide cover for troops. It was just a deadly stone's throw from the Canadians' final objective – Cambrai. On the evening of September 28, thousands of Canadian troops lay in wait as close to the canal as they could without attracting German attention. At 5:20 a.m. the next morning, the battle began. Arthur described the scene:

> The Germans had blown up the canal and there was water all over the countryside. The slit trench we occupied was a sea of mud ankle deep. We were organized to cross a temporary footbridge and the German positions along the canal, but "fritz" had other ideas and raked the road, the only dry place, with heavy machine gun fire. We were pinned down in the ditches in water up to our necks with the bullets throwing gravel into our faces. We managed to crawl out of this mess with only a few casualties. They brought up our 5.9 whiz-bangs and they soon blasted the Germans out of their positions with bricks, concrete and planks flying all over the place. They made a hell of a mess of the canal and we were glad to get out of there for a short time.[31]

Despite the obstacles, the Canadians moved forward quickly, reaching Bourlon Woods by nightfall. The second day would prove less successful. Thick barbed wire defences slowed the troops and made them easy targets for German machine gunners. There were over two thousand casualties that day. Arthur Fraser was among the wounded.

> The following morning, September 29th, 1918 at about 10:30 AM we advanced and I flopped on my stomach, where I was flat as a pancake when a bullet from a German machine gun burst from the buildings of Cambrai and hit me in the right arm. Corporal Percy Hull beside me was killed by several bullets in the neck. Several went through my pack on my back and my mess tin.[32]

Not all Canadian soldiers were facing machine-gun fire in Cambrai. Back in London, Roberta was helping those soldiers who had been given a brief reprieve from the fighting. Despite the demands of her job with the Khaki University, she visited men on leave and those training in camps or recovering in hospital. "I was constantly receiving inquiries and appeals from Albertans both in the army and out of it," she would later tell a reporter.[33] The content of those "appeals" is not clear. What is known is that Roberta ran errands for Canadians serving overseas, sending messages home on their behalf and ferreting out the answers to their questions and concerns. "Her work keeps her in constant touch with Canadian soldiers and she has a steady finger on the pulse of their wants and interests," wrote Beatrice Nasmyth. But no crystal ball could have predicted that the greatest of these "wants and interests" would soon be fulfilled. On November 11, the war would finally be over.

CHAPTER 13

GOING HOME

Going home, going home,
I'm a-going home.
Quiet-like, some still day,
I'm just going home.

It's not far, just close by,
Through an open door,
Work all done, care laid by,
Going to fear no more.

Mother's there, expecting me,
Father's waiting too,
Lots of folk gathered there,
All the friends I knew.

Nothing lost, all is gain,
No more fear or pain.
No more stumbling by the way,
No more longing for the day,
Going to roam no more.

Morning star, lights the way
Restless dreams all done,
Shadows gone, break of day,
Real life has begun.
There's no break, there's no end,
Just a living on…

("Going Home," spiritual)

Trafalgar Square was carpeted in frenzied men and women, soldiers throwing caps into the air, women shouting, children struggling not to get lost in a sea of knees and hips. London had lost its mind and was running naked in the streets. The war was over. The men who had survived the worst carnage the world had ever seen were coming home at last.

Roberta and Beatrice looked down on the square from the window of the fourth-floor office where they had met in the midst of war, two years before. The crowd below had grown all day until it had become one singing, laughing mass. Even the light rain that had begun to fall didn't seem to dampen anyone's spirits. The two women could see children crowded onto the giant lions beneath Nelson's Column, and strangers hugging one another and waving Union Jacks. Their own plans for the day seemed anticlimactic by comparison. As soon as Beatrice put away her typewriter, they were going to make their way through the square to the tube station and take the train to Hastings. Beatrice wanted to store some of her wedding presents at her in-laws' home until Guy came back from France and Roberta – as always – couldn't resist a visit to Guy's father, Harry. Beatrice thrust a pair of two-foot tall brass candlesticks into Roberta's arms and heaved a heavy box into her own.

As they emerged into the cool afternoon, the plaza and the roads that bordered it were filled with people singing war songs. Gone for the moment were the strains of "there's a long, long, trail a-winding," that had captured the fear and longing of the beginning of the war. Instead, people were singing rousing versions of

One of the candlesticks (now a lamp) that Roberta
used as a noisemaker on Armistice Day.
Author's Collection.

"When This Bloody War is Over" and "It's a Long, Long Way to Tipperary."

The two women took a breath and plunged into the crowd. Roberta was soon far ahead of Beatrice, wading through the people, pushed back and forth, candlesticks held high above her head like Roman candles. Swept up in the music, relief coursing through her, Roberta forgot all the dignified manners that her mother had taught her and started banging the candlesticks together like a giant noisemaker, laughing and swirling into the ocean of people.[1]

≈≈≈

The only sound in Jack Hanna's oak-lined study came from his pen scratching quickly along the page and the fire crackling in the hearth. Jack was writing to Neil again, his pen speeding over the page out of sheer relief. The war had been over for ten days – ten long days of waiting and worrying. They hadn't heard from Neil since he had begun training as a pilot in Italy in October. Now, a letter had arrived. Neil had been sick in bed with influenza – a frightening thought – but had managed to pull out of it and was now eager to come home. The letter removed a burden that in recent days had threatened to suffocate Jack Hanna. The knowledge that his son was all right and that he would soon be on his way home meant that Jack and Maud could look ahead, could plan for Neil's return to the comfortable life they longed to give him. Jack signed his letter "With love from all here, Very Sincerely, Your Dad," and set it aside for his secretary to type up in the morning and send by the first post.[2]

Maud was upstairs packing. That night they took the train to New York to visit their daughter Margaret and new-son-in law Harry. After a few days, Jack returned alone to Toronto to attend to legislature business. That was why he was the only member of the family at home on Sunday when the messenger came to the door. Standing in the wide front hall, he carefully turned over the buff-coloured envelope that the man had handed him. Jack knew what it would say, but if he held it for just a little longer, he could still live in a time when the most important things were not being ripped from him, when life was still comfortable and predictable.

There's a long, long night of waiting...

He slipped his silver pen knife under the flap and slowly, oh so slowly, drew it across and opened the envelope.

Until my dreams all come true;

"Deeply regret to inform you Lieutenant W.N. Hanna Royal Air Force is reported to have been killed on November Twentieth. The Air Council express their sympathy..."

Till the day when I'll be going down that long, long trail with you.[3]

❦ ❦ ❦

The bored telegraph clerk stood patiently behind the window as Roberta filled in the form. The pencil clenched between her fingers, Roberta – a lover of books and all things written – must have realized just how inadequate words could be. "All the love in the world, Bert MacAdams" she wrote.[4] In late October, she had received copies of long and worried letters from Jack to Neil. Jack had been concerned that his son hadn't been receiving his mail, and wondered if she might be able to help him get a message to his son. Now there would be no more letters to send or receive.

In the weeks following Neil's death, Roberta wanted to return home and be with her family for as long as she could before the opening of the Alberta legislature. However, with the government struggling to get demobilized men back to Canada as quickly as possible, it wasn't easy to book passage on one of the few troop ships. As luck would have it, an opportunity emerged. On a cold day in mid-January, Roberta found herself standing on a Liverpool dock, someone else's baby balanced on her hip and a heavy suitcase in her other hand. The YWCA had accepted her offer to chaperone a group of several hundred British war brides who were being shipped to Canada along with their war-weary soldier husbands. Around Roberta was a scene of bedlam. Women clutching toddlers and dragging heavy suitcases and boxes were struggling up the gangway onto the *HMT Metagama*. An outsider might have shaken her head at the amount of luggage each woman carried – but most were leaving their country for the first and last time and were bringing their most precious possessions to their new homeland.

After struggling one load of luggage up the ramp onto the ship, the mother of the baby returned to collect him. As Roberta straightened her skirt and lifted her own heavy suitcase, she glanced impatiently at the soldiers lolling on the deck. Despite the fact that the vessel was partially filled with demobilized Canadians, none had been assigned to help the women with their luggage. "If fifty, or at the most, seventy-five soldiers had been delegated to the task of looking after this luggage, it would have proved a great boon, and the women would have gone on board ship feeling more kindly towards the military authorities," she would tell a reporter when she arrived home.[5]

The *Metagama* was a much more utilitarian vessel than the ship that had brought Roberta to England in 1916. It was one of the "two-class" ships that had been built just before the war, with only "cabin class" and "third class" (steerage) accommodations. It had been designed to carry about twelve hundred passengers comfortably, with three decks where they could go when they needed a fresh breath of sea air.[6] Unfortunately, in the interests of saving money and getting the men home fast, it was filled with four hundred more people than its builders had anticipated.[7]

On board, Roberta discovered that conditions for the war brides were primitive. Regular soldiers and their dependents were assigned berths in steerage while civilians (including munitions workers and their wives), officers and their dependents were allowed to travel in "cabin class."[8] Canada's Immigration and Colonization Department had tended to see the wives of regular soldiers as one homogenous group who would be grateful for the government's offer of free transportation. However, as Roberta

Roberta traveled home to Canada aboard the war bride ship *Metagama*.
City of Edmonton Archives; EA-458-86.

quickly learned, many middle- and upper-class women had married regular soldiers. The class divisions among the wives traveling in steerage soon became apparent. Some of the wealthier women complained to her that they would have preferred to travel cabin class, but had been forced to travel in steerage if they wanted to be near their husbands.[9] Although Roberta – herself accustomed to more comfortable accommodations – sympathized with the women, she was more realistic about the limitations the government was under. "On board ship all space was occupied," Roberta later told a reporter. "This, of course, was necessary. The Government rents the troopships, and, as the soldiers and their dependents must be brought back to Canada expeditiously, it is necessary that all the space including that of the steerage, be fully occupied."[10]

Whatever their economic status, the women in steerage had good reasons to feel nervous about the voyage to Canada. Only a month before, soldiers and their families on the troop ship *Scan-*

dinavian had suffered through a nightmarish voyage in which latrines were blocked, women were seasick, and two soldiers and two mothers died as a result of illness.[11] Although one first-class cabin was initially made available to those who were ill, when another cabin was badly needed the ship's captain refused to ask first-class passengers to make any further sacrifices.

The weather during the *Metagama's* crossing was far from ideal, making the crowded voyage even more difficult. To make matters worse, forty-nine passengers became ill with the dreaded Spanish influenza. While all those in the grip of the disease would survive the voyage, several would die soon after reaching Canada.[12] The ship's crew struggled to maintain an atmosphere of calm despite growing fears of a shipboard epidemic. According to Roberta, "all the officers of the ship, from the captain down, were indefatigable in their efforts to make matters pleasant for those on board."[13]

Roberta played her own role in easing tensions. Faced with women who were seasick, homesick, and afraid of what their new country would offer them, she did what she could to keep their minds off their troubles. After Roberta's experience with the Khaki University, she was not surprised to learn that many "were absolutely without knowledge of Canadians in this country. They were unacquainted with the vernacular, so to speak, of the homes, of the stores and of the towns."[14] Roberta reverted back to her old role as domestic-science instructor – gathering women for talks about how to shop for food and supplies in dusty prairie towns and Ontario cities, and the mysteries of using a "modern" North American kitchen range.[15]

◅◆▻

When the *Metagama* finally docked in Halifax on January 19, Roberta was exhausted. A photograph taken soon after reveals a pale and thin woman with deep shadows under her eyes. Although the women had successfully arrived in Canada, her work was still not over. Roberta had to act as a kind of impromptu travel agent, helping many of the women arrange for transportation to their destinations across Canada. She discovered that the federal government had taken creaking colonist cars out of mothballs to transport soldiers and their dependents across the country. Once again, the air was filled with complaints from middle-class women as they faced another uncomfortable, tiring journey in difficult circumstances.

By January 22, Roberta's job was finally over and she was able to accept Jack and Maud's invitation to spend a few days with them in Toronto. The last time she had seen them had been the previous January, en route to her first session in the Alberta legislature. Back then, the house had been filled with the noise of young people – Katherine and Margaret training for Red Cross work, Neil recovering and preparing to return overseas and Harold counting the days until he could join up. Jack had been on the verge of resigning as food controller and was looking forward to his new job as president of Imperial Oil. Caught in the whirlwind, Roberta had ridden the wave of activity and optimism back to Alberta and into her first term in office.

Now the rambling Hanna mansion seemed quiet and empty. Neil and Harold were dead, Margaret married and living in New York, and Katherine studying at Vassar College in the same city.[16] The sudden change in the Hanna's fortunes had taken their toll on Jack. He was pale and ill, and his physician had recommended a warm vacation in the South. He was likely suffering from a heart ailment or other stress-related illness but it was equally clear to family and friends that he was also suffering from a broken spirit. Jack had loved his son deeply. As one of the government's leading war recruiters, he may well have felt personally responsible for losing the child for which Jean Neil had sacrificed her life.

In the weeks following Neil's death, sympathy letters poured into the Hanna homes in Sarnia and Toronto. These were carefully bound together with copies of the many letters that father and son had exchanged during the war. Perhaps the job of compiling this paper memorial comforted Maud and Jack, or maybe it was simply a diversion from a loss that was just too big to comprehend. Among the black-edged sympathy cards was a poem about the loss of a valiant son, neatly folded cards with short, awkward messages of condolence, and letters in which the writers battle their own distress. "Dear Jack: Leslie has just telephoned me of the cable," wrote Mary McBurney, Maud and Roberta's sister. "There is, of course, nothing to be said. If sympathy is of any help be sure it is yours. Bob and I feel a dreadful shock and a great grief. Very much love and all sympathy to you and to Maud. Yours, Mary."[17]

A sombre Roberta returned to Alberta in February. The loss of Neil and the demanding trip to Canada likely fuelled her desire to press the government to listen carefully to the soldiers now flooding home. In a December 1918 article for *The Beaver*, a publication of the Khaki University, she had argued that their experiences overseas had given Canadians a new confidence and a broader view of their nation and its place in the world. "The boys will take back with them something of the wisdom of all the ages stored up in these older, mellower lands – some realisation of the permanency and immutability of the great principles of right and wrong of liberty and honour – some recognition of how ephemeral a thing is a human lifetime or a generation," Roberta mused. "But will they take back too an irritability and impatience, a lack of sympathy with those who have not been permitted the wider horizon, who have not got the larger view?"[18]

A new, progressive, and humanitarian society had to be born out of the ashes of the old. For Roberta, the cornerstone of that society was greater access to health care – many of the soldier's had brought the Spanish influenza back with them from Europe and the province was ill-equipped to deal with a pandemic that would eventually take the lives of over four thousand Albertans[19] and fifty thousand Canadians.[20] Infant mortality was also extremely high – in 1919, Alberta had the highest infant mortality rate in the country.[21] Back in the chilly corridors of the Alberta legislature in February, Roberta actively supported the passage of a bill establishing the province's first Department of Public Health.

Roberta also lobbied for an "inspirational" public school curriculum. According to the *Edmonton Journal*, she maintained that the war "had shown, in its demands upon the soldiers in the line, the value of good homes and the benefits of early health training.

The war had also shown the results of a decadent civilization in certain parts of Europe and it was vitally necessary that conditions in this new land should be made for the creation of a strong citizenship and a healthy people."[22] Such citizenship was the product of "inspirational teaching" that must include greater emphasis on English literature, patriotism and history, as well as music and art. "Frills, I believe they are called," she said drily.[23] Roberta probably shared the views of the early twentieth-century composer Fritz Kreisler (himself a soldier for the Austrian army during the Great War), who argued that "humanity lived more gracefully, more abundantly, and more deeply appreciative of what the arts meant for human uplift during the period before 1914 than it could during and after the ravages of two world cataclysms."[24] Roberta wanted Canadian society to reclaim the possibility of abundant living that she herself had experienced as a child growing up within a cultured family.

These dreams could only be fulfilled if the needs of returning soldiers were addressed, argued Roberta. As she predicted during her first term in the legislature, the government had failed to develop adequate programs to meet the needs of returning soldiers. "She dwelt upon the pressing urgency of having the returned men employed. This was pointed out to the government last session, she contended, but the cry of greater production was the only one that would be listened to," reported the *Edmonton Journal*. "Now there was assurance that a certain number of men would be employed, but she wanted to know what was to be done for the remainder."[25]

Roberta also wondered what kinds of plans might be put into place to help build bridges between those who had stayed at home during the war and those who had served overseas. As events would prove, many soldiers resented those who had kept comfortable jobs or profited financially from the war (benefiting from higher wartime prices for their products) while they risked their lives. Roberta was personally acquainted with that impatience and "lack of sympathy." On previous visits home, she had remarked on the benefits that farmers seemed to be gaining from high wartime prices for their crops at a time when Canadian soldiers earned less than the pay of a farm labourer. She also found it appalling that throughout the war Canadians had enjoyed a seemingly high standard of living with abundant food and fuel while Britons endured severe rationing and the men in the trenches faced death with stomachs filled with food that most Canadians would consider barely fit for their dogs.

Some returned soldiers turned their anger against the slow pace of reconstruction efforts on eastern European immigrants, some of whom had been imprisoned during the war or barred from serving.[26] On April 17, the Great War Veteran's Association (GWVA) petitioned the Alberta government to "disenfranchise aliens for a period of not less than 20 years."[27] It was believed that the fifty thousand "aliens" in the province would offset soldier votes in coming elections and somehow impede soldier rights. The GWVA also demanded that "all aliens, women and slackers in the employ of the government be dismissed to make way for returned soldiers.... They hated the men who had been born in an alien country and it was hard for the men who had fought against them overseas to put up with them here."[28] Premier Stewart reassured the men that all possible was being done to ensure that German immigrants were not working for the government and that "they would be able to accommodate all the stenographers who would apply without displacing the women."[29]

Although Robert Pearson – the other soldier's representative – supported the GWVA, Roberta does not seem to have joined their xenophobic chorus. Instead, on the floor of the legislature she warned that unless the government acted soon to address the concerns of returned soldiers (particularly their need for jobs), there would be negative consequences for Canadian society as a whole. "Unrest is an unwholesome thing in this land but it is only energy out of place," she argued. "The armies at the front had never failed Canada and it must not be said the government failed to obtain a victory in peace after one had been won in war."[30]

Despite such warnings, the Alberta government – like the federal and other provincial governments – was unwilling to embrace comprehensive reconstruction plans. Legislators continued to apply placatory solutions to the problems of post-war reconstruction, arguing that more extensive plans would have to wait until the declining post-war economy improved. Soldier settlement was the only chestnut they left in the fire – and, as events would prove, it would meet the needs of only a small number of demobilized men. Meanwhile, inflation, poor working conditions, and rampant unemployment built discontent among returning soldiers as well as those who had stayed behind.

While most of the MLAs who filled the seats of the sandstone legislature seemed unwilling to begin the hard work of post-war reconstruction, Alberta women were more than eager to take up the task of rebuilding society along new lines. Roberta, the once-hesitant feminist, now actively encouraged women to use their new political muscle to bring about social change. As she would later tell a reporter, "there is the wide awakeness of the women of our Province, and their progressiveness. The sense of social welfare is particularly keen among Western women."[31] What Roberta didn't mention was that she herself had been one of those who had set the wheels of social welfare into motion. Many of the things she argued for in the legislature – city-based Normal Schools to train teachers and the establishment of hospitals and broad-based district nursing – would be established within ten years of her election.[32]

On March 12, the influential Women's Canadian Club of Calgary held a reception in honour of the province's leading women. Nellie McClung, Isabel Noble (president of the provincial Women's Institutes) and various other representatives of Alberta and British Columbia branches of the WI were among the guests of honour. Roberta, Mary Ellen Smith (the first woman elected to the British Columbia legislature), and Emily Murphy were the featured speakers.[33] Although there is no record of what Roberta said, the minutes of the club note that the speakers focused on the importance of women's full participation in electoral politics, from exercising the franchise to running for office.

Just as her life in peacetime Alberta seemed to be settling into a predictable and busy routine of legislative and public work, the Great War again exacted its toll from Roberta and her family. In March, Maud and Jack Hanna had taken his doctor's advice and were vacationing in Augusta, Georgia. The couple was staying at the Partridge Inn, an elegant southern hotel with wide verandas that overlooked a swirl of sandy beach. Jack had begun to feel better and sent a cable home saying he expected to be back at the legislature within a week or ten days. He would never fulfill that promise. On March 20, a warm, humid southern morning, Jack woke up feeling ill. Within hours he was dead, the victim of a massive stroke. He was fifty-seven.

The news made the front page of several major Canadian newspapers. Jack Hanna had been an influential figure in both national and provincial politics, liked and respected by both political friends and enemies. Few doubted that the loss of his son was responsible for Jack's early death. According to *Saturday Night Magazine*, "his health was undermined not merely by his strenuous activities during the past decade, but by grief over the death of his only son Flight-Lieut. Neil Hanna, who was killed in an accident in Italy nine days after the Armistice."[34]

Although newspaper accounts don't say which family members attended the funeral service for Jack Hanna, Roberta probably returned home to grieve the loss of the brother-in-law who had been her political model and had likely enabled her to work at the Ontario Military Hospital. Jack's body was brought by train to Sarnia to lie in state, guarded by four khaki-clad soldiers. Before the service began, hundreds of Sarnians waited in line to pass by the open casket. The funeral was led by ministers of three denominations, including prominent Toronto Presbyterian Rev. Dr. Strachan, Rev. Canon Davis (the MacAdams family priest), and Jack's own minister, Rev. Dr. Manning. The congregation was a "who's who" of Canadian politics and business. Premier William Hearst and future Prime Minister Arthur Meighen were among the pallbearers. Ontario Lieutenant Governor Sir John Hendrie, the president of Standard Oil and vice-presidents of Imperial Oil, judges and members of parliament sat in a roped-off block of pews. Friends and acquaintances filled the remainder of the seats while thousands stood on the road outside the church. Eighty cars formed the cortege that carried Jack's body to the cemetery. All this was of little consolation to his family, who met in the Hanna's Brock Street home for a private service before participating in the public funeral of a very public man.[35]

⁂

While Roberta MacAdams did not save many of the records of her political career, the family of Jack Hanna cherished and preserved his memory. In a fifties-style diner on a well-shaded street in Toronto's Riverview neighbourhood, I pored over a box of Hanna family memorabilia. With me was Neil Spaulding, the great-grandson of Maud and Jack Hanna. A tall, lean man with the deep-set MacAdams eyes, Neil was the namesake of that beloved son who had died at the end of World War I. Within the box we found photographs of Maud and Jack Hanna and early pictures of Roberta and Mary. There were recruiting speeches by Jack Hanna and political cartoons lampooning his work in the Ontario legislature. But most poignant was the carefully bound wartime correspondence between father and son, the many sympathy letters and cards sent after Neil's death, and the obituaries for Jack Hanna. It may have been more than eighty years since the war had ended, but the contents of that box were still permeated with grief.

In the hours that Neil and I sifted through this family archive – our coffee getting cold and the waitress humming Patsy Cline tunes as she leaned on the long Formica counter – I became convinced that loss was a unifying feature of the conflict for most Canadians on the home front and especially women. Like Maud Hanna, most women faced the temporary or permanent absence of friends, lovers, husbands, brothers, and sons. Over sixty thousand Canadian soldiers, sailors, and aircrew died during the conflict, and by the war's end over forty-three thousand were recuperating in hospital beds overseas.[36] Of those who survived, many returned home as changed men. Some were permanently disabled or emotionally damaged. Others were simply exhausted from years of enormous stress and physical hardship.

Politicians and religious leaders expected women to play a central role in helping men readjust to civilian life. However, few were concerned with how women were to do this, nor was there an acknowledgment that women were facing daunting readjustments of their own. Many women had spent the war years doing "men's jobs" or struggling to support families on inadequate soldier incomes. Now they were expected to quietly hand over their jobs to the returning heroes and pour their energies into helping them adjust.

After years of separation, some husbands and wives seemed like strangers to one another. The bonds of affection and mutual dependency that had been the foundation of many marriages often suffered as people struggled to re-establish relationships after four years of harsh experiences. Marriages began to break down, an almost unheard-of occurrence before the war. In March 1919, Emily Murphy would tell a meeting of Women's Institutes that 123 Alberta soldiers had sued their wives for divorce.[37]

Literary critics like Paul Fussell have maintained that the Great War forever altered the political, social, and religious ideals of the men who served in the trenches. The same argument could be made about the experience of many Canadian women during the same period. Their pre-war idealism about honour, duty, and the role of their nation in the world was tempered by the sacrifices the war exacted from them. One prairie woman noted that when her son's regiment was mobilized early in the war, she felt a sense of patriotism and duty. As the war progressed, however, she began to question her faith in government leaders and the principles they promoted. "But gradually through the months when always more of the people's food supply and constantly more men were taken by the government for its military purposes, when I saw the state institutions for defectives closed, the schools abridged or dismissed, women and children put to work in factories under hours and conditions which had been legally prohibited years before, when the very governmental officials who had been so concerned for the welfare of the helpless were bent only upon the destruction of the enemy at whatever cost to their fellow citizens, the State itself gradually became for me an alien and hostile thing."[38]

～～～

In the months following Jack Hanna's death, Roberta embodied that bitter post-war mood. On her return to the legislature in April, her public pronouncements were noticeably sarcastic and tinged with anger and impatience. Gone for the moment was the razor-sharp wit and elegant speeches that had helped her win political arguments during her first term. It didn't help matters that a political skeleton had come out of the closet. In the previous session of the legislature, Robert Pearson had argued that the Alberta Agent General's Office in Britain served only the needs of "London financiers" while doing little for Alberta soldiers serving overseas. It should be closed, argued Pearson, and the exorbitant $15,000 cost of running the office redirected into a department for returned soldiers and their dependents. In response to these criticisms, the provincial government agreed to establish a soldiers department. However, it also kept the London office open, ostensibly to aid potential immigrants interested in settling in Alberta. Not only that, it transferred Agent General Reid (one of Premier Stewart's political cronies) into a well-paid appointment as "efficiency officer" for the Province of Alberta.[39]

Roberta had seconded Pearson's demands for the closure of the London office and his later critique of Reid's new salary. Unfortunately, some politicians considered her support disingenuous at best. Premier Stewart, often under attack from Roberta for not moving quickly enough on soldier's rights, pointed out that "Miss MacAdams had quarters at the agent general's office" during the war and by implication had benefited unfairly from her association with it. Stewart's comments enraged Roberta. According to the *Edmonton Journal*, she responded with "one of the most caustic criticisms of the conduct of that office heard in the house this session." Eager to distance herself from accusations of patronage and cronyism, she asserted that she "had no further connection with the province's London office than any other Albertan overseas."[40]

Roberta didn't just leave the issue there.

> I should be very sorry indeed to be charged with any connection with the office. It was not serving overseas Albertans effectively although it might I am convinced, under different administration, have been of very great value. At this time, indeed, it was occupied by an educationalist from Montreal, a member of the Khaki University staff who had no interest in, and who assumed no responsibility toward Albertans. The only official of the province was the secretary who had no definite authority and no material support from headquarters. When she went out of the office, even for lunch, there was no one there to meet Albertans or to look after their interests. I may say that I was constantly

In her rush to defend herself, Roberta obscured the accomplishments of the Agent General's Office. As she well knew from her own experience working with that institution, the Khaki University had been allowed to use the Agent General's Office for work that presumably aided all interested Canadian soldiers, including Albertans. But more serious was Roberta's implicit dismissal of the contributions to that Office made by her own loyal friend, Beatrice Nasmyth. Roberta obliquely describes her as a "secretary who had no definite authority." This would imply that Beatrice was no more than an office clerk. Yet Beatrice's actual title had been "publicity secretary," and as her wartime correspondence with her family indicated, she worked ten- to twelve-hour days promoting the province. Most blatantly dishonest, however, was Roberta's assertion that she herself had no more connection to the Agent General's office than any other Albertan. According to Beatrice, Roberta had used the office as her "headquarters" and had also gratefully accepted the active support and encouragement of Agent General Reid during her election campaign.

The scandal was one of Roberta's less than shining moments and revealed that she was as susceptible to political expediency as any male legislator. However, her unusually stinging remarks suggested that there was more at work in her response than simple political self-defence. As a woman who had served in an overseas hospital, Roberta had witnessed the horrible outcomes of the war and experienced personal losses of her own. The war had been over for just under four months and in that short period she had lost both her nephew and her brother-in-law in its service. Yet her fellow MLAs did not seem to understand or make any allowances for her.

It must have been a harsh reality for Roberta to accept. It seemed that many of the "stay at homes" in the legislature had forgotten her contributions and those of the men and women with whom she had served. Not only that, but some politicians had even cast her election in a negative light. It is not surprising that her frayed spirit revealed itself in uncharacteristically bitter and dishonest arguments in the legislature.

～～～

As the 1919 legislative term drew to a close, Roberta began to cast about for some new project or direction for her life. Like other veterans, she needed a job. She had given up her commission in the CAMC and her job with the Khaki University was finished. Her only income was the roughly $1,426 annual stipend given to MLAs[42] (worth approximately $20,000 in 2006 dollars[43]). As she once remarked to a reporter, this was "hardly sufficient, in view of the high cost of living in Canada and the good salaries usually paid, to tempt anyone to enter Parliament as a means of livelihood."[44]

In May, Roberta met with her old friend William Carpenter. The Edmonton School Board had promised to keep her job open for her when she went overseas, and she now intended to ensure that they kept their promise. Carpenter was pleased that Roberta was willing to work for the Board again and wanted her to spearhead a new initiative – an opportunity to "work among Ruthenian [Ukrainian] girls."[45] Women's rights leaders had been lobbying for residential schools where female eastern European immigrants could be taught "proper" English-Canadian values and mores and it was this kind of work that Carpenter would have had in mind for Roberta.[46] Such programs were seen as an essential element of post-war reconstruction efforts. Journalist Marjory MacMurchy, head of the Women's Department of the Canadian Reconstruction Association argued: "Aliens already in Canada and incoming immigrants should be Canadianized so that they may respect and love our national ideals and share fully in the future of the nation."[47]

Roberta accepted Carpenter's offer and returned to Ontario to spend the summer with her family. But on August 14 she withdrew her acceptance. She had decided to take a different job – one that would combine her dedication to her soldier constituents and her desire to help Alberta's rural women. There was another factor that undoubtedly influenced her decision: Harvey Price was coming home.

CHAPTER 14

WALKING OUT OF HISTORY

The water is wide, I cannot cross over
And neither have I wings to fly
Build me a boat that can carry two
And both shall row my true love and I.

A ship there is and she sails the seas
She's laden deep, as deep can be
But not so deep as the love I'm in
And I know not if I sink or swim…

(From "The Water is Wide," Traditional)

It was late August when Harvey Price finally stepped off the *RMS Adriatic* onto the dock at Halifax Harbour. After nearly three years overseas, he was glad to be able to stretch his legs in Canada again. Like most demobilized men, he was eager to put the war behind him and pick up where he had left off when it began. He planned to make a short visit to his family in Ontario and then travel back to Alberta to re-establish his northern law office. There was little doubt that he had another compelling motive for returning to the West – the chance to be reacquainted with Roberta MacAdams.

x

One of the most important phases in connection with the work of the land settlement board is to see that the man has a happy home. This will naturally follow if the wife is contented and understands her part in farm life. And it is to help the wife of the soldier settler, particularly in those cases where the wife has been brought from England and finds herself in new and strange surroundings that the soldier land settlement board has organized the home branch.[1]

With these words Roberta summed up her new job, one that would likely take her on many forays into the very Peace River country where Harvey Price was planning to resettle. Roberta had been appointed district director for Alberta of the home branch of the Soldier Settlement Board. It was an ironic appointment – Roberta had once raised concerns about soldier settlement, arguing that not all men were meant to be farmers and that other measures were needed to address the needs of the veterans. However, soldier settlement was now the only broad-based program being offered for soldiers. Between 1918 and 1919, nearly 25 per cent of all returning soldiers applied to participate in this program.[2] Perhaps their enthusiasm persuaded Roberta to alter her views. She may have also had other reasons. Roberta had once criticized farmers for profiting from the agricultural boom while troops sacrificed their health and sometimes their lives. She probably came to believe that through soldier settlement, Canada's fighting men would finally gain the same economic benefits.

Roberta's job was to help the wives of soldier settlers adjust to their new lives in rural Alberta. Government officials recognized that women played a central role on the family farm and believed that one way to ensure the success of soldier settlers was to address the needs of their wives, particularly those women without agricultural experience. As Roberta well knew, many of these war brides had come from towns and cities and were ill prepared for the life they would face in Canada. Canadian writer Miriam Green Ellis described an encounter with one such woman, en route to the Peace River area.

She was a perfect stranger to the country, and almost a stranger to the young husband she was coming so hopefully to meet. She had lived all her life

> in the city of London and I felt I should prepare her a little, so I told her of the long distances and the lack of conveniences, but that the opportunities were equally great in compensation, for those willing to work.
>
> "It costs quite a lot to get a start," I warned.
>
> "Oh, well, but Arthur is going to get help from the government. They are giving a start to all the soldiers that take up homesteads," she replied. "Anyway," she said with the cunning of a girl who had always to look after herself. "I am not afraid, I have my 'tride.'"
>
> "What is that?"
>
> "Making flowers. I was the biggest paid girl in our shop and the boss told me when I left, I was the quickest girl he had."[3]

Roberta knew that women like this young flower maker would experience a profound culture shock when they reached their new homes. "Cast, with little or no preparation into what must seem a veritable maelstrom of bewildering problems, domestic, economic, social – it is small wonder that some, despairing and dissatisfied, returned to the Old Land, and many others, no less discouraged, remained, even to the breaking of health,"[4] she told a reporter.

In some cases, the "breaking of health" included mental and emotional breakdown. In May 1919, the *Edmonton Journal* reported that "Dorothy, wife of H. H. Millward, a returned soldier settler near Vermilion committed suicide Saturday night by hanging herself in a new barn which was being built on their farm. The woman tied a rope to a beam and placing a noose round her neck jumped off a bale of shingles, where she was found shortly after by her husband." Dorothy was an English nurse. During the war, the hospital in which she served was subjected to two air raids. While her suicide was attributed to the after-affects of these raids, the stress of farm life in an unfamiliar country, far away from family and friends, probably contributed to her feelings of desperation.

Roberta wanted to help women like Dorothy. Her own experience as a transplanted easterner and her early work with the Women's Institutes had taught her much about the impact of the rural, pioneer West on the urban women who often moved there. Yet despite her solid résumé some people still objected to her appointment. A letter to the editor of an Edmonton newspaper declared that "as Miss McAdams had never homesteaded, had never been married, kept house, nor brought up a family of children, she had not the necessary equipment for her present appointment."[5] Such criticisms might have had an impact in earlier years, when Roberta's own concerns about her ability had led her to leave her job with the Alberta government. However she was seven years older now and her war work had given her greater confidence in herself and her skills.

Many of the women who lined up outside Roberta's office door each day included novice farm wives seeking information about poultry or dairy work and directions for bread-making and home canning. Their needs were easily met with advice, information pamphlets, and referrals to agricultural extension programs. Other problems required Roberta's on-site intervention. *The Edmonton Journal* reported one such case. "[A] certain little widow came into the board's offices and offered to sell her farm to a soldier. The land was listed and soon afterwards a soldier decided it would suit him. So the board financed the deal. Then the little widow married the very soldier to whom she had just sold her farm. Now she will not let her new husband on the homestead to do any work nor will she listen to the various officials who have tried to visit her and get things straightened out. It has resolved itself into a domestic tangle, and Miss MacAdams has been asked to go out and visit the woman financier and see if she can be persuaded to share her farm with her husband."[6]

There is no record of how Roberta resolved the dispute, but the case was just one of many that demanded her direct assistance. Once again, she was travelling across the province, visiting isolated and lonely women settled on partially cleared quarter sections. Years before, she had focused most of her energy on farms in central and southern Alberta. This time, her journeys were more likely to take her north. Since most of the homestead lands in central Alberta had long since been settled, many of the soldier settlers were establishing farms in the province's Peace River country.[7]

Before the Great War, the "Peace" had mainly been home to Aboriginal and Metis peoples, fur traders, miners, missionaries, speculators, and a handful of hardy settlers. The region was named after the wide river that snaked 1,923 kilometres from the Rocky Mountains eastward across Alberta then north, joining the mighty Athabasca River just north of Lake Athabasca.[8] The river was set in a wide, fertile valley, ideal for farming. Many saw that valley as a land of untapped wealth, in which anyone willing to take the risk could make "black velvet furrows in golden avenues of opportunity."[9] It was also a land isolated from the rest of the province by sand hills, thick forests and swamps. There was no railway into the region, so intrepid pioneers had to begin their journey by blazing a trail north from Edson with ox wagon or horse teams. It was a gruelling journey of muskeg, mud, and mosquitoes in which wagons bogged down, supplies were lost, and people sometimes died from exposure or injury.

While travel conditions had improved by the end of the war, Roberta's trips north would still have been arduous. Train service had been introduced in 1916, when the Edmonton Dunvegan and British Columbia Railway (ED & BC) was completed from Edmonton to Grande Prairie via McLennan. From McLennan, passengers could transfer to a separate line that would take them north to the community of Peace River. Or they could go straight on to Grande Prairie and transfer onto another line back to Edmonton. During her travels, Roberta could stop at various stations and take a car or wagon and visit women in scattered towns and farms. She likely stayed with the women or at one of the new hotels that were springing up in the region. The length of her stay was often unpredictable. Dilapidated trains and frequent derailments (due to poor construction of rail lines) meant that journeys often took much longer than expected. In 1919, the return journey to Edmonton from Grande Prairie was supposed to take thirty-seven hours but occasionally consumed four days.[10] (Roberta would later argue that the provincial government should take action to ensure the improvement of rail line construction in the Peace River country.[11])

During most of her visits, Roberta dispensed friendship and advice, cheering women up and getting them acquainted with the local chapter of the Women's Institute.[12] She had re-established her connection with the WI in 1919, addressing its annual convention in March.[13] There were now over two hundred Institutes in Alberta and many of them had special reception committees for returned soldiers and their wives. They gave banquets and showers for the women and provided demonstrations on canning, use of kitchen equipment, and preparation of local foods.[14] The WI had also begun to respond to the financial needs of some of the new settlers. As early as 1919, local chapters had started to gather money and clothing, bedding, and household linens for those who were having trouble managing to make ends meet. Between December 6, 1919, and January 20, 1920, alone, the group would provide clothing for 744 members of soldier settler families.[15]

Like canaries in a mine tunnel, the charitable activities of the WI hinted that an economic crisis was looming for many soldier settlers. During the war years, prices for agricultural goods had been high. After the war, most believed the boom would continue. Soldiers borrowed money from the Soldier Settlement Board and happily paid top dollar for their farms. They believed that they would have no difficulty paying back their loans. For the first year, it seemed they were right. Although yields from the wheat crop of spring 1919 were terrible – 9.5 bushels to the acre – the price of wheat was the highest in years.[16] 1920 would also be a good year for farmers, as Roberta herself would observe. "Everyone is in great spirits [in Alberta] over the splendid crops, equal to those of 1915, they say," she would tell reporters.[17] The good luck didn't last long. Prices for crops began to tumble. Oats and barley that sold for seed at $1.10 a bushel in 1920 would sell for 45 to 75 cents in 1921.[18] Although the government would revalue many farms in the mid-1920s, it would be too late for many – almost 20 per cent would have abandoned their farms by that time.[19]

In 1919, however, all this was in the future. Soldier settlement still seemed like an economic bonanza. Hundreds enrolled in government-sponsored agricultural training to prepare them for homestead life.

Back in civilian clothes – ladies in the legislature among a sea of male MLAs.
Glenbow Archives; ND-3-971.

Roberta left few letters and no diaries. Newspaper clippings, along with the letters and observations of her close friend Beatrice, provide clues to her public life, but say much less about her personal affairs. Yet it is likely that Roberta resumed her romance with Harvey Price sometime in the fall of 1919. He had opened a new law office in Grande Prairie.[20] Perhaps he accompanied her on trips to communities established by soldier settlers such as Teepee Creek, Bad Heart, Sylvester (later Elmworth), Rio Grande, Goodfare, or Northfield.[21] Or maybe they visited Sexsmith, a town just north of Grande Prairie that would eventually play an important role in their life together. Whatever the case, later events would suggest that somehow or another they managed to keep in touch and deepen their relationship during what was a hectic time in both their lives.

In late January, Roberta returned to the legislature. Some of the seeds she had planted in her first two sessions had begun to take root. In March, the government put forward proposals for a new Normal School (teacher training school) in Edmonton. The population had begun to grow again and so too, had the need for both teachers and schools. Funding for innovative educational programs was also being advocated. On March 18, the Alberta legislature passed second reading of a bill to provide $1,200 each for three university students to do postgraduate work in France. The scholarships were seen as a living memorial to fallen soldiers.

At a time when many towns and cities were putting up marble monuments to their war dead, some of Roberta's fellow legislators – notably Robert Pearson and Louise McKinney – couldn't see how scholarships fulfilled the definition of a memorial. But Roberta saw the awards as a chance to strengthen the relationships built between countries during the war. "Miss MacAdams favored the bill," noted the Edmonton Bulletin, "because of the desirability of promoting the good relationship existing between France and Canada. She spoke gracefully of her experience in France and the hospitality of the French people."[22] While some legislators argued that Canadian accommodations be furnished for the students, Roberta maintained that the recipients should "live the life of the French." It was a view that probably shocked the prejudices of the still very British Alberta legislature.

Education wasn't the only issue on the provincial agenda in March. The Liberal budget was tabled, showing a surplus of $316,990. Beneath the rosy figures lay a growing provincial debt. Members of the Opposition immediately raised the alarm, pointing out that increased taxation lay in the near future if the government did not rein in spending. Roberta sidestepped the debate, praising the government for allocating funds to social needs, including new provisions for the provincial home for the "mentally deficient." (Like most of the province's leading women, it seemed that Roberta supported the new emphasis on institutionalizing those deemed unfit.) She also supported the budget's allocation of $185,000 to mothers' pensions. Roberta attributed these "humanitarian" measures to the fact that "the influence of women electors was being reflected in the increased interest taken in such forms of public welfare.... So long as money was honestly spent along these lines she was sure the new women voters would not object."[23]

A year after her difficult post-war transition back to civilian life, Roberta's optimism and self-assurance had returned. She was now a "real Westerner," proud of her province and even describing it in cosmopolitan terms. As she would tell a reporter during the summer of 1920, "we have people from practically all over the world who contribute their diversified interests to the community and state life. Take our capital city, Edmonton, for example, ten years ago a comparatively small city now numbering a population of 68,000. The rapid growth indicates that people from elsewhere must have come in large numbers, making us a most cosmopolitan group. We thus get the advantage of advances and ideas from other countries more quickly than is possible in more settled countries."[24] Roberta had experienced that growth first hand, beginning with her arrival in 1911.

When asked how it felt to be a woman legislator, her answer was quick. "Just like flying. No sensation at all. Just the same as working on a hospital or any other board with men. It never at any time seemed to me an incongruous position for me to be there, and the men have shown such a splendid spirit of co-operation and companionship, neither Mrs. McKinney nor I have at any time had reason to feel out of our element."[25] In her early years in Alberta, Roberta had successfully adapted to life as a teacher on a staff made up almost entirely of men. During the war she served with a male quartermaster and an all-male kitchen staff. Over 90 per cent of those who had voted her into office were men and she had coped with two terms in an almost all-male legislature. Roberta wasn't "out of" her element – she was once again immersed in it.

Until late in the spring, Roberta juggled her legislative duties with her job with the Soldier Settlement Board. Although her name doesn't appear in the newspaper accounts of the events, the last duty she carried out for the Board may have been to participate in one of the most ambitious programs yet sponsored by the organization.

In April 1920, it hosted a national series of short demonstration courses in domestic science and home nursing for the wives of soldier settlers. These eight-day to six-week programs were held in towns and cities across Canada, including Edmonton, Regina, Swift Current, Yorkton, and Moose Jaw. Instruction was provided free of charge by local universities and colleges while transportation to the events was funded by the Red Cross and other agencies. Local Councils of Women provided billets for the women and free day care for their babies. Seventy-five per cent of those who attended were British-born.[26]

There was a high turnout for the courses. Four hundred women attended the Edmonton event, while seventy-two women attended in Moose Jaw and another forty-seven women participated in the program in Regina.[27] The high turnout was a strong indication of the women's commitment to making their farms successful. It also suggested the desire of many for a break from the rigours of farm life and for the companionship of other women. As one grateful participant noted, "It was a splendid week for me, as I met such lots of nice people, and I won't feel quite so lonely out on the prairie now. I shall always look back on the first week's holiday I've had in Canada."[28]

Perhaps exhausted from carrying out two jobs or simply because she was eager for an extended visit with her family, Roberta resigned from her job soon after this conference and returned to Sarnia for the summer. In late August, Harvey Price joined her there. By now, Robert and Catherine would have realized that he was a central figure in the life of their youngest daughter and it is not difficult to imagine them nervously welcoming him into their formal front parlour. Harvey would have quickly charmed them, telling stories about his adventurous life in the north or describing some of the London air raids that he and Roberta witnessed together. Then, after promising to return for dinner the next day, the two might have taken a walk around the well-kept garden outside. Harvey may have proposed to Roberta under the oak tree that had shaded the house since her childhood or there may have already been an understanding between them, made during passionate meetings on windswept hills in the Peace country. Just how passionate can be gleaned from the wedding plans that soon followed.

On August 31, newspapers in Alberta and Ontario announced Roberta and Harvey's engagement. The wedding was to take place on September 21. There seems to have been no reason for such a short period between engagement and marriage, suggesting that Roberta may have been pregnant. Although pre-marital relations were seen as socially and morally unacceptable in the first part of the twentieth century, they were much more common than might be assumed today. As long as couples married quickly and quietly and later celebrated the "early" birth of a child, society tended to look the other way. Roberta's niece Margaret Hanna had married hastily due to a wartime pregnancy, and it was possible that Maud MacAdams was pregnant before she married Jack Hanna. Roberta could have found herself in a similar position. Although her only child, Robert Price, would not be born until 1924, Roberta would experience two miscarriages in the years before his birth.[29] One of those pregnancies might have been lost sometime in 1920.

If Roberta was pregnant when her engagement was announced, her response to reporters' questions revealed a woman unafraid of overturning social conventions when a higher principle was at stake. "Will you retain your seat in the provincial parliament after your marriage in September?" asked a *Toronto Star* journalist.[30] "Assuredly," she replied with laughter and surprise in her voice. "Why not?" Until that moment it had probably not occurred to Roberta that anyone would expect her to step down. Since she had first taken flight in 1909, Roberta had been setting her own independent course. In the short term, neither marriage (nor possibly pregnancy) would alter her path.

～～～

Although it was 9:00 on a Tuesday morning, St. George's Anglican Church was filled to capacity. The organ played softly as throngs of people poured into the church for what one society journalist called a "wedding of more than usual interest." Asters, gladiolas, and autumn leaves were arranged in deep vases on the communion table. Roberta's brothers and sisters sat in the polished pews, gathered once more in the church of their youth. White-haired Catherine MacAdams was resplendent in her lace trimmed, black silk dress and close fitting gray ostrich hat. Nearby sat Maud Hanna with her daughters Katherine and Margaret. Johnston − finally out of uniform − sat with Robert and Mary McBurney, Leslie and Muriel MacAdams and their little daughter Catherine.[31] Only William was missing − busy with a new job in northern British Columbia.

Roberta entered the church on the arm of her father. She had rejected the traditional virginal white gown and opted to wear what one society reporter described as "a smart crow-blue tailor-made, trimmed with oppossum, a blue crepe blouse, embroidered with chenille, and a henna hat." That hat was really a turban, a pile of rust-coloured velvet trimmed in blue and gold. The deep blue of her dress matched the colour of Roberta's eyes and the dramatic hat framed what was still a remarkably youthful face. On one lapel she wore a glittering platinum and diamond pin (a gift from Harvey) and on the other, a corsage of orchids and lilies of the valley.[32]

After the short service, family members and a small cluster of invited guests walked over to the MacAdams's Brock Street home for a lavish wedding breakfast. A white wedding cake, surrounded by more asters and gladiolas (probably arranged by Maud) sat at the centre of the dining room table where Robert MacAdams had once recited epic poetry to his large family.[33]

The wedding marked one of the last MacAdams family reunions. Within three years, quiet, dignified Catherine MacAdams would pass away and her husband would suffer a debilitating stroke.[34] In 1925, Johnston would marry and settle permanently in California.[35] Three years later, Robert MacAdams − the adventurous Irish Canadian newspaper publisher for whom Roberta's first child would be named − would die in his sleep.[36] That same year, the life of Leslie MacAdams would end prematurely in a tragic accident.[37] Of the remaining members of the family, Bill would continue to raise his family in British Columbia, and Mary and Maud would remain in Sarnia. Mary (widowed in 1928) would eventually move into the family home on Brock Street.[38] Maud would continue to reign over the nearby Hanna mansion, dedicating her considerable wealth to funding public gardens, playgrounds, and beaches.[39]

In 1909, Roberta had left her family behind and begun the journey that would eventually take her halfway around the world. Eleven years later, she was leaving her childhood home again – more aware than ever that her goodbyes could be permanent. As she and Harvey said their farewells on the wide front veranda of the Brock Street house, Roberta must have been keenly aware that her life was changing yet again. At forty years old, the dutiful daughter, dietitian, lieutenant, and ground-breaking politician was setting out on another career path, albeit a more traditional one.

After a short honeymoon in Quebec, Roberta and Harvey spent the remainder of the fall in Toronto before returning to Alberta. In February 1921, Roberta returned to the legislature for her final session as "soldier's representative." The needs of her constituents were still making themselves felt. As Roberta had once predicted, unemployment for those soldiers who couldn't or wouldn't farm was widespread. On March 3, a group of veterans met for a demonstration in Edmonton's Memorial Hall. The Alberta government, they declared, had failed to take action to end unemployment among the members of this group. "That more provision should be made for the employment and re-establishment of the physically fit returned man, was the general consensus of opinion at the meeting," noted *the Edmonton Journal*.[40] The veterans weren't only protesting the lack of jobs. They were making connections between the men's experience overseas and their readjustment to civilian life. "The hardships endured 'over there' could not but have its effect, even though the veteran passed through the conflict presumably unscathed. Because of this fact, he needed assistance in establishing himself in civilian life again. It was the country's duty to see that this well-merited aid was forthcoming."[41]

The Alberta government had few resources to address the soldiers' concerns. It was now facing a financial crisis. Estimates for the provincial debt varied from $18 million to $42 million. There was little money in the provincial budget for initiatives to help returned soldiers. One way of raising money was for the province to gain control of its natural resources from the federal government. Roberta supported resolutions censuring Ottawa's unwillingness to allow Alberta to benefit from its rich timber and oil resources. It would take until 1929 before Alberta would finally win this important debate (although it would resurface decades later during the oil crisis of the 1970s).

Roberta's last major action in the legislature was appropriately enough taken on behalf of Alberta's women. On April 5, 1921, she joined forces with Louise McKinney to help block a regressive motion put forward by opposition member Dr. Stewart [not the premier] of Lethbridge. Stewart wanted to strike out "all actions providing for women to serve as jurors" in the province's Jury Act. In the debate that followed, both Roberta and Louise "spoke many times urging that women be put on juries under the same conditions as men."[42] Probably sensing the defeat of his bill, Stewart moved an amendment demanding that all special exemptions for women in the Jury Act be struck out. He must have known that such an expectation would be unpopular in a province where people were still getting accustomed to women's active participation in public life. While both Roberta and Louise were in essential agreement with the amendment, they knew it was a trap and did not press for its acceptance.

As the legislative session drew to a close, a group of MLAs presented Roberta with a letter and wedding gift. There is no record of what the gift was, but Roberta kept the letter for the rest of her life:

> Dear Mrs. Price: We are asking you to accept the accompanying small wedding gift in the hope that it may at times remind you of our best wishes for your continued happiness and in the hope that by allying yourself to another "party" you may not sacrifice your own "independence."[43]

It was signed by eighteen members of the legislature, including Louise McKinney and Robert Pearson. They knew that Roberta had truly allied herself with another "party." While few of her colleagues, friends, and family members would suggest that she had given up her autonomy, she did plan to give up her political career. The provincial Liberals had almost reached the end of their mandate. On June 23, Premier Stewart called an election, to be held on July 18.[44] Roberta decided not to run. There was no further need for "soldier's representatives" and her friend Beatrice believed that "she did not care to run on a party ticket so she did not run for re-election." There were probably other considerations. She had once told her friend William Carpenter that she was "always more interested in organizing and building than in carrying on a completed routine."[45] In serving one term in the legislature, she had lobbied for soldier's rights, improved health care, and legislation that addressed the needs of women. She had "organized and built." Now it was up to others to carry these dreams forward.

There were probably more personal reasons, as well. Roberta and Harvey wanted to have a family. Roberta may have lost her first pregnancy and become convinced that the stresses of political life had contributed to her miscarriage. Harvey Stinson Price, while supportive of his wife's involvement in public life, may also have wanted his wife to play the more traditional role of homemaker.

There is another compelling reason that Roberta might have chosen this time to leave political life. At the end of the legislative session, she and Harvey moved to a farm just outside Sexsmith. It seems that despite her earlier reservations about the challenges of farming, Roberta had come to believe that she and Harvey might be able to benefit from the government's soldier settlement scheme. Harvey was entitled to benefits under the Soldier Settlement Act and probably wanted to access them before the government chose to withdraw its support. The couple had experienced the beauty of the Peace River country. Now they would try their own hands at homestead life.

≈ ≈ ≈

Sometime in the 1940s, Roberta asked her friend Beatrice to lend her copies of the letters that Beatrice had sent home during the Great War. Roberta wanted her son Robert to read them and get a "glimpse of Old London as you and I knew it, or a bit of it, during that fantastic episode in our mostly forgotten past." Many of the letters described Roberta's famous election campaign and her experiences overseas. After nervously presenting them to her son ("I did not make much comment, just suggested that he might take time out for a bit of amusing reading"), Roberta was pleased to discover that he did not find them "funny and absurd." It was somehow important to her that Robert take seriously what his mother had experienced during those tumultuous years. "Toynbee put it this way," wrote Roberta to Beatrice. "We thought we were out of history."

In 1921, Roberta had chosen to walk "out of history." Although the reasons for her decision aren't entirely clear, she was doing what many women in public life sometimes still do. She traded her briefcase for a life that revolved around being a wife, and later a mother. Yet Roberta left behind a legacy that would have a long-term impact on Canadian society. Before and during her time in office, she had provided tangible aid and support to the rural women who helped to settle the Canadian West. She (along with many others) laid some of the groundwork for government measures to meet the needs of soldiers and their families. Those whom she helped did not forget those contributions. As late as 1944, a woman would approach Johnston MacAdams and say, "I am from Edmonton. I wonder if you are related to Sister MacAdams who did so much for us women who had boys at the front in the last war."[46]

Most important, by running successfully for office, Roberta MacAdams helped push open the door to women's participation in politics. The year she left office would be the same year another woman – Agnes MacPhail – would enter the political ring and become the first woman elected to the federal government. Without Roberta MacAdams and her colleague Louise McKinney, there is little doubt Agnes's journey would have been that much more difficult and lonely.

The purse arrived by courier on a subzero January afternoon.

When I drew it out of the plastic envelope, tiny gold beads cascaded out onto my desk. It was something that we once called an "evening bag," a tiny, impractical fabric concoction with a gold chain strap and brass ball clasp – a purse that would barely hold a hairbrush. Although here and there some threads had come loose, it was still remarkably intact, beautifully beaded in a delicate pattern of blue, green, black, and red arranged against a background of gold. The remnants of a beaded fringe dangled along the bottom of the bag, as if in anticipation of another gala evening. It smelled faintly of face powder and soft perfume.

The purse once belonged to Roberta. She probably purchased it sometime in the 1920s to go with a filmy drop-waist dress and pair of thin-strapped shoes. The bag was discovered by her granddaughter in the bottom of an old trunk in the attic of her parents' home in Calgary. It had probably laid there undisturbed since Roberta's death in 1959. Now it had arrived on my desk, next to the humming computer on which the last chapter of her story was being written. It was as though, at the last minute, Roberta wanted to send me one final message.

I opened the purse to pull out yet another part of Roberta's history. A mixture of badges and buttons spilled out. Most had belonged to Roberta, but a handful had once graced the uniform of Harvey Price. There were two of Roberta's Canadian Medical Corps badges, four brass buttons, and a King George medal with her name inscribed along the edge (given to all military nurses who served overseas). But what drew most of my attention were the four shiny stars from Roberta's uniform. In the centre of each was a garland of green leaves and a circle of scarlet. These stars were the "pips" that were once worn – two on each shoulder – to indicate the rank of lieutenant. They were worn proudly by every nurse in the Canadian Army Medical Corps, and by one dietitian turned politician.

Living in the vastness of western Canada, I long ago learned that every person's life leaves an impression, however faint: a footprint pressed into the mud, a straight row of trees in the middle of a canola field. Roberta's election photograph had been the first "impression" that had started me on the path to find her. Now here, among the stars and badges, was the sign that my journey was coming to an end, the final evidence of a woman whose vital presence had drawn me across the country, to England and France, and back home again. After what seemed like a long time, I put everything back into the bag and clicked it shut, slipping it into an envelope to mail back to those who had entrusted it to me. It was time to say goodbye to Roberta.

NOTES

INTRODUCTION

1　Mary MacLeod Moore, *The Maple Leaf's Red Cross* (London: Skeffington and Sons Ltd., 1919): 11.

2　Marjorie Barron Norris, *Sister Heroines* (Calgary: Bunker to Bunker Publishing, 2002): 147.

CHAPTER 1

1　This description of Mary and William's trip across the Atlantic is a creative reconstruction based on the known facts about the couple: that they were Irish Protestants who had access to some financial resources and therefore had the means to pay for a cabin and that they crossed some time between the birth of their son Robert in England and the first documented appearance of the family in Canada in 1844.

2　David Hollett, *Passage to the New World: Packet Ships and Irish Famine Emigrants 1845–1851* (Abergavenny: P.M. Heaton Publishing, 1995): 121.

3　David Wilson, *The Irish in Canada* (Ottawa: Canadian Historical Association, 1989): 6.

4　Michael Swift, *Historical Maps of Ireland* (Edison: Chartwell Books Inc., 1999): 81.

5　Sean Sexton and Christine Kinealy, *The Irish: A Photohistory* (New York: Thames and Hudson, 2002): 34. Also Wilson, *The Irish in Canada*, 7–8.

6　*Historical Atlas of the County of Wellington, Ontario* (Toronto: Historical Atlas Publishing Company, 1906).

7　Sexton and Kinealy, *The Irish: A Photohistory*, 39.

8　Obituaries, *Ottawa Times*, 24 January 1867.

9　Wilson, *The Irish in Canada*, 3.

10　Ibid., 11.

11　George Stanley, *Canada's Soldiers: 1604–1954* (Toronto: MacMillan Co., 1954): 186–89.

12　Norma Geggie, *Wakefield Revisited* (Chelsea: Castenchel Editions, 2003): 5.

13　Ibid.

14　Samplers, Spaulding Collection.

15　*Historical Atlas of the County of Wellington, Ontario* (Toronto: Historical Atlas Publishing Company, 1906). Marsha Boulton, *Minto Memories: Families Facts and Fables* (Durham: Saugeen Press, 1988).

16   The Chaloner brothers' comments were included in the Census for 1861, National Archives Microfilm, C-1083.

17   Bruce Elliott, *Irish Migrants in the Canadas: A New Approach* (Montreal: McGill-Queen's University Press, 1988): 198.

18   *The Petrolia Advertiser* (Sarnia Public Library). Obituaries, "Death Summons Robt. McAdams, Veteran Sarnian," *Sarnia Canadian Observer*, 20 April 1928.

19   "Mrs. R. MacAdams Passes Away on 80th Birthday," *Sarnia Canadian Observer*, 14 May 1923.

20   Paul Rutherford, *A Victorian Authority: The Daily Press in Late 19th Century Canada* (Toronto: University of Toronto Press, 1982): 84–85.

21   "Death Summons Robt. McAdams, Veteran Sarnian."

22   Wilson, *The Irish in Canada*, 15.

23   *County of Lambton Gazeteer and General Business Directory*, Sarnia Public Library: 10.

24   George Mathewson, "Fenian Scare a Rather Unusual Story," *150 Years of Local News, Sarnia Observer Volume 1* (newspaper insert, 2003): 7.

25   Donald Graves, ed., *Fighting for Canada: Seven Battles 1758–1945* (Toronto: Robin Brass Studio, 2000): 37.

26   Edward Phelps, *Sarnia: Gateway to Bluewaterland* (Sarnia: Windsor Publications, 1987): 28.

27   George Mathewson, "Fenian Scare a Rather Unusual Story," (2003): 7.

28   Phelps, *Sarnia: Gateway to Bluewaterland*, 31.

29   Victor Lauriston, *Lambton's Hundred Years: 1849–1949* (Sarnia: Haines Frontier Printing Company, n.d.): 239.

30   Most of the evidence of the *Canadian's* Conservative leanings is third-hand; only four copies of the newspaper remain in existence – two in the National Archives and two in the Mooretown Museum. These examples of Robert's Conservatism come from a surviving edition dated 17 February 1897.

31   George Mathewson, "A Memorable 1872 Clash of the Titans," *150 Years of Local News, Sarnia Observer Volume 1* (newspaper insert, 2003): 25.

32   *The Canadian Encyclopedia*, entries under Conservative Party, Liberal Party, Sir John A. Macdonald, Sir Alexander Mackenzie.

33   Census of Canada, 1891.

CHAPTER 2

1   Cathy Dobson, "Sarnia Facing Deficit," *Sarnia Observer*, Tuesday, 7 October 2003.

2   Information about MacAdams family servant in letter from Mary Urie Watson, MacDonald Institute, to William Bradey, Edmonton, 17 June 1912, Guelph McLaughlin Archives, University of Guelph.

3   In the 1890s, one out of every eleven Canadian families employed a "girl," according to Janice Acton et al., *Women at Work, Ontario, 1850–1930* (Toronto: Women's Press, 1974): 76.

4   Letter from Mary Urie Watson, MacDonald Institute, to William Bradey, Edmonton, 17 June 1912.

5   Author interviews with Monica Newton, Tom Spaulding, and Robert Price.

6   Wendy Mitchinson, *The Nature of their Bodies: Women and their Doctors in Victorian Canada* (Toronto: University of Toronto Press, 1991): 14–15.

7   Comments about Mary are from a letter from William Hanna to his son Neil, 20 July 1918, Spaulding Collection.

8   Letter from Johnston MacAdams to his niece Evelyn, 15 December 1944, Gormley Collection.

9   "Elected but No Campaigning," *Globe*, 2 February 1918.

10   "Miss Roberta MacAdams," *OAC Review* 31 (March 1919): 334.

11   In the 1901 Canadian census, Leslie MacAdams is listed as a printer and Johnston MacAdams as a reporter.

12   *Sarnia Canadian*, 17 February 1897, Moore Museum Collection.

13   "Well Known Local Newspaper Man Writes from War," *Sarnia Canadian Observer*, 14 September 1918.

14   Letter from Johnston MacAdams to his niece Evelyn, 15 December 1944. Gormley Collection.

15   *Sarnia Canadian*, 17 February 1897, Moore Museum Collection.

16   Ibid.

17   Edward Phelps, *Sarnia: Gateway to Bluewaterland*, 41.

18   Ibid.

19   "The Late Rev. Canon Thomas R. Davis M.A.," one-page biography, Lambton Archives.

20   Sara Jeannette Duncan, *The Imperialist* (1904; Ottawa: Tecumseh Press, 1996).

21   "The Late Rev. Canon Thomas R. Davis M.A.," one-page biography, Lambton Archives.

22   "Miss MacAdams Pleads for More Inspiration in Educational Life," *Edmonton Journal*, 12 February 1919.

23   Quote courtesy of Archdeacon James Broadfoot and Huron Diocese Archivist Diana Coates.

24   *Meals, Tested, Tasted and Approved* (Chicago: John Cuneo Co, 1930).

25   From Alfred, Lord Tennyson's famous poem "The Charge of the Light Brigade" (1864).

26   Donald Harman Akenson, *The Irish in Ontario: A Study in Rural History* (Montreal: McGill-Queen's University Press, 1988): 215.

27   Glen C. Phillips, *History of the Sarnia Public Library* (booklet, 1990).

28   Lorne Bruce, *Free Books for All: The Public Library Movement in Ontario, 1850–1930* (Toronto: Dundurn Press, 1994): 153.

29   M. Starr, "The Gentle Suffragette," *My Golden West Magazine* (November/December 1966): 36.

30   "W.J. Hanna Nominated As Conservative Candidate for West Lambton," *Sarnia Observer*, 5 October 1900.

CHAPTER 3

1   "The Collegiate Institute Opened," *The Sarnia Observer*, 18 December 1891, 4.

2   "The Old Collegiate Building," *The Sarnia Observer*, 28 October 1922, 25.

3   This reconstruction of an average high school day for Roberta is based on several sources, including: "The Collegiate Institute Opened," *The Sarnia Observer*, 18 December 1891, 4; "The Old Collegiate Building," *The Sarnia Observer*, 28 October 1922, 25; late nineteenth century photograph of Roberta MacAdams in the Spaulding Collection; "Old Collegiate Served All of Sarnia," by O.N. Wilson, *Sarnia Observer* (undated), Lambton County Archives; *Merry Times: Sarnia Collegiate Institute Yearbook*, 1902, Lambton County Archives; and *Sarnia: Old Home Week* (Sarnia: Frontier Printing, 1925), Lambton County Archives.

4   The description of Roberta is based on a photograph in the Spaulding Collection.

5   The Collegiate was renowned for its draftiness – see article "Old Collegiate Served All of Sarnia," by O.N. Wilson, *Sarnia Observer* (undated), Lambton County Archives.

6   Descriptions of Mr. Grant are taken from *Merry Times: Sarnia Collegiate Institute Yearbook* and *Sarnia: Old Home Week*, both from the Lambton Archives.

7   *Sarnia Old Home Week*.

8   "The Collegiate Institute Opened," *Sarnia Observer*, 18 December 1891, 4.

9   Franklin Foster, *John E. Brownlee: A Biography* (Lloydminster: Foster Learning, 1996): 7. Brownlee also attended the Sarnia Collegiate in the 1890s, and his biographer includes a description of the courses students were expected to take.

10   *The High Schools Reader* (Toronto: Ontario Department of Education, n.d.).

11   "Novel Lyceum Club Function", *Pall Mall Gazette*, 23 July 1917.

12   *Modern School Geography and Atlas* (Toronto: Canada Publishing Company, 1879): 46.

13   J.M. Bumsted, *The Peoples of Canada: A Post-Confederation History* (Toronto: Oxford University Press, 2004): 146–49.

14   "Miss Roberta MacAdams," *OAC Review*, 335.

15   Roberta MacAdams, "Table Talk," *The Beaver: A Live Weekly for Canadians Overseas*, 28 December 1918, 4.

16   "Believes Government Supervised Clubs Cannot Meet Needs of Girls," *Edmonton Journal*, 1 March 1919.

17   Craig Brown, ed., *The Illustrated History of Canada* (Toronto: Key Porter Books, 2002): 302.

18   Maud's role as housekeeper appears to be the most logical explanation for how she came to know Jack Hanna and how their romance blossomed so quickly, despite what would normally have been a period of mourning for Jack Hanna.

19   Interview with Tom Spaulding, Maud's grandson.

20   This description of Roberta in her sister's bedroom is a reconstruction of what Roberta might have done on the evening following her sister's wedding. The

oak tree next to the house still exists. The description of Maud and her wedding dress is based on photographs in the Spaulding Collection.

21 George Bernard Shaw, *Man and Superman* (1903; Harmondsworth: Penguin, 1946).

22 *Alberta in the 20st Century, Volume 2: The Birth of a Province* (Edmonton: United Western Communications Ltd., 1992): 40.

23 W.A. Craick, "Wanted: Big Job for Hanna," *Maclean's Magazine*, 1908, 108.

24 Ibid., 108–9.

25 Ibid., 114.

26 *The Sarnia Canadian*, 17 February 1897, Moore Museum Collection.

27 Thomas B. Doherty, *Sarnia: A Pictorial History*, 100.

28 "The Carnival of Nations," *Sarnia Observer*, 27 May 1898, 1.

29 In April 1898, the American Government ordered a blockade of Cuba, beginning the Spanish-American War. By December 1898, Spain would relinquish its claim to Cuba. The USA would occupy the country until 1902. (*Encyclopedia Americana*, 1963, Vol. 8).

30 *Sandon Paystreak*, 17 May 1902.

31 *Sandon Paystreak*, 23 August 1902.

32 C.H. Stout, *Backtrack* (Calgary: L. Stout, 1973).

33 Margaret Hanna would one day become a Communist Party activist. For more information, see Ross Lambertson, "The Rosedale Red," *The Beaver*, June/July 2003, 23.

34 This is based on correspondence between Jack Hanna, Roberta MacAdams, and Neil Hanna. During the Great War, Jack Hanna copied all of his son's correspondence to Roberta, keeping her updated on how her nephew was doing at school and later in the military.

35 Linda Ambrose, *For Home and Country: The Centennial History of the Women's Institutes of Ontario* (Guelph: Federated Women's Institutes of Ontario, 1996). 20.

CHAPTER 4

1 According to Darlene Wiltsie of the Guelph McLaughlin Archives, there were nineteen students in Roberta's first year class. Thirteen were under the age of twenty-two. Roberta's arrival at college is reconstructed based on information from retrospective articles by her classmates in the *OAC Review* of October 1911 and the *36th Annual Calendar of the Ontario Agricultural College, 1909–1910*.

2 All student applications included students' fathers' occupations. The examples given come from a list of first-year students (for all programs) compiled by archivist Darlene Wiltsie at the Guelph McLaughlin Archives. It is clear that most of the sixty-one fathers listed were professional men – only one in the list was a farmer.

3 Acton, *Women at Work*, 194, Table 3.

4 Fees are taken from the *36th Annual Calendar of the Ontario Agricultural College, 1909–1910*. According to the Consumer Price Index for the earliest year on record (1914), calculated using the Bank of Canada's inflation guide <http://

www.bankofcanada.ca/en/inflation_calc.htm>, when adjusted for inflation, tuition at the Institute translates into roughly $10,506 in 2006. Room and board at Macdonald Hall would be $3,193 in 2006 dollars.

5   Terry Crowley and Alexander Ross, *College on the Hill* (Toronto: Dundurn Press, 1999): 95.

6   "The Opening Day," *OAC Review*, Vol. 24, No. 1, October 1911, Guelph McLaughlin Archives, University of Guelph, 48.

7   It is not known whether or not Roberta shared a room. (The Hall had thirty-five single and forty double rooms). However, each room included the furnishings I have described. See the *36th Annual Calendar of the Ontario Agricultural College, 1909–1910*, 101.

8   *36th Annual Calendar of the Ontario Agricultural College, 1909–1910*, 103.

9   This reconstruction of Roberta unpacking is based on information about requirements for student dress in the *36th Annual Calendar of the Ontario Agricultural College, 1909–1910*, 96–97. Information about Roberta's likely undergarments and other personal items are taken from the *Autumn and Winter Catalogue No. 58 of the Hudson's Bay Company* (1910–1911; Winnipeg: Watson and Dwyer Publishing Ltd., 1977): 60–64.

10   Macdonald Hall regulations are taken from the *36th Annual Calendar of the Ontario Agricultural College, 1909–1910*, 100–103.

11   Roberta's course load and marks courtesy of the Guelph McLaughlin Archives, University of Guelph.

12   *36th Annual Calendar of the Ontario Agricultural College, 1909–1910*, 93.

13   Ibid, 87.

14   Comments of Grace Greenwood, Critic Teacher in Roberta's school file in the Guelph McLaughlin Archives, University of Guelph. Undated, but probably June 1912.

15   *The OAC Review*, 13 (March 1919): 335.

16   See *Merry Times: Sarnia Collegiate Institute Yearbook* and *Sarnia Old Home Week* for more information. Both available from the Lambton County Archives.

17   James Snell, *Macdonald Institute: Remembering the Past, Embracing the Future* (Toronto: Dundurn Press, 2003): 27. See also Ambrose, *For Home and Country*, 49–51.

18   Snell, *Macdonald Institute*, 27; also photographs of Watson's office in the Guelph McLaughlin Archives, University of Guelph Archives.

19   Letter from Mary Urie Watson, MacDonald Institute, to William Bradey, Edmonton, 17 June 1912. Collection of the University of Guelph Archives.

20   Snell, *Macdonald Institute*, 44.

21   Student Records, Roberta MacAdams, Guelph McLaughlin Archives, University of Guelph.

22   Shelagh S. Jameson, "The Soldier's MLA," *Alberta Historical Review*, 15 (Autumn 1967): 19.

23   Interview with Robert Price, June 2004; also information from Harvey Stinson Price's military records file in the National Archives of Canada.

24   J.M. Bumsted, *The Peoples of Canada: A Post-Confederation History*, 2nd ed. (Don Mills: Oxford University Press, 2004): 170.

25 Cheryl MacDonald, "The Angel in the House, Adelaide Hoodless, Domestic Science Crusader," *The Beaver* (August/September 1986): 27.

26 Macdonald Institute Student Records, Roberta MacAdams file, Guelph McLaughlin Archives, University of Guelph.

27 See entries on Naval Aid Bill and Naval Service Act in the *Canadian Encyclopedia* (Toronto: McClelland and Stewart Inc., 1999). Also see Martin Gilbert, *A History of the Twentieth Century*, Vol. 1 (Toronto: Stoddart Publishing Co., 1997): Chapter 10.

28 *The OAC Review*, 23 (July 1911).

29 In the *Globe* of 27 July 1911, Roberta is listed as the only first-class honours graduate of the MacDonald Institute.

CHAPTER 5

1 *The Stony Plain Advertiser*, 3 February 1912.

2 The description of the interior of Hardwick and Rossell's store was based on their advertisements in the *Stony Plain Advertiser*, and information about general stores of the period.

3 Description of Roberta's coat based on a photograph in the Monica Newton Collection.

4 *Stony Plain Advertiser*, February 1912. Also *Province of Alberta Annual Report 1912*.

5 See *Canadian Encyclopedia* entry "Sifton, Arthur Lewis." See also Howard Palmer with Tamara Palmer, *Alberta: A New History* (Edmonton: Hurtig Publishers, 1990): 148.

6 Linda Rasmussen, Lorna Rasmussen, Candace Savage, Anne Wheeler, *A Harvest Yet to Reap: A History of Prairie Women* (Toronto: The Women's Press, 1976): 228.

7 John G. Niddrie, "The Edmonton Boom of 1911–1912," *Alberta Historical Review* (Spring 1965): 1.

8 Census of Prairie Provinces 1916, in Alan Artibise, "Boosterism and the Development of Prairie Cities, 1871–1913," in R.D. Francis and Howard Palmer, eds., *The Prairie West: Historical Readings* (Edmonton: Pica Pica Press, 1985).

9 Palmer, *Alberta: A New History*, 142.

10 See Gibson Girl entry in *Canadian Oxford Dictionary* (Oxford University Press, Toronto: 1998) and Ann Beth Presley, "Fifty Years of Change: Societal Attitudes and Women's Fashions, 1900-1950," *The Historian* (Winter 1998): 307.

11 Acton et al., *Women at Work*, 268.

12 Ibid., 267. In 1911, the largest number of Canadian women in paid work were employed as servants (Ibid., 98, 128). Women at this time formed 13.4 per cent of the paid labour force.

13 Rasmussen et al., *A Harvest Yet to Reap*, 110.

14 Cornelia R. Wood, *My Memories* (Edmonton: UVISCO PRESS, 1982): 406. See also Province of Alberta's Annual Report, 1912, Alberta Legislature Library.

15 *The Stony Plain Advertiser* mentions that the audiences for the lectures were mostly made up by experienced homemakers.

16   *Along the Fifth: A History of Stony Plain and District* (Stony Plain: Stony Plain and District Historical Society, 1982): 546.

17   *The Alberta Club Woman's Blue Book* (Calgary: Calgary Branch of the Canadian Woman's Press Club Publishers, 1917): 31.

18   Faye Reineberg Holt, *Threshing: The Early Years of Harvesting* (Calgary: Fifth House Publishers, 1999): 33.

19   Elizabeth Mitchell, *In Western Canada Before the War; Impressions of Early Twentieth Century Prairie Communities* (Saskatoon: Western Producer Prairie Books, 1981). See also the comments of Marion Rogers, a former AWI president, in Rasmussen et al., *A Harvest Yet to Reap*, 68.

20   Wood, *My Memories*, 406.

21   *The Boom and The Bust*, Volume 3, *Alberta in the Twentieth Century* (Edmonton: United Western Communications Ltd. 1994): 29.

22   Palmer, *Alberta: A New History*, 166.

23   Shelagh S. Jameson, "The Soldier's MLA."

24   Letter from Roberta MacAdams to W.G. Carpenter, 22 July 1919, Edmonton Public School Archives.

25   Letter dated 17 June 1912 from Mary Urie Watson to Edmonton School Board, collection of the Edmonton School Archives.

26   Teacher's Salary Schedule, Edmonton School Archives.

27   Based on an account of a day in Roberta's classroom, as remembered by one of her students. Grace Sudholme, "Reminiscing," Glenbow Archives, M5977/69.

28   Ibid.

29   Speech by Roberta MacAdams, Glenbow Archives, M1670/43.

30   *The Chinook*, Victoria High School magazine, December 1910.

31   *Town Topics* [a weekly Edmonton tabloid], December 1913, quoted in Michael Kostek, *A Century and Ten: The History of Edmonton Public Schools* (Edmonton: Edmonton Public Schools, 1992).

32   The curriculum for domestic science was described in the Annual Report of the Alberta Department of Education, 1912. It appears that domestic-science teachers either taught without the use of recipe books, or used cookbooks of their own choice. Roberta was known to have enquired about a book entitled "Household Science" by Lines, but little more was known about the book. The cookbooks named in this chapter were in the collection of Cornelia Railey, who taught in a one-room school in Stony Plain around this time and used these books as resources for teaching home economics.

33   Letter from W.G. Carpenter to A.C. MacKay discussing challenges facing city schools, 3 December 1915. Discounting of teacher's salaries began in September 1914.

34   Letter from W.J. Hanna to Neil Hanna, dated 25 July 1912, Spaulding Collection.

35   Tom Wilson, 1913 MLA for Rocky Mountain House, quoting Sifton in an interview recorded in Rasmussen et al., *A Harvest Yet to Reap*, 194.

CHAPTER 6

1   "City Celebrates Dominion Day in A Royal Fashion," *Edmonton Journal*, 2 July 1914.

2   F. C. McConnell, "University Education," *The Chinook*, Easter 1914, 25.

3   "2 Victims of Assassin were Laid at Rest: Archduke Francis Ferdinand and his Wife Buried at Vienna," *Edmonton Journal*, 2 July 1914, 1.

4   "City Teachers Honor Member from Overseas" *Edmonton Journal* (n.d.; possibly 1919).

5   "Grand Farewell to Soldier Boys at the Pantages," *Edmonton Daily Capital*, 22 August 1914.

6   Mike Kostek, archivist, "School Boys in Khaki: The School Cadet Story" (occasional paper); *The Chinook*, Easter 1914 (this issue describes the shield hanging in the hallway and the history of the school cadets).

7   According to Alex Johnston and Andy den Otter, *Lethbridge: A Centennial History* (Lethbridge: Lethbridge Historical Society, 1991), by November 1916, 1,875 Lethbridge men had joined up, 20 per cent of the city's population at the time; 261 of these men died in action. The town had the highest percentage enlistment of any community in Canada. According to the 1916 census, there were 496,525 people living in Alberta that year.

8   Elizabeth Abbott, ed., *Chronicle of Canada* (Montreal: Chronicle Publications, 1990): 567.

9   Johnston MacAdams military records, National Archives of Canada.

10 In a letter dated 20 September 1915 to William Carpenter, the board's superintendent, Roberta notes that girls were sewing Red Cross bandages. Edmonton Public School Archives.

11 Margaret R. Higonnet, ed., *Nurses at the Front: Writing the Wounds of War* (Boston: Northeastern University Press, 2001): vii.

12 Susan Mann, *The War Diary of Clare Gass, 1915–1918* (Montreal: McGill-Queen's University Press, 2000): xvi.

13 Arthur Marwick, *Women at War: 1914–1918* (London: Fontana Paperbacks, 1977): 21.

14 Ibid., 84.

15 Linda J. Quiney, "Hardly Feminine Work! Violet Wilson and the Canadian Voluntary Aid Detachment Nurses of the First World War," in Sharon Anne Cook, Lorna McLean and Kate O'Rourke, eds., *Framing Our Past, Canadian Women's History in the Twentieth Century* (Montreal: McGill-Queen's University Press, 2001): 290.

16 Lyn MacDonald, *The Roses of No Man's Land* (London: Penguin Books, 1980): 197.

17 Marwick, *Women at War*, 167.

18 This takes into account $20.00 separation allowance, $25.00 from the Patriotic Fund, and about half of a private's monthly pay (approximately $15). See Desmond Morton, *When Your Number's Up: The Canadian Soldier in the First World War* (Toronto: Random House, 1993): 12, 50–51.

19 A.B. McCullough, Introduction to Section 6 in Cook, et al., *Framing Our Past*.

20   *The Alberta Club Woman's Blue Book.*

21   This figure has been calculated using the converter provided by the Bank of Canada <http://www.bankofcanada.ca/en/inflation_calc.htm>.

22   Quoted in a letter from Roberta to W.G. Carpenter, 3 January 1916.

23   Several of the staff of the Ontario Military Hospital received their appointments as a result of connections to Ontario cabinet ministers. See "Abuses at Orpington Hospital," *The Globe*, 27 September 1919, 6.

24   Letter from W.G. Carpenter to Roberta MacAdams, 7 January 1916, Edmonton Public School Archives.

25   Letter from Roberta MacAdams to W.D. Bradey, 22 January 1916, Glenbow Archives.

CHAPTER 7

1   For more information about the ways in which the armed forces used the grounds of the Canadian National Exhibition in Toronto, see John Robinson, *Once Upon a Century: 100 Year History of the 'Ex,'* (Toronto: J.H. Robinson Publishing Ltd., 1978).

2   Helen Ball, "Staff and Their Equipment for Hospital and Orpington," *The Daily News*, 9 March 1916.

3   Mann, *The War Diary of Clare Gass*, xix.

4   Ibid., xix.

5   Ball, "Staff and Their Equipment for Hospital and Orpington."

6   *Alberta in the 20th Century, Volume 4: The Great War and Its Consequences* (Calgary: United Western Communications Ltd., 1992): 89.

7   Letter from W.J. Hanna to Neil Hanna, 7 February 1916, Spaulding Collection. The fire was later proven not to be the work of saboteurs.

8   The Ontario Military Hospital was listed on the nominal roll for the Olympic. This was tracked down by Ray White, a volunteer with the Canadian War Museum in Ottawa.

9   Letter from Nurse Isobel Draffin to Dr. Helen MacMurchy, 17 April 1916, Ontario Provincial Archives, RG 8-9 No. 5, File: November 1915–March 1920.

10   Thomas Bonsall, *Titanic: The Story of the Great White Star Line Trio, the Olympic, the Titanic and the Britannic* (New York: Gallery Books, 1987): 19.

11   Letter from Nurse Grace MacPherson to Dr. MacMurchy, 17 May 1916, Ontario Provincial Archives, RG 8-9 No. 5, File: November 1915–March 1920. Before the ship left for France, the nurses were told that they would be traveling with six thousand troops. Once on board, they were informed that there were actually nearly eight thousand troops on the ship.

12   For a brief description of what it was like to travel on the Olympic, see Will Bird, *Ghosts Have Warm Hands* (Toronto: CEF Books, 1997): 3.

13   The Olympic was later covered in "dazzle paint" as a kind of camouflage. However, at this time it was still painted in British warship grey. See Alex Nickerson, "The Lethal Prow of the Famous Olympic," *Halifax Mail Star*, 6 August 1979.

14 "Women Legislators Make Their Maiden Speeches," *Edmonton Journal*, 28 February 1918.·

15 See the entry for the South African War in the *Canadian Encyclopedia* (Edmonton: Hurtig Publishers, 2000): 2216.

16 Letter from Nurse Grace McPherson to Dr. Helen MacMurchy, 17 May 1916, Ontario Provincial Archives, RG 8-9 No. 5, File: November 1915–March 1920.

17 "Canada in England: What Ontario was Doing for the Wounded," *Nursing Times*, 6 May 1916, 531.

18 These dates were found in an undated and untitled newspaper clipping at the Ontario Archives, which cites 29 March as the anniversary of the date when the hospital staff left Toronto for overseas service. April 1 was listed as the departure date of the ship in a profile of Corporal James Powley, a soldier who also travelled on the Olympic <http://www.kingandempire.com/powley1. html>. The date of arrival in England comes from "Canada in England," *Nursing Times*, 6 May 1916.

19 This is a pseudonym; according to Fiona Bourne of the Royal College of Nursing Archives (Scotland), most of the writers for the *Nursing Times* were prominent women from Canada or Britain, but they were never identified by anything but their initials – in this case "G.V."

20 "Canada in England," *Nursing Times*, 6 May 1916, 531.

21 Ibid., 529.

22 Letter from Nurse Isobel Draffin to Dr. MacMurchy, 17 April 1916, Ontario Provincial Archives, RG 8-9 No. 5, File: November 1915–March 1920.

23 Joanna Trollope, *Britannia's Daughters* (London: Hutchinson and Co., 1983): 96–99.

24 "Canada in England," *Nursing Times*, 6 May 1916, 531.

25 Catharine Cole and Judy Larmour, *Many and Remarkable: The Story of the Alberta Women's Institutes* (Edmonton: Alberta Women's Institutes, 1997): 2.

26 *Alberta in the 20th Century, Volume 3: The Boom, The War, and the Bust* (Calgary: United Western Communications Ltd., 1992): 92–95.

27 Carl Mollins, *Canada's Century* (Toronto: MacLean-Hunter Publishing Ltd. 1999): 51.

28 MacDonald, *The Roses of No Man's Land*, 148.

29 Bill Freeman and Richard Nielsen, *Far from Home: Canadians in the First War* (Toronto: McGraw–Hill Ryerson, 1999): 77, 80–81.

30 Desmond Morton and Jack Granatstein, *Marching to Armageddon: Canadians and the Great War, 1914–1919* (Toronto: Lester & Orpen Dennys, 1989): 114.

31 *Orpington from Saxon Times to the Great War* (Orpington: Worker's Educational Association, n.d.): 33. Details concerning the seriously wounded man came from a letter from Nurse Catherine Lawrence to Dr. MacMurchy, 12 June 1916, Ontario Provincial Archives.

32 The Ontario Military Hospital accepted men from all the Allied armies; the largest number of patients were Canadian – 12,483 by the end of the war (12,156 British, 1,626 Australian, 2 Newfoundlanders, 11 New Zealanders). From *Orpington from Saxon Times to the Great War*, 23. See also microfilm "History of Ontario Military Hospital," Ontario Provincial Archives.

33 *Orpington from Saxon Times to the Great War*, 20.

34 Ibid.

35 Captain W. H. Fox, "Our Hospital: A Short History and Description," *The Ontario Stretcher*, undated clipping, Ontario Provincial Archives.

36 Marwick, *Women at War*, 137.

37 This was based on the amount suggested for 1917, listed in Andrew MacPhail, *Official History of the Canadian Forces in the Great War, 1914–1919; Medical Services* (Ottawa, King's Printer, 1925): 307.

38 Roberta MacAdams, speech to the Alberta legislature, February 1918, Collection of Robert Price.

39 April 2002 letter to the author from Rev. Alan Mustoe, Vicar of All Saints Parish Church, Orpington.

40 Conversion from Bank of Canada <http://www.bankofcanada.ca/en/inflation_calc.htm>.

41 *Orpington from Saxon Times to the Great War*, 23.

42 MacPhail, *Official History of the Canadian Forces in the Great War*, 306.

43 From a postcard entitled "Army Stew" in Linda Granfield, *Where Poppies Grow: A World War I Companion* (Toronto: Stoddart, 2001): 13.

44 The recipe was drawn from the *Purity Cook Book* (Western Canada Flour Mills Co., 1936) and interviews with prairie seniors who related their parents' favourite farm recipes.

45 Letter from Catharine Lawrence to Dr. MacMurchy, 12 June 1916, Ontario Provincial Archives.

46 This reconstructed account was based on two articles: the first appeared in *The Daily Province* in late October 1917. It was entitled "Leads Busy Life at Orpington" (by Beatrice Nasmyth) and described the kind of work that Roberta did at the hospital and the tomato soup incident; the second article was "Our Hospital: A Short History and Description" (no date was given for this clipping; nor was information provided about the publication in which the article appeared; possibly August 1917). This article was appended to a report entitled "Report on Building of the Ontario Military Hospital at Orpington, Kent, England," by Col. Dr. R. A. Pyne, Minister of Education and Acting Prime Minister of Ontario, Ontario Provincial Archives.

CHAPTER 8

1 According to *The Ontario Stretcher*, the magazine produced for the Ontario Military Hospital, Roberta was a member of a committee that organized these regular dances. (See *Ontario Stretcher*, 16 September 1916, Ontario Provincial Archives). Information about the dances, including the fact that patients provided the orchestra, is recorded in *Orpington from Saxon Times*, 26.

2 *Orpington from Saxon Times*, 24.

3 Descriptions of London during the summer of 1916 are taken from Michael MacDonagh, *In London During the Great War: The Diary of a Journalist* (London: Eyre and Spottiswoode, 1935): 119.

4 Telegraph message to W.J. Hanna dated 6 October 1916 citing Neil's upcoming arrival in Toronto.

5 Martin Gilbert, *The First World War* (Toronto: Stoddart, 1994): 258–69.

6 Robert Graves, *Goodbye to All That: An Autobiography* (Oxford: Berghahn Books, 1995): 201.

7 The account of Roberta's visit to Neil Hanna in hospital is based on a letter from Col. H.A. Bruce to William Hanna, dated 4 August 1916, Spaulding Collection.

8 John Pateman, *Canadian Corner: A Brief History* (Orpington: Privately published, 1980): 15.

9 Morton and Granatstein, *Marching to Armageddon*, 138–44.

10 Ibid., 143.

11 Pateman, *Canadian Corner*, 15.

12 From Nurse Edith Hudson's war diary, Kerr Collection.

13 Martin Middlebrooke, *The First Day of the Somme, 1 July 1916* (London: Allan Lane, 1971): 252.

14 Desmond Morton, *When Your Number's Up*, 198 and Lyn MacDonald, *The Roses of No Man's Land*, 340. For vivid descriptions of mental breakdown and its treatment during the Great War, read novelist Pat Barker's Great War trilogy (*Regeneration, The Ghost Road, The Eye in the Door*).

15 *Orpington from Saxon Times to the Great War*, 25.

16 Ibid.

17 Jeffrey A. Keshen, *Propaganda and Censorship During Canada's Great War* (Edmonton: University of Alberta Press, 1996): 59.

18 *The Windsor Magazine, Volume XLVII*, London, December–May 1918, 573.

19 Letter from Dr. S. Cummings to William Hanna, 20 October 1916, Spaulding Collection.

20 Letter from W.J. Hanna to Col. Sam Hughes, dated 8 July 1913, Spaulding Collection.

21 "Mr. Hanna's Stirring Call to Arms," *The Orillia Packet*, 20 January 1916.

22 Hilda Ridley, "Pen Portraits of Progressive Women," *The Christian Guardian*, 16 February 1921, 11.

23 Ibid.

CHAPTER 9

1 These Orpington shops were advertised in "The Ontario Stretcher," a magazine of the Ontario Military Hospital, September 1916.

2 The description of the interior of the nurses' sitting room is based on descriptions and a photograph in an article entitled "Our Hospital: A Short History and Description" by Captain W.H. Fox, Quartermaster at the Ontario Military Hospital, published in "The Ontario Stretcher" (clipping, no date), Ontario Provincial Archives.

3 According to *GWL Nicholson's Canadian Expeditionary Force 1914–1919*, (Ottawa : Queen's Printer, 1962) this office was the predecessor of the famous Canadian War Records Office established by Max Aitken/Lord Beaverbrook.

4 Letter from Beatrice Nasmyth to her father dated 25 September 1915, Monica Newton Collection.

5   Letter from Beatrice Nasmyth to her father dated 16 August 1917, Monica Newton Collection.

6   Ibid.

7   "Elected, But No Campaigning," *The Globe*, 2 February 1918.

8   Beatrice Nasmyth, "Leads Busy Life at Orpington," *Daily Province*, October 1917.

9   *An Act to Provide for Representation in the Legislative Assembly of Alberta's Soldiers and Nurses in the Present War*, 5 April 1917, Alberta Legislature.

10   Letter from Beatrice Nasmyth to her father, 16 August 1917, Monica Newton Collection.

11   See A.J.P. Taylor, *Beaverbrook: A Biography* (New York: Simon and Schuster, 1972).

12   Letter from Beatrice Nasmyth to her father, 16 August 1917, Monica Newton Collection.

13   From correspondence with and biographical description provided by Graham Howe, Director of Curatorial Assistance Inc., Pasadena, California. Howe is a specialist on Hoppé.

14   Letter from Beatrice Nasmyth to her father, 16 August 1917, Monica Newton Collection.

15   Letter of Harold McGill to Emma, 24 September 1917, Glenbow Archives (M742 File 7).

16   Lt. Col. G.R. Stevens, *A City Goes to War: The History of the Loyal Edmonton Regiment* (Edmonton: Edmonton Regiment Association, 1964): 96.

17   Letter of Harold McGill to Emma, Glenbow Archives (M742 File 7).

18   Stevens, *A City Goes to War*, 96.

19   Beatrice Furniss (Nasmyth), *The Fundless Campaign: The Election of Roberta MacAdams, Armed Services Representative, 1917, to the Alberta Legislature* (Vancouver: privately published booklet, 1966).

20   Letters dated 31 July and 2 August 1917 between Matron In Chief Margaret MacDonald and Capt. Mary Plummer. Available in the National Archives of Canada, C148683 and C148684.

21   *The Scottish Women's Suffrage Movement* (Glasgow: People's Palace Museum, 1978): 16.

22   Midge Mackenzie, *Shoulder to Shoulder* (Harmondsworth: Penguin Books Ltd., 1975): 280.

23   Ibid., 283.

24   Ibid., 305.

25   "What Women are Doing," *The Daily Sketch*, London, 31 July 1917.

26   "Woman MP for Alberta: Nurses May Vote," *British Journal of Nursing*, 4 August 1917, 75.

27   "Alberta Stands at Head in Re-educational Work for Returned Soldiers: Miss Roberta MacAdams Pays Tribute to the Vocational Training System, But Sounds Note of Warning in Legislature as to Real Needs After the War," *Edmonton Journal*, 28 February 1918. One of Roberta's first fights in the Alberta legislature was over the issue of soldier retraining.

28   Quoted in Margaret MacMillan, *Paris 1919* (New York: Random House, 2001): 55.

29   Fetherstonhaugh, *The Royal Montreal Regiment 14th Battalion CEF* (Montreal: The Gazette Printing Company, 1927): 161.

30   Morton and Granatstein, *Marching to Armageddon*, 161.

31   Letter from Roberta MacAdams to Beatrice Nasmyth, 16 August 1917, Monica Newton Collection.

32   See the War Diary of the 3rd Infantry Brigade, online at the National Archives of Canada <http://www.collectionscanada.ca>.

33   Ibid.

34   In his book *No Place to Run: The Canadian Corps and Gas Warfare in the First World War* (Vancouver: UBC Press, 1999), historian Tim Cook says that by the last year of the war, artillery dumps used by German forces sometimes contained 50 per cent gas shells.

35   On 7 November 1917, Haig submitted names of those deserving special mention to the London Gazette. The list of names (including Lt. J. M. MacAdams) was published on 18 December 1917.

36   Beatrice Nasmyth, "Leads Busy Life at Orpington," *Daily Province*, October 1917.

37   This letter is mentioned in *The Fundless Campaign* and is also mentioned in a letter sent from Beatrice Nasmyth to her father, 8 September 1917, Monica Newton Collection.

38   Ernest Marshall, *Justice on the Peace: The Law and Lawyers in Alberta's Northwest* (Edmonton: Juriliber, 2003): 60.

39   Information about Harvey Price taken from interviews with Robert Price, and from his military records, held in the National Archives of Canada.

40   Interview with Robert Price.

41   Letter from Beatrice Nasmyth to her parents dated 15 February 1918. Monica Newton Collection.

42   Letter from Beatrice Nasmyth to her father, 8 September 1917. Monica Newton Collection.

43   Ibid.

44   Ibid.

45   Letter from Roberta MacAdams to Beatrice Nasmyth, 16 September 1917. Monica Newton Collection.

46   Letter from Gladys Hoyt to William Bradey, dated 19 September 1917. Edmonton Public Schools Archives, 84.1.1666.

47   Beatrice Nasmyth, "Leads Busy Life at Orpington," *Daily Province*, October 1917.

48   The unnamed British newspaper was quoted in "Alberta's Women M.P.P.'s" in the 29 December 1917 issue of *The Globe* (Toronto).

49   Beatrice Nasmyth, "Leads Busy Life at Orpington," *Daily Province*, 12 October 1917.

50   Ibid.

51   "A Curiously Democratic Election," *The Woman Citizen*, Boston, 22 December 1917.

52   Information from *Knowles and Son Until 1860* and *A History of the Grovesnor Hotel* (paper produced by Merit Hotels) and Priscilla Boniface, *Hotels and Restaurants 1830 to the Present Day* (London: Royal Commission on Historical Monuments, 1981).

CHAPTER 10

1   Roland Andre, *Memoire en Images Boulogne-sur-Mer* (Bouglogne: Alan Sutton, 1997): 36.

2   *Boulogne-sur-Mer Tourist Guide* (Boulogne: Office de Tourisme, 2001): 9.

3   Beatrice Nasmyth, "Leads Busy Life at Orpington," *Daily Province*, 12 October 1917.

4   Henry Morgan, ed., *Canadian Men and Women of the Time* (Toronto: William Briggs, 1912): 819.

5   *Montreal Gazette*, 4 February 1918.

6   Fetherstonhaugh, *No. 3 Canadian General Hospital*, 148.

7   Mary MacLeod Moore, "Somewhere in France: The Veil Lifted," *Saturday Night Magazine*, 26 January 1918.

8   For more on the process of allowing journalists into France, see Keshen, *Propaganda and Censorship*, 29.

9   Higonnet, *Lines of Fire*, xlvii.

10   Beatrice Nasmyth, "Lifts the Curtain on Life of Canadian Troops on Soil of France," *Daily Province*, 16 February 1918, 16.

11   Elizabeth Montizambert (pseudonym "Antoinette"), "Causerie de Paris," *Montreal Gazette*, 4 February 1918.

12   Morton and Granatstein, *Marching to Armageddon*, 170–73; see also Morton, *When Your Number's Up*, 245.

13   Palmer, *Alberta: A New History*, 186.

14   Morton and Granatstein, *Marching to Armageddon*, 169.

15   Beatrice Nasmyth, "Lifts the Curtain on Life of Canadian Troops on Soil of France," *Daily Province*, 16 February 1918, 16.

16   Ibid.

17   Mary MacLeod Moore, "Somewhere in France: The Veil Lifted," *Saturday Night Magazine*, 26 January 1918.

18   MacPhail, *Official History of the Canadian Forces in the Great War*, 307.

19   E.H.A. Watson, *History of the Ontario Red Cross* (Toronto: Ontario Divisional Headquarters, 1946): 4.

20   MacLeod Moore, *The Maple Leaf's Red Cross*, 167.

21   Beatrice Namsyth, "Red Cross Has An Army All Its Own," *Daily Province*, 18 February 1918.

22   Quoted in Richard van Emden and Steve Humphries, *Veterans, The Last Survivors of the Great War* (Barnsley: Leo Cooper, 1998): 118.

23   Beatrice Nasmyth, "Once Cow-shed; Now Modern Operating Room with all Equipment," *Daily Province*, 6 March 1918.

24   Ibid.

25   Dianne Graves, *A Crown of Life: The World of John McCrae* (St. Catharines: Vanwell Publishing Ltd., 1997): 218–47.

26   Mann, *The War Diary of Clare Gass*, xxx.

27   Mary MacLeod Moore, "Somewhere in France: The Veil Lifted," *Saturday Night Magazine*, 26 January 1918.

28   Ibid.

29   H. Essame, *The Battle for Europe 1918* (New York: Charles Scribner's Sons, 1972):
      24.

30   Douglas Gill and Julian Putkowski, *The British Base Camp at Etaples: 1914–
      1918* (Etaples: Musee Quentovic, 1997): 59–60.

31   Beatrice Nasmyth, "Once Cow-shed; Now Modern Operating Room With
      All Equipment," *Daily Province*, 6 March 1918.

32   Mary MacLeod Moore, "Somewhere in France: The Veil Lifted," *Saturday
      Night Magazine*, 26 January 1918.

33   Ibid.

34   Mary MacLeod Moore, *The Maple Leaf's Red Cross*, 167.

35   Beatrice Nasmyth, "Once Cow-shed; Now Modern Operating Room With
      All Equipment," *Daily Province*, 6 March 1918.

36   Beatrice Nasmyth, "Canadian Girls Drive Ambulances and Think It Fun,"
      Daily Province, 2 March 1918.

37   Gill and Putkowski, *The British Base Camp at Etaples*, 51–53.

38   Ibid., 65–67.

39   Ibid., 49–50

40   Beatrice Nasmyth, "Candian Girls Drive Ambulances and Think It Fun,"
      Daily Province, 2 March 1918.

41   Mary MacLeod Moore, *The Maple Leaf's Red Cross*, 187.

42   Beatrice Nasmyth, "Canadian Girls Drive Ambulances and Think It Fun,"
      Daily Province, 2 March 1918.

43   Ibid.

44   Ibid.

45   Gill and Putkowski, *The British Base Camp at Etaples*, 69–73.

46   Ibid.

47   Mary MacLeod Moore, "Our Doctors and Nurses in War Time," *Saturday
      Night Magazine*, 4 May 1918.

48   Ibid.

49   Gill and Putkowski, *The British Base Camp at Etaples*, 54.

50   Mary MacLeod Moore, "Our Doctors and Nurses in War Time," *Saturday
      Night Magazine*, 4 May 1918.

51   Quoted in van Emden and Humphries, *Veterans, The Last Survivors of the Great War*,
      120.

52   See "Professional Identities and Nurses' Training, 1914–1930" in Elizabeth
      Smyth, Sandra Acker, Paula Bourne, and Alison Prentice, eds., *Challenging
      Professions: Historical and Contemporary Perspectives on Women's Professional Work*
      (Toronto: University of Toronto Press, 1999): 178.

53   Norris, *Sister Heroines*, 136–37.

54   The closing of the St. John Ambulance Hospital is described in Janine Watrin,
      British Military Cemeteries in the Region of Boulogne-Sur-Mer (Lewes: The Book
      Guild Ltd., 1987): 29–32.

55   Norris, *Sister Heroines*, 130.

56   Mann, *The War Diary of Clare Gass*, 26.

57   Mary MacLeod Moore, "Our Doctors and Nurses in War Time," *Saturday Night Magazine*, 4 May 1918.

58   Letter from Johnston MacAdams to his niece Evelyn, dated 15 December 1944, Gormley Collection.

59   Mary MacLeod Moore, "Somewhere in France: The Veil Lifted," *Saturday Night Magazine*, 26 January 1918.

60   "Just the Soldier's Representative," *Edmonton Journal*, 7 February 1918.

61   Marriages, *Toronto Star*, 4 May 1918.

CHAPTER 11

1   "Women Members of Legislature Applauded at House Opening," 8 February 1918 newspaper article reproduced in *Pioneer Women of Western Canada* (Toronto: OISE, 1978): 108.

2   Grace Studholme, "Reminiscing," Glenbow Archives, M5977/69.

3   "Women Members of Legislature Applauded at House Opening," 8 February 1918 newspaper article reproduced in *Pioneer Women of Western Canada* (Toronto: OISE, 1978): 108.

4   "Women Members of Legislature Applauded at House Opening," contemporary newspaper report in *Pioneer Women of Western Canada* (Toronto: OISE, 1978): 103.

5   "The North Side," *Edmonton Journal*, 7 February 1918.

6   "Elected but no Campaigning," *Globe*, 2 February 1918.

7   *The Alberta Club Woman's Blue Book* (Calgary: Calgary Branch of the Canadian Woman's Press Club Publishers, 1917): 101.

8   "Miss MacAdams Introduces First Bill," *Edmonton Bulletin*, 9 February 1918, 1.

9   Fact Sheet, *The Regimental Colours*, Alberta Legislature Occasional Paper.

10   Morton and Granatstein, *Marching to Armageddon*, 50.

11   Desmond Morton and Glenn T. Wright, *Winning the Second Battle: Canadian Veterans and the Return to Civilian Life, 1915–1930* (Toronto: University of Toronto Press, 1987): 102.

12   Ibid., 144.

13   Speech by Roberta MacAdams, Robert Price Collection.

14   Ibid.

15   Ibid.

16   Ibid.

17   "Women Legislators Make Their Maiden Speeches," *Edmonton Journal*, 28 February 1918.

18   Holger Herwig, "The German Victories: 1917–1918," in Hew Strachan, ed., *The Oxford Illustrated History of the First World War* (Oxford: Oxford University Press, 1998): 260.

19   James McWilliams and R. James Steel, *Amiens: Dawn of Victory* (Toronto: Dundurn Press, 2001): 13–14.

20 "Raiders Come In Dark: Bombs Dropped on London," *Daily Province*, 8 March 1918, 2.

21 Mary MacLeod Moore, "London Letters," *Saturday Night Magazine*, 27 April 1918.

22 Untitled article, *Toronto Star*, 4 May 1918; also letter dated 15 February 1918 from Beatrice Nasmyth to James Nasmyth (Monica Newton Collection).

23 Ibid.

24 S.F. Wise, *Canadian Airmen and the First World War: The Official History of the RCAF, Volume I* (Toronto: University of Toronto Press, 1980): 645–46.

25 Letter from W.J. Hanna to Neil Hanna, 30 May 1918, Spaulding Collection.

26 Ibid.

27 "Problems of Soldiers Under Separate Branch Promises Premier Stewart," *Edmonton Journal*, 9 April 1918.

28 "Alberta Has Best Soldier Laws Says Capt. R. Pearson," *Calgary Albertan*, 29 April 1918.

29 "Secures the Promise that Any Future Normal School Will be Located in Edmonton: Miss Roberta MacAdams, MLA, Proves More than a Match for Hon. Geo. Smith in Debate – Causes Much Merriment in Legislature," *Edmonton Journal*, April 1918.

30 Ibid.

31 Kostek, *A Century and Ten*, 113.

32 "Just the Soldier's Representative," *Edmonton Journal*, 7 February 1918.

33 Hilda Ridley, "Pen Portraits of Progressive Women," *Christian Guardian*, 16 February 1921, 11.

34 "Greatest Enemy to Progress is the Comfortable Woman," undated clipping, Louise McKinney Fonds, Glenbow Archives.

35 "Miss Roberta MacAdams," *The OAC Review*, June 1918, 335.

36 Linda Rasmussen, Lorna Rasmussen, Candace Savage, Anne Wheeler, *A Harvest Yet to Reap* (Toronto: Women's Press, 1979): 230.

37 "Women's War Conference at Ottawa and Women's Enfranchisement," *Saturday Night Magazine*, 27 April 1918.

38 "Inspiration for Canadian Women," *Daily Province*, Tuesday, 5 March 1918.

39 Ceta Ramkhalawansingh, "Women During the Great War," in Acton, et al., *Women at Work*, 285–87.

40 *Minute Book*, Women's Canadian Club of Calgary, Entry for 18 April 1918, Glenbow Archives.

41 Beatrice Nasmyth, "Miss MacAdams Has Interesting Career in View," *Daily Province*, 27 August 1918.

42 City Teachers Honors Member from Overseas, undated, unattributed clipping, Edmonton Public Schools Archives.

43 G.W.L. Nicholson, *Canada's Nursing Sisters* (Toronto: Samuel Stevens, Hakkert and Company, 1975): 95.

CHAPTER 12

1   "Big British Smash Launched at Dawn," *The Sarnia Canadian Observer*, 8 August 1918, 1.

2   Morton and Granatstein, *Marching to Armageddon*, 198–204; see also Daniel G. Dancocks, *Sir Arthur Currie: A Biography* (Toronto: Methuen, 1985): 149–56.

3   Ibid.

4   "Well-Known Local Newspaper Man Writes From War," *Sarnia Canadian Observer*, 14 September 1918, 1.

5   Ibid.

6   Beatrice Nasmyth, "Miss MacAdams Has Interesting Career in View," *Daily Province*, 27 August 1918.

7   Col. H.M. Tory, "The Birth of a University," *The Beaver*, 14 December 1918, 5.

8   E.A. Corbett, *Henry Marshall Tory: A Biography* (Edmonton: University of Alberta Press, 1992): 138–56.

9   *Canada's War Effort 1914–1918* (Ottawa: Director of Public Information, 1918).

10   Corbett, *Henry Marshall Tory*, 144.

11   Walter Johns, *A History of the University of Alberta* (Edmonton: University of Alberta Press, 1981): 66.

12   Lt. Col. J. Obed Smith, "Repatriation: Its Reality and Romance," in *The Beaver*, 22 February 1919, 8.

13   See correspondence between Mildred Cunningham and Mary Urie Watson, Guelph McLaughlin Archives, RE1 MAC A0014, Box 5.

14   Letter from Mildred Cunningham to Mary Urie Watson, 1 February 1919, Guelph McLaughlin Archives, University of Guelph, REI MAC A0014, Box 5.

15   Beatrice Nasmyth, "Tells of Life in London Suburb," *Daily Province*, 1 April 1918.

16   War Diary, Eleventh Company, Canadian Forestry Corps, National Archives of Canada.

17   Letter from Beatrice Furniss to Miss Jameson, 4 March 1967, Newton Collection.

18   Beatrice Nasmyth, "Enemy Alien Question in England," *Daily Province*, 30 August 1918.

19   Ibid.

20   Winston Churchill, quoted in the British House of Commons, 20 December 1912. Quote provided by Richard Langworth, Editor, The Churchill Centre, Moultonborough, New Hampshire, in email correspondence with the author, dated October 20, 2006.

21   Beatrice Nasmyth, "Enemy Alien Question in England," *Daily Province*, 30 August 1918.

22   Ibid.

23   Edward Preston, *A Brief Guide to the Plaques, Commemorative Tablets and Public Memorials in Hastings and St. Leonard's* (Hastings: Hastings Borough Council, nd).

24   Interview with James Wheeler, current owner of the former Furniss home in Hastings.

25   References to Harry Furniss from <http://www.victorianweb.org/art/illustration/furniss/pva319.html>. Information provided by Philip Allingham, Contributing Editor, Victorian Web, Faculty of Education, Lakehead University, Canada.

26   Interview with James Wheeler.

27   Letter from Beatrice Furniss to Miss Jameson, 4 March 1967, Newton Collection.

28   M. Bryan and S. Heneage, *Dictionary of British Cartoonists and Caricaturists*, 1730–1980 (London: Scholar Press, 1994): 84–85.

29   Plus-fours are three-quarter-length pants worn with high socks.

30   *Memoirs of Arthur Fraser*, n.d., Corinne Marshall Collection.

31   Ibid

32   Ibid

33   "Miss MacAdams Criticises Alberta Office Administration," *Edmonton Journal*, 9 April 1919.

CHAPTER 13

1   Letter from Beatrice (Nasmyth) Furniss to Miss Jameson, 4 March 1967, Monica Newton Collection.

2   Letter from W.J. Hanna to Neil Hanna, 21 November 1918, Spaulding Collection.

3   Stoddard King, "The Long, Long, Trail," 1914, quoted in Max Arthur, *When This Bloody War is Over: Soldiers' Songs of the First World War* (London: Piatkus, 2001): 54.

4   Telegram from Roberta MacAdams to W.J. Hanna, 9 December 1918, Spaulding Collection.

5   "Need Instruction Regarding Canada: Miss McAdams Speaks of Plight of Englishwomen Coming to This Country," *The Mail and Empire*, 22 January 1919.

6   Jim Wilkie, *Metagama: Journey from Lewis to the New World* (Edmonton: Birlinn Ltd., 2001): 49–50.

7   "Just a Day: The Sights and Scenes at the Landing Stage When the War Brides Come Home," *Saturday Night Magazine*, 8 March 1919.

8   Lt. Col. J. Obed Smith, "Repatriation: Its Reality and Romance," 22 February 1919, 7.

9   "Need Instruction Regarding Canada: Miss McAdams Speaks of Plight of Englishwomen Coming to this Country," *The Mail and Empire*, 22 January 1919.

10   Ibid.

11   Morton and Wright, *Winning the Second Battle*, 111.

12   "Just a Day: The Sights and Scenes at the Landing Stage When the War Brides Come Home," *Saturday Night Magazine*, 8 March 1919.

13   "Land Settlement Board Names Miss MacAdams to Undertake Delicate Task," *Edmonton Journal*, 4 September 1919, 1.

14   Ibid.

15   Ibid.

16   "Lt. W. Neil Hanna Killed in Italy," *The Globe*, 26 November 1918, 8.

17   Letter from Mary McBurney to W.J. Hanna, Sunday, 25 November 1918, Spaulding Collection.

18   Roberta MacAdams, "Table Talk," *The Beaver*, December 1918, 4.

19   Palmer, *Alberta: A New History*, 188.

20   *The Canadian Encyclopedia* (Toronto: McClelland and Stewart Inc., 1999): 1164.

21   See comments by historian Sharon Richardson in "Eighty Years Filled With Firsts," <http://www.ualberta.ca/~publicas/folio/35/10/09.htm>

22   "W.A. Rae, Member for Peace River, Deals with Railway Development in the North: Higher Type of Education Advocated by Miss Roberta MacAdams, Who Also Points to Need of Concerted Action to Handle Returned Soldier Problem Properly," *Edmonton Journal*, 12 February 1919.

23   "Miss MacAdams Pleads for More Inspiration in Educational Life," *Edmonton Journal*, 12 February 1919.

24   Liner notes to *Fritz Kreisler* CD, James Ehnes and Eduard Laurel (Analekta Records, 2001).

25   Ibid.

26   Roberta MacAdams, "Table Talk," *The Beaver*, December 1918, 4.

27   "Disenfranchise Enemy Aliens Veterans Ask," *Edmonton Bulletin*, 17 April 1919.

28   "Government Preference to Returned Men," *Edmonton Bulletin*, 9 April 1919, 1.

29   Ibid.

30   "Miss MacAdams Pleads for More Inspiration in Educational Life," *Edmonton Journal*, 12 February 1919.

31   "Marriage Won't Take Her from Public Life," *Toronto Star*, 31 August 1920.

32   The Provincial Normal School would be established in Edmonton in 1930. See Kostek, *A Century and Ten*, 113.

33   Minute Book of the Women's Canadian Club of Calgary, Glenbow Archives, 23.

34   "The Late Hon. W.J. Hanna," *Saturday Night Magazine*, 29 March 1919.

35   Further details of the death and funeral of W.J. Hanna taken from "Hon. W.J. Hanna Dies Suddenly at Augusta, Georgia," *Sarnia Canadian Observer* (undated clipping, Lambton Archives) and "Many Mourn Big Canadian," *The Globe*, March 26 1919.

36   Morton and Granatstein, *Marching to Armageddon*, 250.

37   Cole and Larmour, *Many and Remarkable*, 17.

38   Rasmussen et al., *A Harvest Yet to Reap*, 116.

39   "Opposition Makes Strong Fight in Legislature on Vote for Salary of Efficiency Officer," *Edmonton Bulletin*, 8 April 1919.

40   "Miss MacAdams Criticises Alberta Office Administration," *Edmonton Journal*, 9 April 1919.

41   Ibid.

42   "Alberta Soldiers' Member on Her Election," *The Times*, 22 September 1917, 9.

43   See Bank of Canada web site <http://www.bankofcanada.ca/en/inflation_calc.htm>.

44   "Alberta Soldiers' Member on Her Election," *The Times*, 22 September 1917, 9.

45   Letter from William Carpenter to Roberta MacAdams, 1 August 1919, Edmonton Public Schools Archives and Museum.

46   See the report of the Local Councils of Women of Calgary in *The Alberta Club Woman's Blue Book*.

47   "A Woman's Reconstruction Programme," *Maclean's Magazine*, December 1918, 80.

CHAPTER 14

1   "Land Settlement Board Names Miss MacAdams to Undertake Delicate Task," *Edmonton Journal*, 4 September 1919.

2   Morton and Wright, *Winning the Second Battle*, 145.

3   Miriam Green Ellis, "War Brides from Abroad Eagerly Making Good Here," *Maclean's Magazine*, 1 October 1921, 54.

4   "This Woman M.P.P. Is Official Mother to Lonely War Brides," *Toronto Star*, 14 February 1920.

5   Ibid.

6   "Land Settlement Board Names Miss MacAdams to Undertake Delicate Task," *Edmonton Journal*, 4 September 1919.

7   Donald Wetherell and Irene Kmet, *Alberta's North: A History, 1890–1950* (Edmonton: University of Alberta Press, 2000): 243.

8   David Munro, *Oxford Dictionary of the World* (Oxford: Oxford University Press, 1995): 477.

9   Beatrice Nasmyth, "Greater Than Any Yet Told is to be Future Story of Last of Last Great west – Peace River District," *Daily Province*, 14 October 1916.

10   *Alberta in the 20th Century, Volume 4: The Great War and Its Consequences* (Calgary: United Western Communications Ltd., 1992): 249.

11   "Budget Debate Is Not Critical of Government," *Edmonton Bulletin*, 18 March 1921, 3.

12   Ibid.

13   "Alberta Women's Institute Annual Convention Program," *Edmonton Journal*, 1 March 1919, 6.

14   Cole and Larmour, *Many and Remarkable*, 17.

15   Ibid.

16   Morton and Wright, *Winning the Second Battle*, 151.

17   "Marriage Won't Take Her from Public Life," *Toronto Star*, 31 August 1920.

18   Markham Hislop, "Returning War Vets Put to Work as Part of Farm Settlement Plan," *Western People*, 11 November 1986, 6.

19   Ibid.

20   Marshall, *Justice on the Peace*, 60.

21   Names of soldier settlement communities were drawn from a chronology by David Leonard developed for Alberta Community Development.

22   "Alberta Legislature," *Edmonton Bulletin*, 18 March 1920, 5.

23   "Alberta Legislature," *Edmonton Bulletin*, 22 March 1920, 4.

24   "Marriage Won't Take Her from Public Life," *Toronto Star*, 31 August 1920.

25   Ibid.

26   "Short Demonstration Courses for Wives of Soldier Settlers," *Edmonton Journal*, 1 April 1920.

27   Miriam Green Ellis, "War Brides from Abroad Eagerly Making Good Here," *Maclean's Magazine*, 1 October 1921, 54.

28   "Short Demonstration Courses for Wives of Soldier Settlers," *Edmonton Journal*, 1 April 1920.

29   Interview with Robert Price, Calgary 2002.

30   "Marriage Won't Take Her from Public Life," *Toronto Star*, 31 August 1920.

31   Wedding reception description from two sources: article by Mrs. Edmund Phillips, "Society News," *Toronto World*, 22 September 1920, 5; also "Miss Roberta MacAdams Becomes Bride of Major Harvey S. Price," *Edmonton Journal*, 22 September 1920, 18.

32   Ibid.

33   Ibid.

34   "Mrs. R. MacAdams Passes Away on 80th Birthday," *Sarnia Canadian Observer*, 14 May 1923.

35   "Weddings: MacAdams-Moore," *Sarnia Canadian Observer*, 10 July 1925, 5.

36   "Death Summons Robt. McAdams, Veteran Sarnian" in *Sarnia Canadian Observer*, 20 April 1928.

37   "Deep Regret at Sudden Death of L. M. MacAdams" *Sarnia Canadian Observer*, 21 May 1928, 1.

38   "Deaths: Mrs. Mary McBurney," *Sarnia Observer*, 1 April 1958.

39   George Mathewson, "The Inspiring Story of Canatara Park," *150 Years of Local News: Volume 4* (Sarnia: Sarnia Observer, 2003): 106.

40   "Veterans Out of Employment Will Urge Upon Government Immediate Action for Relief," *Edmonton Journal*, 3 March 1921.

41   Ibid.

42   "Amendments to New Jury Act Defeated in Committees," *Edmonton Journal*, 5 April 1921.

43   Letter to Roberta Price dated 18 April 1921, Robert Price Collection.

44   *Alberta and the 20th Century: Volume 4, The Great War and Its Consequences 1914–1920*, 354.

45   Letter from Roberta MacAdams to W.G. Carpenter, 22 July 1919, Edmonton Public School Archives.

46   Letter from Johnston MacAdams to his niece Evelyn, 15 December 1944, Sheila Gormley Collection.

SELECTED BIBLIOGRAPHY

ARCHIVES AND LIBRARIES

Alberta Legislature Library
British Coledale Newspaper Archives
Edmonton Public Schools Archives and Museum (Lori Clark)
Glenbow Archives (Lynette Walton)
Guelph McLaughlin Archives, University of Guelph (Darlene Wiltsic)
Imperial War Museum Archives
Lambton Archives (Anne Ashton)
Moore Museum (Laurie Mason)
National Archives of Canada
Ontario Provincial Archives
Orpington Public Library
Provincial Archives of Alberta (Marlena Wyman)
Royal College of Nursing Archives
Sarnia Public Library (John Rochon and Jeffrey Beeler)
Women's Studies Library, Ohio State University (Linda A. Krikos)

NEWSPAPERS AND MAGAZINES

British Journal of Nursing (London)
Calgary Albertan (Calgary)
Christian Guardian (unknown)
Daily Province (Vancouver)
Daily Sketch (London)

Daily News (Toronto)
Edmonton Bulletin (Edmonton)
Edmonton Daily Capital (Edmonton)
Edmonton Journal (Edmonton)
Globe (Toronto)
Maclean's Magazine (Toronto)
The Mail and Empire (Toronto)
The Montreal Gazette (Montreal)
My Golden West Magazine (Calgary)
Nursing Times (London)
O.A.C. Review (Guelph)
Orillia Packet (Orillia)
Ottawa Times (Ottawa)
Pall Mall Gazette (London)
Petrolia Advertiser (Petrolia)
Sarnia Canadian (Sarnia)
Sarnia Canadian Observer (Sarnia)
Sarnia Observer (Sarnia)
Saturday Night Magazine (Toronto)
Stony Plain Advertiser (Stony Plain)

PRIVATE COLLECTIONS

Corinne Marshall Collection (Edmonton)
Douglas MacAdams Collection (Vancouver)
Kerr Collection (Edmonton)
Monica Newton Collection (Vancouver)
Robert Price Collection (Calgary)
Sheila Gormley Collection (Sarnia)
Spaulding Collection (Toronto)

BOOKS

Abbott, Elizabeth, ed. *Chronicle of Canada*. Montreal: Chronicle Publications, 1990.

Acton, Janice, Penny Goldsmith, and Bonnie Shepard, eds. *Women at Work, Ontario, 1850–1930*. Toronto: Women's Press, 1974.

Akenson, Donald Harman. *The Irish in Ontario: A Study in Rural History*. Montreal: McGill-Queen's University Press.

The Alberta Club Woman's Blue Book. Calgary: Calgary Branch of the Canadian Woman's Press Club Publishers, 1917.

Alberta in the 20th Century. Volumes 1–4. Edmonton: United Western Communications Ltd., 1992.

Along the Fifth: A History of Stony Plain and District. Stony Plain: Stony Plain and District Historical Society, 1982.

Ambrose, Linda. *For Home and Country: The Centennial History of the Women's Institutes of Ontario*. Guelph: Federated Women's Institutes of Ontario, 1996.

Andre, Roland. *Memoire en Images: Boulogne-sur-Mer*. London: Alan Sutton, 1997.

Bird, Will. *Ghosts Have Warm Hands*. Toronto: CEF Books, 1997.

Boniface, Priscilla. *Hotels and Restaurants 1830 to the Present Day*. London: Royal Commission on Historical Monuments, 1981.

Bonsall, Thomas. *Titanic: The Story of the Great White Star Line Trio, the Olympic, the Titanic and the Britannic*. New York: Gallery Books, 1987.

Boulton, Marsha. *Minto Memories: Families, Facts, and Fables*. Durham: Saugeen Press, 1988.

Brown, Craig, ed. *The Illustrated History of Canada*. Toronto: Key Porter Books, 2002.

Bryan, M., and S. Heneage. *Dictionary of British Cartoonists and Caricaturists, 1730–1980*. London: Scholar Press, 1994.

Bumsted, J.M. *The Peoples of Canada: A Post-Confederation History*. Toronto: Oxford University Press, 2004.

Cole, Catharine, and Judy Larmour. *Many and Remarkable: The Story of the Alberta Women's Institutes*. Edmonton: Alberta Women's Institutes, 1997.

Cook, Sharon Anne, Lorna McLean, and Kate O'Rourke, eds. *Framing Our Past, Canadian Women's History in the Twentieth Century.* Montreal: McGill–Queen's University Press, 2001.

Cook, Tim. *No Place to Run: The Canadian Corps and Gas Warfare in the First World War.* Vancouver: UBC Press, 1999.

Corbett, E.A. *Henry Marshall Tory: A Biography.* Edmonton: University of Alberta Press, 1992.

Dancocks, Daniel G. *Sir Arthur Currie: A Biography.* Toronto: Methuen, 1985.

Duncan, Sara Jeannette. *The Imperialist.* Ottawa: Tecumseh Press, 1996.

Elliott, Bruce. *Irish Migrants in the Canadas: a New Approach.* Montreal: McGill–Queen's University Press, 1988.

Essame, H. *The Battle for Europe 1918.* New York: Charles Scribner's Sons, 1972.

Fetherstonhaugh, R. C. *No. 3 Canadian General Hospital (McGill) 1914–1919.* Montreal: The Gazette Printing Company, 1928.

Francis, R.D., and Howard Palmer, eds. *The Prairie West: Historical Readings.* Edmonton: Pica Pica Press, 1985.

Freeman, Bill, and Richard Nielsen. *Far from Home: Canadians in the First War.* Toronto: McGraw-Hill Ryerson, 1999.

Geggie, Norma. *Wakefield Revisited.* Chelsea: Castenchel Editions, 2003.

Gilbert, Martin. *The First World War.* Toronto: Stoddart, 1994.

Gill, Douglas, and Julian Putkowski. *The British Base Camp at Etaples: 1914–1918.* Etaples: Musee Quentovic, 1997.

Granfield, Linda. *Where Poppies Grow: A World War I Companion.* Toronto: Stoddart, 2001.

Graves, Dianne. *A Crown of Life: The World of John McCrae.* St. Catharines: Vanwell Publishing Ltd., 1997.

Graves, Robert. *Goodbye to All That: An Autobiography.* Oxford: Berghahn Books, 1995.

Higonnet, Margaret R., ed. *Lines of Fire: Women Writers of World War I.* New York: Plume/Penguin Books Ltd., 1999.

Historical Atlas of the County of Wellington, Ontario. Toronto: Historical Atlas Publishing Company, 1906.

Hollett, David. *Passage to the New World: Packet Ships and Irish Famine Emigrants 1845–1851.* Abergavenny: P.M. Heaton Publishing, 1995.

Holt, Faye Reineberg. *Threshing: The Early Years of Harvesting.*
        Calgary: Fifth House Publishers, 1999.

Jameson, Shelagh. "The Soldier's MLA." *Alberta
        Historical Review* 15 (Autumn 1967).

Johns, Walter. *A History of the University of Alberta.* Edmonton:
        University of Alberta Press, 1981.

Keshen, Jeffrey. *Propaganda and Censorship During Canada's Great
        War.* Edmonton: University of Alberta Press, 1996.

Kostek, Michael. *A Century and Ten: The History of Edmonton Public
        Schools.* Edmonton: Edmonton Public Schools, 1992.

Lauriston, Victor. *Lambton's Hundred Years: 1849–1949.*
        Sarnia: Windsor Publications, 1987.

MacDonald, Lyn. *The Roses of No Man's Land.*
        London: Penguin Books Ltd., 1993.

MacDonagh, Michael. *In London During the Great War: The Diary
        of a Journalist.* London: Eyre and Spottiswoode, 1935.

Mackenzie, Midge. *Shoulder to Shoulder.* Harmondsworth:
        Penguin Books Ltd., 1975.

MacMillan, Margaret. *Paris 1919.* New York: Random House Inc., 2001.

MacPhail, Andrew. *Official History of the Canadian Forces in the Great War
        1914–1919; Medical Services.* Ottawa: King's Printer, 1925.

Mann, Susan, ed. *The War Diary of Clare Gass, 1915–1918.*
        Montreal: McGill-Queen's University Press, 2000.

Mann, Susan. *Margaret Macdonald, Imperial Daughter.* Kingston:
        McGill-Queen's University Press, 2005.

Marshall, Ernest. *Justice on the Peace: The Law and Lawyers in
        Alberta's Northwest.* Edmonton: Juriliber, 2003.

Marwick, Arthur. *Woman at War 1914–1918.* London:
        Fontana Paperbacks, 1977.

McWilliams, James, and R. James Steel. *Amiens: Dawn of
        Victory.* Toronto: Dundurn Press, 2001.

Middlebrooke, Martin. *The First Day of the Somme, 1
        July 1916.* London: Allan Lane, 1971.

Mitchell, Elizabeth. *In Western Canada Before the War; Impressions
        of Early Twentieth Century Prairie Communities.*
        Saskatoon: Western Producer Prairie Books, 1981.

Mitchinson, Wendy. *The Nature of their Bodies: Women and their Doctors in Victorian Canada.* Toronto: University of Toronto Press, 1991.

Mollins, Carl. *Canada's Century.* Toronto: MacLean-Hunter Publishing Ltd., 1999.

Moore, Mary MacLeod. *The Maple Leaf's Red Cross.* London: Skeffington and Sons Ltd., 1919.

Morgan, Henry, ed. *Canadian Men and Women of the Time.* Toronto: William Briggs, 1912.

Morton, Desmond. *When Your Number's Up: The Canadian Soldier in the First World War.* Toronto: Random House of Canada Limited, 1993.

Morton, Desmond, and Jack Granatstein. *Marching to Armageddon: Canadians and the Great War 1914–1919.* Toronto: Lester & Orpen Dennys Limited, 1989.

Morton, Desmond, and Glenn T. Wright. *Winning the Second Battle: Canadian Veterans and the Return to Civilian Life, 1915–1930.* Toronto: University of Toronto Press, 1987.

Munro, David. *Oxford Dictionary of the World.* Oxford: Oxford University Press, 1995.

Nicholson, G.W.L. *Canada's Nursing Sisters.* Toronto: Samuel Stevens, Hakkert and Company, 1975.

Norris, Marjorie. *Sister Heroines: The Roseate Glow of Wartime Nursing 1914–1918.* Calgary: Bunker to Bunker Publishing, 2002.

Orpington from Saxon Times to the Great War. Orpington: Worker's Educational Association, n.d.

Palmer, Howard, and Tamara Palmer. *Alberta: A New History.* Edmonton: Hurtig Publishers, 1990.

Pateman, John. *Canadian Corner: A Brief History.* Orpington: Privately Published, 1980.

Phelps, Edward. *Sarnia: Gateway to Bluewaterland.* Burlington: Windsor Publications, 1987.

Phillips, Glen. *History of the Sarnia Public Library.* Sarnia: 1990.

Preston, Edward. *A Brief Guide to the Plaques, Commemorative Tablets and Public Memorials in Hastings and St. Leonards.* Hastings: Hastings Borough Council, n.d.

Rasmussen, Linda, Lorna Rasmussen, Candace Savage, and Anne Wheeler. *A Harvest Yet to Reap: A History of Prairie Women.* Toronto: The Women's Press, 1976.

GIVE YOUR OTHER VOTE TO THE SISTER

Robinson, John. *Once Upon a Century: 100 Year History of the 'Ex'*.
Toronto: J.H. Robinson Publishing Ltd., 1978.

Rutherford, Paul. *A Victorian Authority: The Daily Press in Late 19th
Century Canada*. Toronto: University of Toronto Press, 1982.

The Scottish Women's Suffrage Movement. Glasgow:
People's Palace Museum, 1978.

Sexton, Sean, and Christine Kinealy. *The Irish: A Photohistory*.
New York: Thames and Hudson, 2002.

Smyth, Elizabeth, Sandra Acker, Paula Bourne, and Alison
Prentice, eds., *Challenging Professions: Historical and
Contemporary Perspectives on Women's Professional Work*.
Toronto: University of Toronto Press, 1999.

Smith, George. *A History of Sarnia in Pictures*.
Sarnia: Self-Published, 1970.

Snell, James. *Macdonald Institute: Remembering the Past, Embracing
the Future*. Toronto: Dundurn Press, 2003.

Stevens, Lt. Col. G.R. *A City Goes to War: The History
of the Loyal Edmonton Regiment*. Edmonton:
Edmonton Regiment Association, 1964.

Strachan, Hew, ed. *The Oxford Illustrated History of the First World
War*. Oxford: Oxford University Press, 1998.

Swift, Michael. *Historical Maps of Ireland*. Edison:
Chartwell Books Inc., 1999.

Taylor, A.J.P. *Beaverbrook: A Biography*. New York:
Simon and Schuster, 1972.

Trollope, Joanna. *Britannia's Daughters*. London:
Hutchinson and Co., 1983.

van Emden, Richard, and Steve Humphries. *Veterans: The Last
Survivors of the Great War*. Barnsley: Leo Cooper, 1998.

Watrin, Janin. *The British Military Cemeteries in the Region of
Boulogne-sur-Mer*. Lewes: The Book Guild Ltd., 1987.

Watson, E.H.A. *History of the Ontario Red Cross*. Toronto:
Ontario Divisional Headquarters, 1946.

Wetherell, Donald and Irene Kmet. *Alberta's North: A History,
1890–1950*. Edmonton: University of Alberta Press, 2000.

Wilkie, Jim. *Metagama: A Journey from Lewis to the New
World*. Edinburgh: Berlinn Limited, 2001.

Wilson, David. *The Irish in Canada*. Ottawa: Canadian
  Historical Association, 1989.

Wise, S.F. *Canadian Airmen and the First World War: The
  Official History of the RCAF, Volume I*. Toronto:
  University of Toronto Press, 1980.

Wood, Cornelia. *My Memories*. Edmonton: UVISCO Press, 1982.

INDEX

Page numbers in **bold**
refer to photographs.

LEGACIES SHARED SERIES

Janice Dickin, series editor
ISSN 1498-2358

The Legacies Shared series preserves the many personal histories and experiences of pioneer and immigrant life that may have disappeared or have been overlooked. The purpose of this series is to create, save, and publish voices from the heartland of the continent that might otherwise be lost to the public discourse. The manuscripts may take the form of memoirs, letters, photographs, art work, recipes or maps, works of fiction or poetry, archival documents, even oral history.

Memories, Dreams, Nightmares: Memoirs of a Holocaust Survivor Jack Weiss · No. 13

The Honourable Member for Vegreville: The Memoirs and Diary of Anthony Hlynka, MP Anthony Hlynka, translated by Oleh Gerus · No. 14

The Letters of Margaret Butcher: Missionary-Imperialism on the North Pacific Coast Margaret Butcher, edited by Mary Ellen Kelm · No. 15

The First Dutch Settlement in Alberta: Letters from the Pioneer Years, 1903–14 edited by Donald Sinnema · No. 16

Suitable for the Wilds: Letters from Northern Alberta, 1929–31 Mary Percy Jackson edited by Janice Dickin · No. 17

A Voice of Her Own edited by Thelma Poirier, Doris Bircham, JoAnn Jones-Hole, Patricia Slade and Susan Vogelaar · No. 18

What's All This Got to Do with the Price of 2 x 4's? Michael Apsey · No. 19

Zhorna: Material Culture of the Ukrainian Pioneers Roman Fodchuk · No. 20

Behind the Man: John Laurie, Ruth Gorman, and the Indian Vote in Canada Ruth Gorman, edited by Frits Pannekoek · No. 21